THE BATTLE OF THE DENMARK STRAIT

THE BATTLE OF THE
DENMARK STRAIT

A Critical Analysis of
the Bismarck's *Singular Triumph*

ROBERT J. WINKLARETH

CASEMATE
Philadelphia & Oxford

Published in the United States of America and Great Britain in 2012 by
CASEMATE PUBLISHERS
908 Darby Road, Havertown, PA 19083
and
10 Hythe Bridge Street, Oxford, OX1 2EW

ISBN 978-1-61200-123-4
Digital Edition: ISBN 978-1-61200-135-7

Cataloging-in-publication data is available from the Library of Congress and
the British Library.

10 9 8 7 6 5 4 3 2 1

Printed and bound in the United States of America.

For a complete list of Casemate titles please contact:

CASEMATE PUBLISHERS (US)
Telephone (610) 853-9131, Fax (610) 853-9146
E-mail: casemate@casematepublishing.com

CASEMATE PUBLISHERS (UK)
Telephone (01865) 241249, Fax (01865) 794449
E-mail: casemate-uk@casematepublishing.co.uk

All maps and diagrams were created by the author.

All combat photographs taken during the Battle of the Denmark Strait were
filmed by *Prinz Eugen* photographer Lagemann.

CONTENTS

APPENDICES

ACKNOWLEDGMENTS

THE AUTHOR IS DEEPLY INDEBTED TO PROF. DR. JÜRGEN Rohwer for his continued guidance and support, without which this book would not have been possible. The early recognition of the validity of the so-called "reversed photo theory" by Sir Ludovic Kennedy is also appreciated. To the many others who gave encouragement for my efforts to seek the truth about the Battle of the Denmark Strait, I also extend my heartfelt thanks.

The author wishes to thank Internet webmasters John Asmussen of the Bismarck-class Forum, José Rico of the KBismarck Forum, and Frank Allen of the HMS Hood Association for allowing the free exchange of information and viewpoints on the subject and for providing on their websites copies of many of the source documents so essential for the proper evaluation of the battle.

The entire naval history community is grateful to Ulrich Rudofsky for his translation of related German documents into English for the benefit of us all. The author also thanks Marc Mindnich for providing the *Bismarck* battle film in digital form so that the last two minutes or so of the battle could be analyzed in detail on a frame-by-frame basis.

The author is also indebted to Michael W. Pocock of MaritimeQuest for providing many of the photographs used in this book. Thanks also to ThyssenKrupp Marine Systems AG for their photos of the *Bismarck* under construction at the Blohm & Voss shipyard.

The author appreciates the contribution of the many individuals who took the time and effort to respond to questions and comments on the subject on Internet forums and by private communications, and which thereby enhanced my understanding of how the Battle of the Denmark

Strait was fought. Of particular value were the exchanges I had with Antonio Bonomi and Vic Dale that explored the minutest details of the battle in light of the existing documentary and photographic evidence.

Information provided by Fridthor Eydal on Royal Air Force and Royal Navy operations in Iceland in general, and especially during Operation Rhine Exercise, was particularly helpful in understanding the contribution of those forces in the efforts made to locate the *Bismarck* and *Prinz Eugen* after their escape.

Robert J. Winklareth
Woodbridge, Virginia
September 2012

DEDICATION

This book is respectfully dedicated to the memory of all of the gallant seamen on both sides who lost their lives during the Battle of the Denmark Strait and in subsequent actions related to the *Bismarck* operation. Every effort was made to make this account of the battle as accurate as humanly possible in their honor.

PREFACE

THE BATTLE OF THE DENMARK STRAIT WAS UNDOUBTEDLY one of the most famous and most important naval battles of World War II. It was fought on the morning of 24 May 1941 in the waters between Iceland and Greenland when a British naval force, consisting of the venerable battle cruiser HMS *Hood* and the recently completed battleship HMS *Prince of Wales,* intercepted the German battleship *Bismarck* and her heavy cruiser consort *Prinz Eugen* as they were attempting to break out into the North Atlantic for raiding operations against Allied shipping. The Battle of the Denmark Strait is perhaps the most documented event in naval history.

On the British side, there are several official reports detailing the action, including Admiralty reports ADM 116-4351, Final Report on First Enquiry into the Loss of HMS Hood; ADM 116-4352, Report on Second Enquiry into the Loss of HMS Hood; ADM 234-509, Official Dispatch of Admiral Tovey on the Pursuit of Bismarck; and ADM 199-1187, Prince of Wales Salvo Plot, and Air Ministry report, AIR 14-415, Report on the Sinking of the Bismarck. There are also authoritative books on the subject, including *Loss of the Bismarck,* written by Vice-Admiral B.B. Schofield with the assistance of the staffs of the Admiralty, Imperial War Museum, and Royal United Service Institute, and *The Bismarck Episode*, written by Captain Russell Grenfell of the Royal Navy in consultation with many of the commanders involved in the operation.

On the German side, there are the *Prinz Eugen's* war diary (Kriegstagebuch), the *Prinz Eugen's* battle diagram (Gefechtsskizze), the *Prinz Eugen's* speed chart, and books written by Baron Burkard von Müllenheim-Rechsberg, surviving fourth gunnery officer of the *Bismarck*; Paul Schmalenbach, second gunnery officer of the *Prinz Eugen*; and Fritz Otto Busch, an official observer on the *Prinz Eugen*. *Prinz Eugen's* staff photographer, Lagemann, took about 20 still photographs during the battle, mostly of the *Bismarck* in action against the British force, and there were also segments of motion-picture film taken from the *Prinz Eugen* during the battle.

Despite the wealth of information contained in those documents, there has been considerable confusion and even some controversy as to how the battle was fought. Part of the problem was due to the fact that the photographs taken of the *Bismarck* from the *Prinz Eugen* during the battle show the *Bismarck* on both the port and starboard sides of the *Prinz Eugen* without any supporting evidence to show how this cross-over occurred. One theory was that there was no cross-over at all, but that some of the photographs had merely been printed in reverse.

The so-called "reversed photo theory," however, seemed so implausible that it has never been universally accepted by the naval community, even in the face of strong supporting evidence that this was actually the case. The noted German naval historian, Prof. Dr. Jürgen Rohwer, has accepted that theory as being correct, and Sir Ludovic Kennedy, author of the book *Pursuit—The Chase and Sinking of the Battleship Bismarck*, has also concluded that the several photographs in question had been printed in reverse.

Instead of being just a compilation of facts, information, and quotations from various sources, this book attempts to provide a narrative description of how the Battle of the Denmark Strait was fought and the significance of pertinent events leading up to the battle and in its aftermath. It clarifies the technical terminology often used in official reports so that its meaning can be readily understood by the average reader. In doing so, however, the book in no way compromises the essence of those documents and the accuracy of the information contained therein.

The scenario of the Battle of the Denmark Strait, as presented herein, is based on a comprehensive and detailed technical analysis of all of the documentary and photographic evidence currently available on the subject. Every item of data obtained from primary source documents was carefully evaluated in the development of this narrative of the battle. Any discrepancies found in the information derived from different sources were studied in-depth to determine which version was most likely to be correct in relation to the other evidence.

In developing the narrative for the events described in this book, the author consolidated and integrated all of the data and information from both sides into a single cohesive account of the event. Earlier descriptions of those events were amplified in this scenario with additional information where it seemed desirable to enhance the understanding of that event for the benefit of the reader. Additional information is also provided on the key participants in the battle and in subsequent actions to provide a personal perspective to the story of the battle.

Except for the timing of certain events associated with the Battle of the Denmark Strait and other material that was developed on the basis of a detailed technical analysis of the circumstances by the author, all of the other data and information contained in this book were derived from the bibliography and the other sources of information identified herein. The contribution of the author in this regard was to consolidate and integrate all of the data and information associated with each specific event into a single cohesive description that could be readily understood by the reader.

Specific references for all of the information contained in this book would be too numerous to mention, especially since certain facts may be included in multiple references, and therefore, such references are not included in this book. Suffice it to say that every fact mentioned in this book can be traced back to one of those references or to the technical analysis performed by the author, as fully explained herein.

This book is amply illustrated with photographs, not only of the *Bismarck* taken from the *Prinz Eugen* during the battle, but also of the other ships that participated in the overall operation or had historical significance related to the operation. The numbers in parentheses after the names of ships indicate the year in which they entered service. Photographs of some of the key personnel involved in the operation are also included. The photographs are supplemented by pencil sketches and diagrams prepared by the author to enhance the reader's understanding of the events that happened at the time.

The maps provided in this book are intended merely to graphically illustrate the movements of the ships involved in the various aspects of the overall operation. The landmasses shown on the maps are only approximate renditions of the actual configuration of the nations that they represent. Mercator projections with parallel meridians were used for small geographical areas, but conical projections were used for larger geographical areas for more realistic representation of horizontal distances at higher latitudes. Conical projections, however, result in some distortion of land-masses at the left and right sides of the maps. Where significant, latitude and longitude degrees are shown along the inside edges of the maps.

German terms are subject to a variety of translations, but in general, the interpretations are sufficiently similar to convey substantially the same meaning. For example, the term "Seekriegsleitung" refers to the office responsible for the direction of sea warfare in the German Naval High Command. The person in charge of that office can be called the "Chief of Staff of the Directorate of Sea Warfare", but in this book, that person is referred to as merely the "Director of Sea Warfare." The Collins German-English Dictionary was the primary source of English translations of German terms used in referenced German documents.

In addition to the *Prince of Wales* salvo plot, which shows the relative position of the *Bismarck* to that of the *Prince of Wales* throughout most of the battle, there are several other facts that tie the opposing forces together at certain points in time. It is well documented from Admiralty reports that the *Prince of Wales* opened fire on the *Bismarck* at 0553:00 at a range of 25,000 yards and a bearing of 335°. Testimony at the Admiralty enquiry into the sinking of the *Hood* reported that the *Prince of Wales* received a heavy hit shortly after firing its 12th salvo, most likely from *Bismarck's* second salvo, and this would place her 12th salvo at sometime after 0601.

Admiralty reports place the hit on the compass platform of the *Prince of Wales* at 0602, probably from the *Bismarck's* third salvo. The *Prince of Wales* began to turn away from the scene of battle at 0605, at which time the *Bismarck* was at a range of 14,500 yards and a bearing of 328°. The *Bismarck* battle film also includes the splashes from the last two single-shot salvos fired by the *Prince of Wales*, giving a good indication of when those shots were fired in relation to the *Bismarck* firing her last salvo just before she ceased fire at about 0610.

Within those parameters, a comprehensive, salvo-by-salvo description of the battle was painstakingly developed. The estimated timing of each salvo was based on the time of flight of the shells at the specific range fired, the average reaction time of the gunners to make azimuth and range corrections based on the fall of shot, and the recycle time for each gun system based on its rate of fire. Many iterations of this procedure were necessary to arrive at a scenario that best fit all of the facts and parameters in the case.

It is ludicrous to believe that the events that took place during the Battle of the Denmark Strait could be reconstructed down to the very last second. However, certain factors, such as the flight time of projectiles at specific ranges, are accurate to within a second or two. The average recycle time of the various gun systems and the reaction time for the gunners to readjust the aiming of the guns after each salvo, while somewhat less precise than flight times, can also be expressed in terms of seconds.

On the other hand, leaving all times rounded out to the nearest full minute would not allow for the description of events in the detail actually possible. The timing of the events described herein is therefore presented in multiples of five-second intervals. This provides clock times that are reasonably accurate for the purpose of describing how the battle was fought, and it greatly facilitates the telling of the story. Purists may object to this technique, but the only other alternative is to avoid completely coming up with a detailed scenario of the battle, as most others have done.

Time and distance constraints, often overlooked in other versions of the battle, were carefully considered in this scenario. Of particular importance was the relative speed between the *Bismarck* and the *Prinz Eugen*. The *Prinz Eugen's* speed chart shows that the cruiser sailed at a constant speed of 27.0 knots throughout the battle, and the maximum speed of the *Bismarck* was known to be 30.0 knots. Therefore, the *Bismarck* with a 3.0 knot speed advantage could gain at the most only 100 yards per minute on the *Prinz Eugen* with both ships traveling in the same general direction.

At that rate, it would have taken nearly three minutes for the *Bismarck* to gain one ship length on the *Prinz Eugen*, and this limitation is vital in assessing the progress of the *Bismarck* in successive photographs. The track of the *Prinz Eugen* during the battle is firmly established by her battle diagram, and it is known that the *Bismarck* came directly in the line of fire from the *Prinz Eugen* to the *Prince of Wales* at about 0608, as indicated in the *Prinz Eugen's* war diary. Therefore, the *Bismarck* must have been about 1500 yards astern of the *Prinz Eugen* at 0555, when the *Bismarck* opened fire on the *Hood*, allowing for a 200-yard loss in forward travel by the *Prinz Eugen* as a result of her turns between 0603 and 0608.

Those circumstances completely rule out any possibility that the *Bismarck* could have initially come up on the port side of the *Prinz Eugen*, turned to starboard at 0602, crossed the wake of the *Prinz Eugen*, circled around to the rear of the *Prinz Eugen*, moved up on the cruiser's starboard side for over two minutes, fallen back and re-crossed the wake of the *Prinz Eugen*, moved all the way up on the port side of the *Prinz Eugen* again, and then finally come between the *Prinz Eugen* and the *Prince of Wales* on the port side of the cruiser, all in six minutes or by 0608, as other versions of the battle suggest.

Timewise, the *Bismarck* could only have come between the *Prinz Eugen* and *Prince of Wales* at 0608 by sailing a straight-line course throughout the battle. After the war, Paul Schmalenbach, the second gunnery officer of the *Prinz Eugen*, prepared a battle diagram that showed the *Bismarck* on the port side of the *Prinz Eugen* from 0600 until after 0609, when the *Prinz Eugen* ceased fire. This diagram was based on his personal observation of the *Bismarck* coming up on the *Prinz Eugen*'s port side during the battle, and it gives additional credence to the concept of the battle as described herein.

In addition to the documentary and photographic evidence, great reliance was placed on the first-hand accounts by eyewitnesses on the scene. Baron von Müllenheim-Rechberg, the fourth gunnery officer of the *Bismarck* and one of her survivors, describes the battle in some detail, but makes no mention of any deviation from the *Bismarck*'s course during the action. Captain Brinkmann of the *Prinz Eugen* makes no mention of any turns by the *Bismarck*, even though the turns attributed to the *Bismarck* in other accounts of the battle would have put the *Prinz Eugen* in great jeopardy, not only from enemy fire but also by the *Bismarck* coming in close proximity to the cruiser.

Reports by Paulus Jasper and Paul Schmalenbach, the first and second gunnery officers of the *Prinz Eugen*, in the ship's war diary clearly place the *Bismarck* on the port side of the cruiser during the final phase of the battle. Flight Lt. Vaughn, an observer on board the RAF Sunderland flying boat that flew over the battle, reported on the action as seen from his vantage point. He described the *Prince of Wales* as coming under heavy and accurate fire from the *Bismarck* and subsequently turning away from the battle, but he made no mention of any turns by the *Bismarck*.

The scenario of the Battle of the Denmark Strait, as described herein, also fully considers the viewpoints of others as presented in exchanges on Internet forums and in private communications. Every effort was made to check out all points of view, especially the ones that differed with those of the author, to ensure that there was nothing of substance that had been overlooked. In the end, however, the author is solely responsible for the contents of this book, but with great appreciation for those who have earlier researched the available documentation, interviewed the combatants, and made that information available to the rest of us.

• PART ONE •

EVENTS LEADING UP
TO THE BATTLE

CHAPTER 1

IMPERIAL GERMAN NAVAL
CHALLENGE TO GREAT BRITAIN

A LTHOUGH THE BATTLE OF THE DENMARK STRAIT WAS not fought until 1941, events that took place as much as half a century earlier had an influence on certain aspects of the battle. During the reign of Kaiser Wilhelm I, the first emperor of the new German Empire (Second Reich) that was established in 1871 after the Franco-Prussian War, the Imperial German Navy (Kaiserliche Marine) had a modest number of ships, primarily for coastal defense purposes. At the time, Germany had only a few colonies, mostly in Africa and on certain islands in the Pacific, so there was no need for a huge navy.

When Kaiser Wilhelm I died in 1888, the German fleet consisted of 15 armored frigates, 3 cruising frigates, 15 corvettes, 6 protected cruisers, 7 light cruisers, and a number of other smaller vessels. Many of these ships were sailing vessels, and some had even been purchased from foreign shipyards. In contrast, by 1888 the British Royal Navy had already produced six first-line battleships, 25 turret ships (the precursor to the battleship), 22 central-battery ironclads, 16 broadside-ironclads, 12 armored cruisers, 26 protected cruisers, and a host of smaller warships of all descriptions.

Great Britain and Germany were on good terms during this period after having combined forces to defeat Napoleon at Waterloo in 1815. Their royal households had since been united by the marriage in 1856 of Crown Prince Friedrich of Prussia to Princess Victoria, the eldest daughter of Queen Victoria of England, and Britain looked forward to a partnership with a more liberal Germany under Friedrich when he ascended to the Imperial throne. Crown Prince Friedrich did become Emperor of Germany upon the death of his father, Wilhelm I, but his reign was short-lived. Already suffering from terminal throat cancer, he died only 99 days later, and was succeeded by his son, Crown Prince Wilhelm, who then became Kaiser Wilhelm II of Germany.

Wilhelm II did not share his parent's liberal and pro-Anglican views, and he soon embarked on a course of action that eventually led to war with Great Britain. One of the first actions that he took was to dismiss Otto von Bismarck, the first Chancellor of the German Empire, whose agenda was too conservative for his taste. Wilhelm II was a naval enthusiast, and he soon undertook a naval expansion program, building eight battleships of the *Siegfried*-class, four battleships of the *Brandenburg*-class, and five battleships of the *Kaiser Friedrich III*-class. Following the practice of Great Britain, the names of ships in the Kaiserliche Marine were preceded by the initials "SMS," which stood for "Seiner Majestät Schiff" (His Majesty's Ship).

In June 1897, Wilhelm II appointed Rear-Admiral Alfred von Tirpitz as State Secretary of the Imperial Navy Office (Reichsmarineamt) with the express purpose of creating a fleet that would challenge the supremacy of the Royal Navy, at least in the North Sea. Wilhelm II never expected Germany to reach parity with the Royal Navy, but if they could build one-third as many ships as Great Britain, Germany would have a fleet at least equal to her greatest antagonist, the British Home Fleet. He reasoned that the remaining two-thirds of the Royal Navy would be needed to defend Britain's far-flung possessions throughout the world.

Admiral von Tirpitz soon obtained Reichstag approval for the construction of five battleships of the *Wittelsbach*-class, then five battleships of the *Braunschweig*-class, and finally five of the *Deutschland*-class. In the meantime, Great Britain had completed nine battleships of the *Majestic*-class, five of the *Canopus*-class, eight of the *Formidable*-class, five of the *Duncan*-class, two of the *Triumph*-class, eight of the *King Edward VII*-class, and two of the *Lord Nelson*-class (39 battleships in all). These ships on both sides generally displaced up to 15,000 tons and had a main armament of four 11-inch guns (German) or four 12-inch guns (British) in two double turrets, one forward and one aft, with smaller caliber guns mounted along their sides.

In 1906, Great Britain completed HMS *Dreadnought*, the first all-big-gun battleship with its main armament consisting of guns of the same caliber, i.e., ten 12-inch guns, and this type of ship became the standard for all capital ship construction throughout the world thereafter. The *Dreadnought* was followed by three battleships of the *Bellerophon*-class, three of the *St. Vincent*-class, and three of the *Neptune*-class, all of which also carried ten 12-inch guns. These ships had a displacement of up to 20,000 tons.

In 1910, Great Britain increased the caliber of its naval guns to 13.5 inches, and it subsequently produced four battleships of the *Orion*-class, four of the *King George V*-class, and four of the *Iron Duke*-class, all with ten 13.5-inch guns and displacing up to 26,000 tons. Britain also completed three additional battleships intended for foreign nations and incorporated them into the Royal Navy, making a total of 25 Dreadnought-type battleships completed by 1914.

Britain's First Sea Lord at the time, Admiral of the Fleet John A. "Jackie" Fisher, not only devised the concept of the all-big-gun battleship, but he also came up with the idea of the battle cruiser, a ship with main armament guns the same caliber as that of a battleship, but with the speed of a cruiser, sacrificing armor protection to attain the speed desired. He believed that if more big guns could be quickly brought to the scene of battle, they would defeat the enemy before any serious damage could be done to their own ships. The first battle cruiser to enter the Royal Navy was the *Invincible*, with eight 12-inch guns, and she was followed by three battle cruisers of the *Indefatigable*-class, also with eight 12-inch guns. Britain then built three battle cruisers of the *Lion*-class, and the *Tiger*, all with eight 13.5-inch guns. These battle cruisers were all completed by 1914.

Germany followed suit with four *Dreadnought*-type battleships of the *Nassau*-class with twelve 11-inch guns and four of the *Helgoland*-class with twelve 12-inch guns. These were followed by five battleships of the *Kaiser*-class and five of the *König*-class, all with ten 12-inch guns. Germany also built several battle cruisers in answer to those produced by the Royal Navy, beginning with the *Von der Tann* with eight 11-inch guns. She was followed by two battle cruisers of the *Moltke*-class and the *Seydlitz*, all with ten 11-inch guns, and the *Derfflinger* with eight 12-inch guns. All of these German battleships and battle cruisers were completed by 1914.

In the meantime, the Armstrong-Whitworth Co., Great Britain's major arms producer at the time, had developed the 15-inch naval gun, which became the standard on the next generation of battleships and battle cruisers. In 1912-13, the keels were laid for five new battleships of the

German pre-dreadnought battleship SMS *Schleswig-Holstein* (1908).
Photo courtesy of MaritimeQuest

Queen Elizabeth-class, and in 1913-14, the keels were laid for five new battleships of the *Royal Sovereign*-class, each of which would carry eight 15-inch guns in four double turrets, two forward and two aft, and displace nearly 30,000 tons. The British also laid down two battle cruisers of the *Renown*-class in 1915, and these ships would carry six 15-inch guns in three double turrets, two forward and one aft, and displace nearly 28,000 tons.

Not to be outdone by the British, the Germans countered by laying down four battleships of the *Bayern*-class from 1913 to 1915. These ships were also designed to have eight 15-inch guns in four double turrets, two forward and two aft, and displace 28,000 tons. Four battle cruisers of the *Mackensen*-class were also laid down in 1915. These ships were to mount eight 14-inch guns in answer to the British 13.5-inch guns of the previous generation of battleships and battle cruisers. Like the *Bayern*-class of battleships, their guns were also arranged in four double turrets, two forward and two aft.

The ships on both sides would soon be put to the test in the Battle of Jutland. The Kaiserliche Marine had the advantage of selecting the time when it was most favorable for them to come out of its base and challenge

German battleship SMS *Ostfriesland* (1911) with naval zeppelin L-31 overhead.
Photo courtesy of MaritimeQuest

the Royal Navy. Its base at Wilhelmshaven on the Jade Bay (Jadebusen) was too well protected by shore batteries on both sides of the inlet to permit a preemptive strike by the Royal Navy, so the British had to wait for the Germans to make the first move. Vice-Admiral Reinhard Scheer, Commander of the German High Seas Fleet (Hochseeflotte), composed of 16 battleships, finally chose to come out on the morning of 31 May 1916.

Scheer sent out Vice-Admiral Franz Hipper's scouting squadron of five battle cruisers in advance in an attempt to lure smaller elements of the Royal Navy into combat with his superior force. The British had broken the German naval code, however, and they became aware in advance of the planned movements of the German fleet. Vice-Admiral David Beatty's battle cruiser force, consisting of his flagship, the *Lion*, and three battle cruisers of the First Battle Cruiser Squadron, sailed out of its base at Rosyth on the Firth of Forth near Edinburgh, Scotland to intercept the German fleet. At about the same time, Admiral John Jellicoe set sail with the British Grand Fleet, consisting of 28 battleships and three battle cruisers, from its base at Scapa Flow in the Orkney Islands off the northern coast of Scotland to engage the German High Seas Fleet.

The opposing battle cruiser squadrons made contact at about 1600, and within a few minutes, the Germans drew first blood when the battle cruiser *Von der Tann* scored five hits on the battle cruiser *Indefatigable* and sank the British ship. Hipper was initially successful in drawing Beatty's squadron toward Scheer's High Seas Fleet, and he was able to sink the British battle cruiser *Queen Mary* in the process at 1625. Upon seeing the superior enemy force, Beatty turned north and led the German ships toward Jellicoe's oncoming Grand Fleet. Soon the major forces on both sides became engaged in a furious battle before Scheer realized the he was now facing the entire British Grand Fleet. Scheer was finally able to extricate himself from combat with the far superior force and escape back to his base, but not without loss.

A couple of hours later, at 1833, the British lost an additional battle cruiser, the *Invincible*, flagship of the Third Battle Cruiser Squadron attached to the Grand Fleet, taking its commander, Rear-Admiral Horace Hood, down with the ship. Additional British losses included the armored cruisers *Defence*, *Warrior*, and *Black Prince*, all of First Cruiser Squadron, which was commanded by Rear-Admiral Robert Arbuthnot, who went down with his flagship, the *Defence*. The British also lost a destroyer flotilla

German battleship SMS *Grosser Kurfürst* (1914). *Photo courtesy of MaritimeQuest*

leader and seven additional destroyers. A total of over 6,000 officers and men of the Royal Navy lost their lives in the battle of Jutland with an additional 500 being wounded.

On the German side, the Kaiserliche Marine lost the battle cruiser *Lützow*, the pre-Dreadnought battleship *Pommern*, four light cruisers and five destroyers. In addition, several German ships suffered heavy damage and were out of service for a considerable period of time. Personnel losses included over 2,500 killed and 500 wounded. Although the numbers would indicate that the Germans came out better than the British in terms of ships sunk and casualties, the British achieved their objective in keeping the German High Seas Fleet bottled up at its base.

Four 15-inch gun battleships of the *Queen Elizabeth*-class, the *Barham*, *Malaya*, *Valiant*, and *Warspite*, participated in the battle of Jutland as part of the Fifth Battle Squadron of the Grand Fleet. During the battle, the *Barham* was hit five times and suffered 26 fatalities, the *Malaya* was hit eight times and had 65 of her crew fatally wounded, and the *Warspite* was hit 15 times and suffered 14 killed in the battle. The *Revenge* and *Royal Oak*, 15-inch gun battleships of the *Royal Sovereign*-class, served in the First Battle Squadron at the battle of Jutland, but like the *Valiant* of the

German battleship SMS *Bayern* (1916) scuttled at Scapa Flow. *Photo courtesy of MaritimeQuest*

Fifth Battle Squadron, they suffered no damage or casualties.

Much has been written about the demise of the three British battle cruisers at Jutland since they all sank as a result of catastrophic explosions of their magazines. Many attributed their sinking to inadequate deck armor, allowing enemy shells to plunge through their decks into the ammunition magazines below. However, others believe that they were victims of shell hits on their turrets, which caused a chain reaction of fire and explosions down to the ammunition handling rooms and finally to the magazines. In any event, the circumstances were carefully analyzed by explosives experts and naval architects to determine what actions could be taken to avoid a recurrence of these incidents in the future.

British naval designers had just completed the design of a super battle cruiser that would have the same armament as the latest British battleships, i.e., eight 15-inch guns, and would also have the speed of a cruiser, 32 knots. To meet these requirements, the ship would have to be 680 feet long, have a beam of 104 feet, and have a standard displacement of 36,300 tons. The keels of four such vessels of the *Hood*-class were laid down in 1916, but with the lessons learned from the battle of Jutland, their specifications were changed to improve the armor protection of those ships. Over 5,000 tons of additional armor was specified, increasing the displacement of the vessels to 41,200 tons and reducing their speed to 31 knots.

With the war's increasingly high demand for competing resources, Germany had to begin cutting back on naval construction in 1916. Of the four battleships of the *Bayern*-class laid down, only the *Bayern* and *Baden* were completed in 1916. All work on the four *Mackensen*-class battle cruisers was suspended in 1917, even though three of those ships had already been launched. With the cutback in heavy German naval construction, the British could afford to reduce the level of their own costly naval expansion efforts as well. Four of the five *Hood*-class battle cruisers were cancelled before they could even be launched. Work on the *Hood* itself, however, was allowed to proceed, and she was launched in August 1918 and completed in March 1920 at the John Brown shipyard on the Clyde River at Clydebank near Glasgow in Scotland.

The armistice of 11 November 1918 ended hostilities in World War I and caused the Kaiserliche Marine to surrender all of its ships to the Allied powers. The British directed that the German High Seas Fleet be interned at the British naval base at Scapa Flow, and the Germans com-

British battleship HMS *Ramillies* (1917). *Photo courtesy of MaritimeQuest*

British battle cruiser HMS *Repulse* (1916). *Photo courtesy of MaritimeQuest*

plied with the order by sailing their ships into the anchorage. Without a peace treaty, however, Germany and Great Britain were technically still at war despite the armistice, and the German crews, fearing that the ships might still be distributed to France and Italy, their other arch rivals, decided to scuttle them in place.

In defiance of their captors, on 21 June 1919, the Germans raised the

Imperial naval ensign and opened the seacocks of their ships upon a pre-arranged signal from their commander, Admiral Ludwig von Reuter. The 74 German warships at Scapa Flow, including 11 battleships, 5 battle cruisers, 8 cruisers, and 50 destroyers, were all anchored at the western end of the harbor between the islands of Hoy and Mainland. The British guarding force took immediate action to board the sinking ships in an attempt to stop the scuttling, killing and wounding a number of German sailors who tried to interfere with their actions. The British succeeded in beaching the battleship *Baden*, three cruisers, and 18 destroyers, allowing them to be evaluated and then used as targets or scrapped.

Most of the sunken ships were eventually salvaged and broken up for their steel, but three battleships and four cruisers remain on the bottom of Scapa Flow where divers may visit them after receiving a permit to do so. The British strongly protested the scuttling of the German ships, and they reacted harshly to those responsible for it, including the crewmembers of the ships involved, but they were secretly relieved by the action taken. Their allies in the war, France and Italy, had each hoped to obtain a quarter of the German vessels under the peace treaty, but that would have decreased the numerical advantage that the British had over those other navies and which they wanted to keep.

The Treaty of Versailles was finally signed by the Germans on 28 June 1919 and ratified by the German National Assembly on 9 July 1919 after heated protests against what they considered to be overly harsh terms. Under the treaty, German naval forces would be limited 15,000 men. Germany could retain six pre-*Dreadnought* battleships, but new construction of capital ships could not exceed 10,000 tons displacement each. Germany could also have six cruisers not to exceed 6,000 tons displacement each, twelve destroyers not to exceed 800 tons displacement each, twelve torpedo boats not to exceed 200 tons displacement each, and no submarines.

In 1920 the German battleship *Ostfriesland*, which was not among the ships of the German High Seas Fleet interned at Scapa Flow, was turned over to the United States as war reparations. The ship was subsequently used as a target for the demonstration of air power over warships conducted by Brig. Gen. William "Billy" Mitchell of the U.S. Army Air Corps in cooperation with the U.S. Navy off Cape Hatteras, North Carolina in July 1921.

CHAPTER **2**

INTERNATIONAL NAVAL DEVELOPMENTS
AFTER WORLD WAR I

THE END OF WORLD WAR I LEFT THE ALLIED POWERS WITH large numbers of warships that they no longer had any need for, but there was also a desire to upgrade their fleets with more modern warships, especially in capital ships. With an eye toward the future, a concerted disarmament program was undertaken by the major powers to reduce the size of their fleets and curtail new construction of warships. The Washington Naval Conference, which was concluded in February 1922, resulted in an agreement by Great Britain, the United States, Japan, France, and Italy that no new capital ships would be built for the next ten years, with the exception of two new ships for Great Britain as replacements to compensate for the age of its fleet. Capital ships would be limited to 35,000 tons in displacement and guns of a caliber not to exceed 16 inches.

The Washington Naval Treaty also specified the total tonnage that each nation was allowed in capital ships and aircraft carriers in accordance with the established ratio of 5:5:3:1.67:1.67 for Great Britain, the United states, Japan, France, and Italy, respectively. Under this formula, Great Britain was allocated 525,000 tons in capital ships and 135,000 tons in aircraft carriers. In recognition of the United States becoming the second largest naval power in the world, America was allocated the same tonnage in capital ships and aircraft carriers as Great Britain. Japan's earlier defeat of the Russian fleet in 1905 established that country as a major naval power, and therefore, Japan was allocated 315,000 tons in capital ships and 81,000 tons in aircraft carriers. France and Italy were each allocated 175,000 tons in capital ships and 60,000 tons in aircraft carriers.

Great Britain was allowed to keep the *Hood* as an exception to the 35,000-ton limit for capital ships, but Britain could not justify any more ships of that size, which was considered to be the minimum size for an acceptable battle cruiser. There were two new battleships on the drawing board, the *Nelson* and the *Rodney*, and their design was altered to meet the 35,000-ton limitation. In the end, they were to be 710 feet long, have a beam of 106 feet, and displace 34,000 tons. The *Nelson* and *Rodney* would have turbine engines that could develop 45,000 SHP and drive the ships at their maximum speed of 23 knots with two shafts. They would carry nine 16-inch guns in three triple turrets, all forward with the center turret above the forward and rear turrets, twelve 6-inch guns in three double mounts on either side of the ships, a number of antiaircraft guns, and two submerged 24.5-inch torpedo tubes.

The arrangement of the main armament turrets of the *Nelson* and *Rodney* would be unique to naval construction throughout the world, and the guns of their main armament would be of the largest caliber ever used on British capital ships. Both ships were laid down on 28 December 1922 at private shipyards, the *Nelson* at Armstrong-Whitworth on the Tyne River

British battle cruiser HMS *Hood* (1920).
Photo courtesy of U.S. Naval History and Heritage Command

at Newcastle, and the *Rodney* at Cammell Laird on the River Mersey at Birkenhead near Liverpool. The *Nelson* was launched in September 1925 and completed in June 1927 while the *Rodney* was launched in December 1925 and completed in August 1927.

In addition to the *Hood*, Great Britain retained all of its other 15-inch gun capital ships, including the five battleships of the *Queen Elizabeth*-class, five battleships of the *Royal Sovereign*-class, and two battle cruisers of the *Renown*-class, to complete its allocation of 15 capital ships. All of its huge fleet of 12-inch gun and 13.5-inch gun ships were relegated to the scrap heap. Great Britain, like the United States and Japan, converted several excess battle cruisers or battle cruiser hulls into aircraft carriers.

With the capital ship situation well in hand, Great Britain then looked toward replacing its obsolete armored cruisers with more modern heavy cruisers. From 1925 to 1930, Britain built a total of 13 County-class heavy cruisers named mostly for English counties (shires), except for the *Berwick*, named for a county in Scotland, and the *Australia* and *Canberra*, built for the Royal Australian Navy. These ships were actually of three different classes with minor differences between each, but they were all about 630 feet long, had a beam of 66-68 feet, and displaced about 9,500 tons. Their geared turbine engines developed 80,000 SHP and could drive the ships at a maximum speed of 32 knots. They all carried eight 8-inch guns in four double turrets, two forward and two aft, four 4-inch antiaircraft guns, and eight 21-inch torpedo tubes in two quadruple mounts.

From 1927 to 1931, the British also built two smaller heavy cruisers, the *Exeter* and *York*. These ships were 575 feet long, had a beam of 57-58 feet, and displaced about 8,500 tons. Their geared turbines produced 80,000 SHP and could drive these ships at a maximum speed of 32 knots. They carried only six 8-inch guns in three double turrets, two forward and one aft, four 4-inch antiaircraft guns, and six 21-inch torpedo tubes in two triple mountings.

The London Naval Conference, which ended in April 1930, extended the moratorium on capital ship construction for five more years to the end of 1936. Existing capital ships would still be limited in size to 35,000 tons, but further reduced in number to 15 each for Great Britain and the United States and 9 for Japan. France and Italy refused to sign the London Naval Treaty and therefore were not included in any specific numerical limitation. The powers agreed to reconvene in 1935 to reconsider the situation as it existed at that time, but in the meanwhile, only modernization of their existing assets could be undertaken.

An extensive modernization of Britain's World War I-vintage battleships and battle cruisers was instituted in 1930, and this extended to the outbreak of World War II in 1939. For the most part, this modernization involved the increase in antiaircraft protection with the installation of dual 4-inch gun mounts and rapid fire pom-pom guns as well as fire control improvements with the installation of high-angle control system (HACS) directors. Some ships received additional underwater protection and a variety of other improvements. The *Hood* received some improvements over the years, and she was scheduled for a complete refit after the modernization of the *Queen Elizabeth*-class battleships had been completed.

When Britain's heavy cruiser program was well on its way, the nation turned its attention to modernizing its light cruiser fleet. From 1930 to 1935, Great Britain constructed five light cruisers of the *Leander*-class. These ships were 554 feet long, had a beam of 56 feet and displaced about 7,000 tons. Their geared turbines produced 72,000 SHP and could drive the ships at a maximum speed of 32.5 knots. They carried eight 6-inch guns in the traditional arrangement of four double turrets, two forward and two aft, four 4-inch antiaircraft guns, and eight 21-inch torpedo tubes in two quadruple mounts. These ships were followed by three modified *Leander*-class light cruisers with the same basic features built for the Royal Australian Navy from 1933 to 1935.

Great Britain then built four somewhat smaller light cruisers of the *Arethusa*-class from 1933 to 1937. These ships were 506 feet long, had a beam of 51 feet, and displaced a little over 5,000 tons. Their turbine engines produced 64,000 SHP and could drive the ships at their maximum speed of 32 knots. They carried six 6-inch guns in three double turrets, two forward and one aft, four 4-inch antiaircraft guns, and six 21-inch torpedo tubes in two triple mounts.

From 1934-1939, Britain constructed eight Town-class light cruisers, often referred to as the *Southampton*-class. These ships were 591 feet long, had a beam of 64 feet, and displaced about 9,000 tons. Their turbine engines generated 75,000 SHP and could drive these ships at a maximum speed of 32 knots. They carried twelve 6-inch guns in four triple turrets, two forward and two aft, eight 4-inch guns in four twin mounts, and six 21-inch torpedo tubes in two triple mounts.

British battleship HMS *Nelson* (1927). *Photo courtesy of MaritimeQuest*

The Town-class cruisers were followed by two modified Town-class light cruisers, the *Edinburgh* and *Belfast*, built in 1936-39. The *Edinburgh* and *Belfast* were slightly larger than their predecessors, being 613 feet long, having a beam of 63 feet, and displacing 10,300 tons. Their turbines developed 82,500 SHP providing a maximum speed of 32.5 knots. Their main armament was the same as on the *Southampton*-class ships, i.e., twelve 6-inch guns, but they had twelve 4-inch antiaircraft guns in six twin mounts, two mounts more with four additional guns. They also had the same number of torpedo tubes, six 21-inch tubes in two triple mounts.

During World War I, the Japanese laid down two new 33,000-ton battleships, the *Nagato* and *Mutsu*. The unique feature of these ships would be the installation of 16-inch guns in lieu of the 14-inch size previously used, and they would be the first battleships in the world that would mount guns of that caliber. The United States also developed a 16-inch gun, and the last three battleships to be started during World War I (i.e., the *Colorado*, *Maryland*, and *West Virginia*) were equipped with eight 16-inch guns in lieu of the twelve 14-inch guns used on its earlier battleships, i.e., the *Pennsylvania*, *Arizona*, *New Mexico*, *Mississippi*, *Idaho*, *Tennessee*, and *California*).

British County-class heavy cruiser *Devonshire* (1929).
Photo courtesy of U.S. Naval History and Heritage Command

Before the next London Conference could take place in 1936, the secondary naval powers (i.e., France, Italy, and Germany) began capital ship building programs that would soon eclipse that of the Royal Navy. France laid down the battleships *Dunkerque* in 1931 and *Strasbourg* in 1934. These ships displaced 26,500 tons, carried eight 13-inch guns in two quadruple mounts, both forward, and had a speed of almost 30 knots. Germany had renounced the Versailles Treaty, and in 1934, she began building two battleships, the *Gneisenau* and the *Scharnhorst*. These ships displaced 32,000 tons, carried nine 11-inch guns, and had a speed of over 30 knots.

In 1934, Italy laid down the 35,000-ton battleships *Littorio* and *Vittorio Veneto,* which carried nine 15-inch guns in three triple mounts and had a speed of 30 knots. These ships would be followed by the *Roma* in 1938. France countered the next year with the 35,000-ton battleship *Richelieu,* which carried eight 15-inch guns in two quadruple turrets, both forward of the bridge structure. The *Richelieu* would be followed by a sister ship, the *Jean Bart,* in 1936. Based on the separate Anglo-German Naval Treaty of 1935, Germany laid down the battleships *Bismarck* and *Tirpitz* in 1936. These ships were intended to displace 35,000 tons, carry eight 15-inch guns in four double turrets, two forward and two aft, and have a speed of 30 knots.

The Admiralty rushed plans to complete the design of their new

35,000-ton entry into the battleship race. Several alternative armament systems were under consideration, including guns ranging in size from 14 to 16 inches and a variety of mounting configurations. Difficulty had been experienced with the 16-inch guns of the *Nelson* and *Rodney*, so that caliber was rejected. The 15-inch gun was the current standard of the Royal Navy and the selection of that caliber for the new ships would minimize logistics problems with respect to ammunition and spares. Besides the traditional arrangement of eight 15-inch guns mounted in four double turrets, nine 15-inch guns mounted in three triple turrets was another possibility that was considered.

The Admiralty finally decided on 14-inch guns of an improved type that had a much longer service life than earlier guns of that caliber. The 14-inch shells to be used with these guns were also of an improved type that would have better ballistic performance and greater armor-penetrating power than the 14-inch projectiles used before. These 14-inch projectiles, however, would each weigh only 1,600 pounds compared with 1,920 pounds for the standard 15-inch shell. Although a 14-inch shell did not pack as much of a wallop as a larger caliber shell, that caliber allowed a larger number of guns to be employed, and a salvo of nine to twelve 14-inch guns would have a correspondingly greater probability of a hit than an eight 15-inch gun salvo.

At first, the Admiralty specified twelve 14-inch guns to be mounted in three quadruple turrets, two forward and one aft. The quadruple turret had been chosen by the French for their battle cruisers with 13-inch guns and later for their battleships with 15-inch guns, but with only two turrets, both forward. With weight becoming an issue in the final design of these ships, two guns were sacrificed in the interests of improved armor protection and speed. It was decided that the second forward turret superimposed over the foremost turret would be only a twin turret rather than a quadruple turret. Ten 14-inch guns would still give these ships a broadside weight of about 7.9 tons, which is somewhat greater that the broadside weight of eight 15-inch guns mounted on other British battleships (7.7 tons) and on the *Bismarck* (7.1 tons).

The 14-inch gun system turned out to be a poor choice for the Admiralty. The system was plagued with technical problems from the beginning, and it would seriously affect the performance of the *Prince of Wales* in her battle against the *Bismarck*. The rate of fire of the 14-inch gun system was about the same as with the standard British 15-inch gun system, i.e., two rounds per minute (one round every 30 seconds), but not as fast as the 2.5 rounds per minute (one round every 25 seconds) for the *Bismarck*. For their final battleship, the *Vanguard*, which was begun in 1941, the British reverted back to the eight 15-inch gun system used on their earlier battleships, taking advantage of surplus turrets and guns available.

The British waited for the expiration of the London Naval Treaty on 31 December 1936, which would end the moratorium on capital ship construction, and on the following day, they began construction on their new 35,000-ton battleships, the *King George V* and *Prince of Wales*. The *King George V* was laid down at Vickers-Armstrong (Tyne) near Newcastle on 1 January 1937, launched on 21 February 1939 and completed on 11 December 1940. During the first part of 1941, she was assigned to the Home Fleet stationed at Scapa Flow and was involved in escorting convoys from North America to the British Isles. The *Prince of Wales* was laid down at the Cammell Laird Shipyard at Birkenhead near Liverpool on 1 January 1937, launched on 3 May 1939, and completed on 31 March 1941.

The *King George V* and *Prince of Wales* were followed in the same year by three more ships of the *King George V*-class, i.e., the *Duke of York*, *Howe*, and *Anson*. The *Duke of York* was laid down on 5 May 1937 at the John Brown Shipyard at Clydebank near Glasgow, Scotland, which had built the *Hood* and more recently the Cunard ocean liners *Queen Mary* and *Queen Elizabeth*. The *Howe* was laid down on 1 June 1937 at the Fairfield Shipyard at Govan on the Clyde near Glasgow, Scotland, and the *Anson* was laid down on 20 July 1937 at the Swan Hunter Shipyard at Wallsend on the Tyne near Newcastle.

The *King George V*-class of battleships had an overall length of 745 feet and a beam of 104 feet. While the British made a sincere effort to hold down the displacement of these ships to the prescribed limit of 35,000 tons, their actual standard displacement slightly exceeded that figure at first and increased with wartime modifications. At completion, the *King George V* had a standard displacement of 36,700 tons, while the *Prince of Wales* displaced 38,000 tons in 1941. Their turbine engines generated 125,000 SHP and could drive these ships at a maximum speed of 29 knots. In addition to their main armament of ten 14-inch guns, the *King George V*-class of battleships also carried sixteen 5.25-inch dual-purpose guns in eight dual mounts and a host of antiaircraft guns.

CHAPTER **3**

THE GERMAN NAVY UNDER
THE WEIMAR REPUBLIC

K AISER WILHELM II ABDICATED THE GERMAN IMPERIAL
Throne on 8 November 1918 and fled with his family to
Holland. On the following day, Philipp Scheidemann, head of the Social
Democratic coalition in the Reichstag, proclaimed the German Republic
with Friedrich Ebert as its first President. On 11 November, an armistice
was signed by representatives of the new German government, ending
hostilities in World War I. The official end of the war came with the sign-
ing of the Treaty of Versailles on 28 June 1919, and immediately thereafter
the German political leaders held a convention in Weimar to establish a
constitution for the new republic, which then became popularly known
as the Weimar Republic. The constitution was approved on 11 August
1919, and subsequent elections confirmed Friedrich Ebert as the first President of the Deutsches Reich, as the new republic was known in Germany.

On 1 September 1919, Vice-Admiral Adolf von Trotha was appointed
as the first Director of Naval Affairs (Chef der Marineleitung) in the new
government. The ships that Germany was allowed to keep under the
Treaty of Versailles became part of the provisional navy (Vorläufige Reichsmarine) of the new republic. The navy included six pre-Dreadnought battleships of the *Braunschweig* and *Deutschland* classes, each of which was
398 feet long, had a beam of 73 feet, and displaced 13,200 tons. They
carried four 11-inch guns in two double turrets, one forward and one aft,
and a number of guns of different calibers in their secondary armament.
Their three-cylinder triple-expansion engines developed 16,000 SHP and
could drive the ships at a maximum speed of 18 knots. Also included were
six light cruisers of the *Gazelle* and *Bremen* classes, which displaced about

3,000 tons and carried ten 10.5 cm (4-inch) guns, plus twelve destroyers, and twelve torpedo boats.

Of the capital ships allowed, only two were actually placed in service, the *Deutschland*-class battleships *Schlesien* and *Schleswig-Holstein*. These ships had been laid down in 1905 and completed in 1908, and they were now only suitable for coastal defense purposes. The *Schleswig-Holstein* became the flagship of the Reichsmarine and held that position until 1932, when she was converted into a training vessel. The *Schlesien* then took over that function until later replaced by newer warships. The *Schleswig-Holstein* had the distinction of firing the opening shots of World War II when she bombarded the Polish fortress of Westerplatte guarding the harbor of Danzig in the early morning hours of 1 September 1939.

Vice-Admiral William Michaelis succeeded Admiral von Trotha as Director of Naval Affairs on 1 March 1920, and he in turn was succeeded by Vice-Admiral Paul Behnke seven months later on 1 October 1920. In March 1921, the Reichsmarine was formally established by the Reichstag, allowing the adjective "Vorläufige" (provisional) to be dropped, and effective 1 April 1921, the Navy of the Weimar Republic became known as just the "Reichsmarine."

The German government wanted to keep up its naval shipbuilding capability, so it ordered the construction of a new light cruiser at its Wilhelmshaven Naval Shipyard. The *Emden* was laid down on 8 December 1921, launched on 7 January 1925, and completed on 15 October 1925. The *Emden* was 508 feet long, had a beam of 47 feet, and displaced 5,600 tons. Her turbine engines developed 46,500 SHP, and she had a top speed of 29.5 knots. The *Emden* carried eight 15cm (5.9-inch) guns in single mounts, two forward, two aft, and two on either side of the ship, and four 21-inch torpedo tubes in two double mounts.

On 1 October 1924, Admiral Hans Zenker became the Director of Naval Affairs, a post that he held until 30 September 1928. Under his leadership, German naval architects began designing more modern cruisers and capital ships to replace the obsolete ships that the Navy was allowed to retain under the Treaty of Versailles. The first of these ships were the "K"-class light cruisers, of which the *Königsberg* was laid down at Wilhelmshaven Naval Shipyard on 12 April 1926, launched on 26 March 1927, and completed on 17 April 1929. The *Königsberg* was followed by the *Karlsruhe*, which was laid down at the Deutsche Werke ship-

German pre-dreadnought battleship *Schlesien* (1908). *Photo courtesy of MaritimeQuest*

German light cruiser *Königsberg* (1929). *Photo courtesy of MaritimeQuest*

yard in Kiel on 27 July 1926, launched on 20 August 1927, and completed on 6 November 1929, and the *Köln*, which was laid down at the Wilhelmshaven Naval Shipyard on 7 July 1926, launched on 23 May 1928, and completed on 15 January 1930.

The "K"-class light cruisers were 571 feet long, had a beam of 50 feet, and displaced 6,650 tons. Their turbine engines produced 68,000 SHP, and their top speed was 32.5 knots. They were also equipped with two ten-cylinder, four-stroke MAN diesel engines for cruising purposes at 10 knots. The "K"-class cruisers carried nine 15cm (5.9-inch) guns in three triple turrets, one forward and two aft, with their after turrets offset from the centerline of the ships, the foremost to starboard and the rearmost to port. They also carried six 8.8cm (3.5-inch) antiaircraft guns in three twin mounts and twelve 21-inch torpedo tubes in four triple mounts.

The "K"-class cruisers were followed by two similar light cruisers, the *Leipzig* and the *Nürnberg*, which had the same armament as the "K"-class cruisers. The *Leipzig* was laid down at the Wilhelmshaven Naval Shipyard on 18 April 1928, launched on 18 October 1929, and completed on 8 October 1931. She was 581 feet, had a beam of 53 feet, and displaced 6,515 tons. Her turbine engines, which developed 60,000 SHP, were connected to her two outboard shafts while her four seven-cylinder, double-acting MAN diesel engines, which developed a total of 12,400 bhp, were connected to her center shaft. Together, they could drive the ship up to 32 knots.

After the *Leipzig* had been completed, there were differences of opinion in the Naval High Command regarding the design of the next light cruiser in the series, with some favoring a larger ship to provide better protection and increased speed, but in the end, it was decided to remain with the *Leipzig* design. The *Nürnberg* was laid down on 4 November 1933 at the Deutsche Werke shipyard in Kiel, launched on 8 December 1934, and completed on 12 November 1935. She was 594 feet long, had a beam of 54 feet, and displaced 6,980 tons. Her engines and speed were similar to the original *Leipzig*.

Germany was allowed to build replacement capital ships, but they could not exceed 10,000 tons in displacement, and they could not have guns exceeding 11 inches in caliber. This posed quite a challenge to German naval architects. How could they design a capital ship with those limitations, squeezing the features of a battleship into the hull of a cruiser?

They considered all of the factors involved, came up with several alternative designs, and finally decided on a very unique solution. No such ship had ever before been conceived, so the Germans merely called it "Panzerschiff" (armored ship). The world would soon come to know that type of vessel by the term "pocket battleship."

The Panzerschiff would nominally displace 10,000 tons, but would achieve that displacement by having a fully welded hull and other weight-saving features. They would be propelled by eight diesel engines that could generate a total of 56,800 HP and could drive the ships through two shafts at a speed of up to 26.5 knots. They would have an overall length of 610 feet, beam of 69 feet, and draught of 19 feet. These ships would carry six 11-inch guns in two triple mounts, one forward and one aft, and a secondary armament of eight 5.9-inch guns in single mounts, four on either side of the ship along the main deck. The ships would also carry eight 21-inch torpedo tubes in two quadruple mounts on the afterdeck and two aircraft.

On 1 October 1928, Admiral Erich Johann Albert Raeder succeeded Admiral Zenker as Director of Naval Affairs. Raeder, like his predecessors, began his naval career in the Kaiserliche Marine, and in 1912 he became the Chief of Staff for Admiral Franz von Hipper, Commander of the First Scouting Group of battle cruisers involved in the battle of Jutland. Raeder was of the same mind as Zenker, and he pushed for the construction of the new Panzerschiffe.

The first Panzerschiff, the *Deutschland*, was laid down on 5 February 1929 at the Deutsche Werke shipyard in Kiel, launched on 19 May 1931, and completed on 1 April 1933. The *Deutschland* was followed by two ships of an improved design. The *Admiral Scheer* was laid down at the Wilhelmshaven Naval Shipyard on 25 June 1931, launched on 1 April 1933, and completed on 12 November 1934, and the *Admiral Graf Spee* was also laid down at Wilhelmshaven 15 months later on 1 October 1932, launched on 30 June 1934, and completed on 6 January 1936. The *Deutschland* had a curved bridge structure that made it look more like a cruise ship than a warship. It also had a relatively thin cylindrical structure behind the bridge to support its forward range finder. In contrast, the *Admiral Scheer* and *Admiral Graf Spee* had massive square-shaped towers to support their forward range finders. They also had their forward fire control directors placed on a second deck ahead of the bridge tower instead of behind the bridge as in the case of the *Deutschland*.

German pocket battleship *Deutschland,* bow view (1933). *Photo courtesy of MaritimeQuest*

German pocket battleship *Deutschland,* stern view.
Photo courtesy of U.S. Naval History and Heritage Command

The tower design for the bridge structure of the *Admiral Scheer* and the *Admiral Graf Spee* also accommodated searchlights, communications equipment, and a variety of other combat support functions previously relegated to spaces below deck. This tower design was carried forth into all subsequent major German warships built before and during World War II. A similar design tower structure was also incorporated into all of the new battleships and battle cruisers built by the United States in lieu of the wire-cage and tripod designs used on earlier battleships for their forward and aft fire control stations. Several of the American battleships refitted during World War II were also modified to incorporate a forward tower structure.

The characteristics of these pocket battleships seemingly made them ideal hit-and-run raiders, being able to outrun any battleship with superior armament and outshoot any cruiser with superior speed. These characteristics would be put to the test early in World War II when two of the pocket battleships were immediately sent out on raiding missions. The *Deutschland*, operating in the North Atlantic, had only limited success in sinking two merchant ships and capturing a third before she had to be recalled for mechanical problems.

The *Admiral Graf Spee* sank nine merchant ships before she was finally intercepted by a force of three British cruisers in the South Atlantic off the coast of Uruguay in December 1939. Although she damaged the heavy cruiser HMS *Exeter* during the initial stage of the battle, the *Graf Spee* was subsequently overwhelmed by the combined firepower of the light cruisers HMS *Ajax* and HMNZS *Achilles*. Driven to seek shelter in the port of Montevideo, the *Admiral Graf Spee* was scuttled in that harbor on 17 December 1939 rather than face the force of British warships mustered at the mouth of the River Plate.

On 22 April 1930, Great Britain, the United States, Japan, France, and Italy signed the London Naval Treaty, which established guidelines for submarine warfare and placed limits on the construction of cruisers by the powers affected. Light cruisers were defined as ships having guns of a caliber not to exceed 6.1 inches (155mm) and heavy cruisers were defined as ships having guns of a caliber not to exceed 8 inches (203mm). The United States was permitted to have 18 heavy cruisers with a combined displacement of 180,000 tons and an unspecified number of light cruisers with a total displacement of 143,500 tons.

Under the Treaty, Great Britain was allowed to have 15 heavy cruisers with a total displacement of 147,000 tons and an unspecified number of light cruisers with a total displacement of 192,200 tons. Japan was allowed to have 12 heavy cruisers totaling 108,000 tons displacement and an unspecified number of light cruisers with a total displacement of 100,450 tons. In addition, displacement limits were established for various warship categories for each of the nations subject to the treaty provisions.

The Allies tried to argue Germany out of building any more pocket battleships after the *Deutschland*, but she refused on the basis of not being allowed to be a signatory to the London Naval Treaty. France responded by building two new battleships, the *Dunkerque* and *Strasbourg*, that would be superior to any Panzerschiff in both armament and speed. These ships carried eight 13-inch guns and had a speed of nearly 30 knots, compared with only six 11-inch guns and a speed of 26 knots for the pocket battleships.

CHAPTER **4**

GERMAN NAVAL EXPANSION
UNDER THE THIRD REICH

IN THE UNREST THAT ACCOMPANIED THE WORLDWIDE economic depression beginning in 1929, the traditional political parties in Germany, led by the Social Democrats, lost ground to the more extreme parties, including the Communist Party and the National Socialist German Worker's (Nazi) Party. The Nazi Party, led by Adolf Hitler, gained popular support from the masses after promising to lead them out of the depression, and they won additional seats in the Reichstag. Under increasing political pressure, then President Paul von Hindenburg appointed Adolf Hitler to become the Chancellor (akin to prime minister) of Germany on 30 January 1933.

When Hindenburg died a year and a half later on 2 August 1934, Hitler took complete control of the government as the Führer (leader) of Germany. He soon renounced the Treaty of Versailles and began a rearmament program to reestablish Germany as a major power. Hitler retained Admiral Raeder as the Commander-in-Chief of the Reichsmarine, and he ordered the German Naval High Command to initiate a major naval shipbuilding program, including battleships, cruisers and destroyers.

The destroyer program got under way first with the laying of the keel of the *Leberecht Maass* (Z-1), at the Deutsche Werke Kiel in October 1934. The *Leberecht Maass* was 391 feet long, had a beam of 37 feet, and displaced 2,232 tons standard. Her turbine engines produced 70,000 SHP and her top speed was 38 knots. The *Leberecht Maass* carried five 128mm (5-inch) guns in single mounts along the centerline of the ship and eight 21-inch torpedo tubes in two quadruple mounts. The *Leberecht Maass* was quickly followed by three additional destroyers of the same class (Z2-Z4), all built by Deutsche Werke Kiel, and twelve almost identical destroyers of the *Paul Jacobi*-class (Z5-Z16) built by the Deutsche Schiffs und Maschinenbau AG (Deschimag) Bremen, Germania Werft Kiel, and Blohm & Voss Hamburg.

In 1936, Deschimag produced six destroyers of the *Diether von Roeder* class (Z17-Z22), which were slightly larger vessels displacing 2,800 tons, but otherwise the same as their predecessors. The next group of eight destroyers of the *Narvik* class (Z23-Z30) and four destroyers of the 36A (Mob)-type (Z31-Z34) were equipped with 150mm (5.9-inch) guns, the earlier ones in four single mounts and the latter with a double mount on the foredeck and three single mounts in the center and to the rear. Three additional vessels of the latter type vessels (Z37-Z39) were built by Germania Werft Kiel. Further wartime construction of destroyers reverted back to the use of five 138mm (5-inch) guns.

The Germans finalized plans for two new 26,000-ton battleships and ordered the materials for their construction. The battleship *Gneisenau* was laid down at the Deutsche Werke shipyard at Kiel on 6 May 1935, launched on 8 December 1936, and commissioned on 21 May 1938. She was followed by a sister ship, the *Scharnhorst*, which was laid down on 15 June 1935 at the Wilhelmshaven Naval Shipyard, launched on 3 October 1936, and commissioned on 7 January 1939. At time of their completion, the ships had an overall length of 742 feet, a beam of 98 feet, and a standard displacement of 31,000 tons. Their steam turbines geared to three shafts

German destroyer *Hans Lody* (Z-10) (1938). *Photo courtesy of MaritimeQuest*

German battleship *Gneisenau* (1938). *Photo courtesy of MaritimeQuest*

could develop 160,000 SHP and drive the ships at a speed of 32 knots.

The *Gneisenau* and *Scharnhorst* each carried nine 11-inch guns in three triple turrets, two forward and one aft. The Germans had considered other main armament configurations for the *Gneisenau* and *Scharnhorst*, but decided to stay within the caliber limitations of the Versailles Treaty, primarily for political considerations. They were already exceeding the size limitations, and they did not want to further antagonize the Allies by also increasing the caliber of the guns these ships would carry. Actually, their decision to stay with 11-inch guns had the advantage of using the same type of guns and turrets as those used on their pocket battleships. By standardizing the armament among all of those ships, the Germans minimized the logistics burden associated with ammunition supplies, spares, and repair parts, operating and technical manuals, and training.

In addition to their main armament, the *Gneisenau* and *Scharnhorst* also carried twelve 5.9-inch guns in six double mounts, three on each side of the ship along the main deck, a multitude of AA guns, and six 21-inch torpedo tubes in two triple mounts. The ships were also equipped with a catapult and could carry up to four aircraft, the latest of which were Arado Ar-196 floatplanes.

The Germans continued to complain about the injustices of the Versailles Treaty and tried to obtain concessions from the Allies by diplomatic means. Great Britain realized that the provisions of the Versailles Treaty were harsh, and they were now willing to consider some relaxation of the terms of that treaty. Since Germany was not allowed to be a signatory to the 1930 London Naval Treaty, Great Britain negotiated a separate Anglo-German Naval Agreement with Germany on 18 June 1935. Under this agreement, Germany could build up to 35 percent of the strength of the Royal Navy but her ships would still be limited to the same international restrictions as all other naval powers, i.e., displacement no greater than 35,000 tons and guns no larger than 16 inches in caliber.

The British, however, also stipulated that the percentage figure applied to all categories of warships, which would cause Germany to build a balanced fleet of conventional warships. Britain believed that it would be easier to defeat a balanced German fleet in case of war due to her numerical superiority. Some German naval tacticians opposed the agreement on the basis that Germany should place a greater emphasis on cruiser-size vessels for commerce raiding in the event of war, but Hitler himself favored a balanced fleet, even with inferior numbers compared with the Royal Navy.

France and Italy were outraged by the Anglo-German Naval Agreement since they were not consulted in advance. Also, the terms of the treaty placed Germany on a par with them based on the 5:5:3:1.67:1.67 ratio agreed to at the Washington Naval Conference, which allowed those countries 33 percent of the strength of the Royal Navy.

The year 1935 also saw some changes intended to increase the prestige of the German Navy under the Third Reich. On 21 May 1935, the name of the German Navy was changed from the Reichsmarine to Kriegsmarine (war navy). The position of Admiral Raeder, the Director of Naval Affairs for the Reichsmarine, was upgraded to Supreme Commander of the German Navy (Oberbefehlshaber der Marine). Raeder was promoted to the rank of General Admiral on 20 April 1936, and on 1 April 1939, he achieved the ultimate rank of Grand Admiral (Grossadmiral).

Germany had agreed to a balanced fleet under the terms of the Anglo-German Naval Agreement of 1935, so the construction of conventional heavy cruisers was ordered in lieu of additional Panzerschiffe (pocket battleships). The first of these heavy cruisers, the *Admiral Hipper*, was laid down at the Blohm & Voss shipyard in Hamburg on 6 July 1935, launched on 2 June 1937, and completed on 29 April 1939. Her sister ship, the *Blücher*, was laid down on 15 August 1935 at the Deutsche Werke Kiel, launched on 6 August 1937, and completed on 20 September 1939, shortly after the outbreak of World War II.

German battleship *Scharnhorst* (1939) after refit with Atlantic bow.
Photo courtesy of U.S. Naval History and Heritage Command

German heavy cruiser *Admiral Hipper* (1939) being fitted out at Blohm & Voss shipyard in Hamburg. *Photo courtesy of ThyssenKrupp Marine Systems AG*

The *Admiral Hipper* and *Blücher* were 666 feet long, had a beam of 70 feet, and displaced 14,250 tons. Their turbine engines could generate 133,600 SHP and drive the ships at a maximum speed of 32.5 knots. The ships carried eight 20.3cm (8-inch) guns in four double turrets, two forward and two aft, twelve 10.5 cm (4.1-inch) guns in six twin mounts, three on either side of the ship, and twelve torpedo tubes in four triple mounts. The *Admiral Hipper* and *Blücher* were also equipped with a catapult and could store three Arado Ar-196 floatplanes in a single hanger.

A third ship of the *Admiral Hipper*-class, the slightly larger *Prinz Eugen*, was laid down at the Krupp Germania shipyard in Kiel on 23 April 1936, launched on 8 June 1937, and completed on 1 August 1940. The *Prinz Eugen* had an overall length of 681 feet, a beam of 72 feet, a standard displacement of 14,300 tons and a full load displacement of 18,700 tons. The *Prinz Eugen* had three turbine engines that delivered a total of 133,000 SHP and drove the ship at her maximum speed of 32.5 knots.

Like her sister ships, the *Prinz Eugen* carried eight 20.3cm (8-inch) guns in four double turrets, two forward and two aft. Each 20.3cm SKC/34 gun had a barrel length of 41 feet (60 calibres), and with a muzzle velocity of over 3000 ft/sec, it could fire a 270-lb. projectile 36,000 yards at its maximum elevation of 37°. The *Prinz Eugen* also carried twelve 10.5cm (4.1-inch) antiaircraft guns in six twin mounts, twelve 21-inch torpedo tubes, and three Arado Ar-196 floatplanes.

The principal fire control components of the *Prinz Eugen* were gyrostabilized, and therefore they could give good results even at the foretop where her main fire control station was located. The foretop fire control station was equipped with a 7-meter (23-foot) rangefinder and two C/38K directors, one port and the other starboard. The *Prinz Eugen's* forward and after fire control stations each had a 7-meter rangefinder and one C/38K director. In addition, the *Prinz Eugen* had four High Angle (HA) directors atop columns and with domed tops, and each director had a 4-meter (13-foot) rangefinder.

To have a viable balanced fleet, a nation must also have aircraft carriers. While Great Britain, the United States, and Japan showed great interest in aircraft carriers as part of their navies, this interest was not shared by France and Italy. Germany made a feeble attempt to add aircraft carriers to the Kriegsmarine after the Anglo-German Naval Agreement of 1935 allowed the nation to build ones of up to 38,500 tons displacement.

The *Graf Zeppelin* was laid down at the Deutsche Werke Kiel on 28 December 1936 and launched on 8 December 1938, but never completed. The keel for a second aircraft carrier was laid down but never got to the point of even being launched. The *Graf Zeppelin* would have been 861 feet long, had a beam of 103 feet, and displaced 33,550 tons. Her turbine engines would have generated 200,000 SHP and could have driven the ship at a speed of 35 knots. She was designed to carry 30 modified Messerschmitt Me-109 fighters and 12 modified Junkers Ju-87 dive-bombers.

With the go-ahead granted by the Anglo-German Naval Treaty of 1935, Germany proceeded with its plans to build 35,000-ton battleships of its own. The *Bismarck* was laid down on 1 July 1936 at the Blohm & Voss shipyard in Hamburg and launched on 14 February 1939. She was followed by her sister ship, the *Tirpitz*, which was laid down at the Wilhelmshaven Naval Shipyard on 24 October 1936 and launched on 1 April 1939. These ships were to have an overall length of about 800 feet, beam of 118 feet, and draught of 30 feet. Their steam turbines were to produce 160,000 SHP and drive these ships through three shafts at a speed of 30.1 knots. They would also be equipped with twin rudders directly behind their outboard screws and tilted slightly outward.

The main armament of the *Bismarck* and *Tirpitz* was to consist of eight 15-inch guns in the traditional arrangement of four double turrets, two forward and two aft. Their secondary armament included twelve 5.9-inch guns in six double mounts, three on each side of the ship along its main deck, and a multitude of antiaircraft guns. As with all navies, considerable thought was given to the main armament configuration of the *Bismarck* and the *Tirpitz*. Although Germany could go up to 16-inch guns based on the provisions of the original London Naval Treaty, she had no experience with guns of that size and would need a considerable amount of time to develop such a gun system with a corresponding turret.

The maximum size naval gun ever used by the Germans was the 15-inch gun that was installed on the latest and most powerful ships in her High Seas Fleet of World War I, the battleships *Baden* and *Bayern* (Bavaria). The use of three triple turrets to give the *Bismarck* and *Tirpitz* nine 15-inch guns was also a serious consideration. Germany had considerable success with the triple 11-inch gun turrets employed on her pocket battleships and battle cruisers, but these would need extensive redesign to accommodate the much more powerful 15-inch gun. In the end, Ger-

Stages in the construction of the German battleship *Bismarck*, under construction at Blohm & Voss Shipyard. *Photo courtesy of ThyssenKrupp Marine Systems AG*

many took the safe approach by adopting the configuration developed and proven on her World War I battleships rather than accept any further delay in the construction of the *Bismarck* and *Tirpitz*.

The launching of the *Bismarck* on 14 February 1939 was turned into a major national event that was capitalized on by the Nazi regime. It was attended by high officials of the government and a host of international observers. The event symbolized the return of Germany as a naval power, and it was used to demonstrate the success of National Socialist policies. On his way to the launching, Hitler made a courtesy visit to Friedrichsruh near Hamburg to pay his respects at the crypt of the "Iron Chancellor," for whom the ship was named. The ship was christened by a granddaughter of Prince Otto von Bismarck, and Hitler used the occasion to deliver a political speech extolling the strength and virtues of the Third Reich.

After the *Bismarck* was launched and while she was still being fitted out at the Blohm & Voss Shipyard in Hamburg, her square bow was replaced with a newly designed clipper-style bow that would give her better sea-keeping characteristics for operating in the rough waters of the

Bismarck being launched at Blohm & Voss Shipyard in Hamburg.
Photo courtesy of ThyssenKrupp Marine Systems AG

Stern view of *Bismarck* being launched.
Photo courtesy of ThyssenKrupp Marine Systems AG

North Sea and stormy North Atlantic. The new bow also incorporated new features for storing the bow anchors. One anchor was stored high in the front edge of the bow directly below the peak, while the other two anchors were nestled in shallow wells at the top edge of the deck on either side of the bow. This kept the anchors clear of the waves where they could cause excessive spray and slow the progress of the ship. This bow was also installed on the *Tirpitz* before she was launched and retrofitted on other major warships built earlier.

On 27 April 1939, Hitler repudiated the Anglo-German Naval Treaty of 1935, giving Great Britain notice that Germany intended to build warships without regard to any international treaty limitations. When viewed in the context of other events that were taking place, it became rather obvious that Germany and Great Britain were heading toward a confrontation in the not far distant future.

CHAPTER 5

THE OUTBREAK OF WORLD WAR II

HITLER'S PROGRAM FOR THE TERRITORIAL EXPANSION OF the Third Reich began with the annexation of his native land of Austria in March 1938. This was followed by the annexation of the German-speaking Sudeten region of Czechoslovakia, as agreed to at the four-power conference in Munich on 29 September 1938. According to British Prime Minister Neville Chamberlain, the Munich Pact was to secure "peace in our time," but these hopes were soon dashed when German troops occupied the rest of Czechoslovakia in March 1939. Britain then began seriously to prepare for the war which now seemed inevitable. Hitler's next goal was the reunification of German territory by elimination of the Polish Corridor that separated East Prussia from the rest of the nation.

On 23 August 1939, Hitler signed a non-aggression pact with Stalin, which paved the way for Germany's invasion of Poland. On the morning of 1 September, German troops crossed the Polish border and began their conquest of the country. The old battleship *Schleswig-Holstein* aided in the capture of the free city of Danzig by bombarding the Westerplatte fortification guarding its harbor. Great Britain and France, which had mutual defense agreements with Poland, demanded the immediate withdrawal of German troops from the country, and when this ultimatum was ignored, they declared war on Germany on 3 September. This was the beginning of World War II. On 16 September, Russia invaded Poland from the east, and after Warsaw surrendered on 27 September, Poland was divided between the two conquering powers, Germany and Russia.

Anticipating a declaration of war from Great Britain and France, Germany had pre-positioned submarines and surface raiders in the Atlantic Ocean to begin commerce raiding operations as soon as war broke out.

On 19 August 1939, 14 U-boats sailed from their bases to take up war stations in the North Atlantic, and these were followed by two more U-boats that left Germany five days later on 24 August. The armored cruiser (pocket battleship) *Admiral Graf Spee* left its base at Wilhelmshaven on 21 August and headed for a holding area in the South Atlantic. On 24 August, the armored cruiser *Deutschland* took up her position in the North Atlantic.

In naval actions, the Germans drew first blood when on 17 September 1939, just two weeks after the beginning of the war, the German submarine U-29, commanded by Lieutenant Otto Schuhart, sank the British aircraft carrier *Courageous* southwest of Ireland. This was followed a month later on 14 October 1939 by the sinking of the World War I-vintage battleship *Royal Oak* at Scapa Flow when U-47, commanded by Lieutenant Günther Prien, penetrated the defenses of the eastern approaches to the British naval base.

German surface warships soon added their weight to the fight against the British. The *Deutschland* began raiding operations in October 1939, but she sank only two freighters before being heavily damaged while refueling from the German tanker *Westerwald* during a severe storm, and she had to return to her base. On 23 November 1939, the German battleship *Scharnhorst* sank the British auxiliary cruiser *Rawalpindi* south of Iceland.

The *Admiral Graf Spee* had greater success, sinking 11 vessels before she was intercepted by a task force of three British cruisers under the command of Commodore Henry Harwood on 13 December 1939. The *Graf Spee* was able to score several hits on the *Exeter* and force the heavy cruiser to withdraw from the engagement, but the *Graf Spee* herself was so badly damaged in the battle that she had to seek safe haven at Montevideo, Uruguay. Four days later, on 17 December 1939, the *Graf Spee* was scuttled by her crew just outside the harbor of Montevideo.

On 9 April 1940, German forces invaded Denmark and Norway. During the invasion, the German heavy cruiser *Blücher* was sunk by Norwegian defense forces in Oslo Fjord, and the light cruiser *Karlsruhe* was torpedoed by the British submarine *Truant* off Kristiansand, Norway. On the following day, the badly damaged *Karlsruhe* was put out of her misery by the German torpedo boat *Grief.* Also on 10 April, the light cruiser *Königsberg* was sunk by British aircraft while docked in Bergen, Norway.

On 10 May 1940, German troops invaded Holland, Belgium and

France. Holland capitulated on 17 May after a devastating German air attack on Rotterdam, and the Belgians followed suit on 28 May. Attacking through the Ardennes Forest between Belgium and France, German forces outflanked the French Maginot Line and drove for the English Channel, forcing the evacuation of British troops at Dunkirk in early June. On 10 June, Italy declared war on Great Britain and France, and then invaded southern France. German troops occupied Paris on 14 June, and on 22 June 1940, France signed an armistice with Germany ending all hostilities in the country.

Under the terms of the armistice, Germany would occupy the northern half of the country, including Paris, and a wide strip of land along the Atlantic coast down to the Spanish border. The remainder of the country, including its Mediterranean coast, would be ministered by a collaborationist government with its capital at Vichy. The French fleet was to be interned and demilitarized at ports under German or Italian control. Despite verbal assurances by the French authorities that the French fleet would never be surrendered, Great Britain felt that this was not sufficient to guarantee that units of the fleet would not fall into German hands, so they took prompt action to prevent such an occurrence.

At the end of June 1940, the British assembled Force H, a task force consisting of the battle cruiser *Hood*, the battleships *Valiant* and *Resolution*, the aircraft carrier *Ark Royal*, the light cruisers *Arethusa* and *Enterprise*, and eleven destroyers at Gibraltar to settle the matter of the French fleet. Under the code name "Operation Catapult," the task force, commanded by Vice-Admiral Sir James F. Somerville, was ordered to sail for the French naval base of Mers-el-Kebir near Oran on the coast of Algeria and neutralize the elements of the French navy stationed there. The French force consisted of the modern battleships *Dunkerque* and *Strasbourg*, the old battleships *Provence* and *Bretagne*, the seaplane tender *Commandant Teste*, and six destroyers.

The French were issued an ultimatum to choose between three options: (1) sail their ships to British harbors whereupon the sailors could either continue the fight against the Germans or be repatriated; or (2) sail their ships to a French port in the West Indies where the ships would be demilitarized or entrusted to U.S. jurisdiction; or (3) sink their ships. Although the British tried to negotiate with the French commander, Admiral Gensoul, for several hours, he rejected all alternatives on the basis of the French government's promise not to let their ships fall into German hands, and his intent to obey the orders of his government and Admiral Darlan. Since Admiral Somerville had been directed to use force if the French did not accept any of the alternatives, he had no choice but to order the destruction of the French ships at the base.

At 1754 on the evening of 3 July 1940, the ships of Force H opened fire on the French ships at a range of 17,500 yards. The battleship *Bretagne* was soon hit and blew up with some 1,000 casualties. The French ships and shore batteries returned fire, but scored no direct hits on the British task force. The French battleships *Dunkerque* and *Provence* were damaged and run aground, and three destroyers were also damaged in the attack. The French battleship *Strasbourg* and the remaining three destroyers managed to raise steam and escape to the French naval base of Toulon on the southern coast of France, but not before being attacked by bomb-carrying Swordfish aircraft from the *Ark Royal* shortly after leaving Mers-el-Kabir.

In the meantime, German surface raiders had encouraging successes. On 8 June 1940, the battleships *Scharnhorst* and *Gneisenau* came across the British aircraft carrier *Glorious* in northern Norwegian waters and sank her with the two destroyers escorting her. In October 1940, the armored cruiser *Admiral Scheer* broke out into the North Atlantic and sank or captured 14 merchant ships. She also sank the British auxiliary cruiser *Jervis Bay* on 5 November 1940. Early in 1941, the battleships *Gneisenau* and *Scharnhorst* sortied into the North Atlantic under Operation "Berlin" and sank 19 merchant ships and captured three more with a total displacement of over 115,000 tons.

The *Bismarck* was commissioned on 24 August 1940 and placed under the command of Captain Ernst Lindemann. She had a standard crew of 2,060 naval officers and men, plus a number of Luftwaffe pilots and mechanics for the aircraft on board. Lindemann had entered the Imperial German Navy as a midshipman in 1913, and during World War I he served as a wireless telegraphy officer on the battleships *Lothringen* and *Bayern*. Between wars, Lindemann served as a gunnery officer on a number of ships, including first gunnery officer on the *Admiral Scheer*. Shortly after the outbreak of World War II, Lindemann became commander of the Naval Gunnery School at Kiel, and a year later he was assigned to be captain of the battleship *Bismarck*, then under construction at the Blohm & Voss shipyard on the Elbe River in Hamburg.

New Atlantic bow being installed on *Bismarck* at Blohm & Voss shipyard.
Photo courtesy of ThyssenKrupp Marine Systems AG

Fitting out of *Bismarck* nearing complettion at Blohm & Voss shipyard.
Photo courtesy of MaritimeQuest

At the time of her completion, the *Bismarck* had a standard displacement of 41,700 tons and full load displacement of 50,900 tons. She had an overall length of 822 feet and a waterline length of 793 feet. Her beam was 118 feet, and her draught at full load was 33 feet. That made her about the same size as the *Hood,* which had an overall length of 860 feet, a beam of 105 feet, and a standard displacement of 41,200 tons. The *Hood* was 40 feet longer than the *Bismarck,* but the *Bismarck* had a beam that was 13 feet wider, giving her greater stability for gunfire and greater protection than the *Hood.*

The *Bismarck* had three turbines that generated a total of 150,000 Shaft Horsepower (SHP) and drove the ship at a maximum speed of 30.1 knots. The *Bismarck* had one aircraft catapult located across her main deck amidships, and she could launch aircraft in either direction. She carried four Arado Ar-196 floatplanes in hangers located in the forward part of her after superstructure.

The *Bismarck's* main armament consisted of eight 38cm (15-inch) guns in four double turrets, two forward and two aft. Each 38cm SKC/34 gun had a barrel length of 58.6 feet (47 calibers), and with a muzzle velocity of 2,690 ft/sec, it could hurl a 1,764-lb. armor-piercing (AP) shell

Bismarck leaves Blohm & Voss shipyard for sea trials. *Photo courtesy of MaritimeQuest*

40,000 yards at the maximum elevation of 35°. The *Bismarck's* secondary armament consisted of twelve 15cm (5.9-inch) guns in six double turrets, three on each side of the ship. In addition, the *Bismarck* was equipped with sixteen 105mm (4.1-inch) anti-aircraft guns in eight dual mounts, four on each side of the ship, and a number of smaller antiaircraft guns.

The *Bismarck* had three main armament fire control stations. The primary fire control station was on the foretop, i.e., atop the tower battle mast some 110 feet above the water level. That station was equipped with a 10.5-meter (34.5-foot) rangefinder and three C/38S directors, one forward and one on each the port and starboard sides of the station. The forward fire control station, located above the conning tower in the forward superstructure, was equipped with a 7-meter (23-foot) rangefinder and three C/38S directors with the same arrangement as on the foretop. The aft fire control station, located atop the after superstructure of the ship, was equipped with a 10.5-meter rangefinder, but only two C/38S directors, one port and one starboard. These fire control components were gyro-stabilized for maximum effectiveness.

In addition to the above rangefinders, each main armament turret of the *Bismarck* had a 10.5-meter rangefinder, except that the one for the fore-

Bismarck as completed after sea trials. *Photo courtesy of ThyssenKrupp Marine Systems AG*

most turret, Anton, had to be removed due to water damage before the operation. The center secondary 150mm gun turret on each side of the ship was equipped with a 6.5-meter (21-foot) rangefinder.

For antiaircraft fire control, the *Bismarck* had two forward high-angle (HA) directors mounted on columns and with domed tops, one column on the port side and the other on the starboard side of the tower battle mast. These directors, each of which also encompassed a 4-meter (13-foot) rangefinder, were also gyro-stabilized. The *Bismarck* also had two open HA director positions aft, each with a 3-meter (10-foot) rangefinder.

In September 1940, the *Bismarck* left Hamburg for a period of training and sea trials in the Baltic before returning to Blohm & Voss in December for final yard work. Upon correction of the deficiencies detected during her sea trials and completion of her fitting out, the *Bismarck* left Hamburg for the final time in March 1941, sailing eastward through the Kiel Canal to the naval base at Kiel. After taking on ammunition, fuel, and supplies and being painted in a camouflage pattern for protection against British submarines, the *Bismarck* headed into the Baltic Sea for gunnery practice and final crew training. The Polish port of Gdynia (renamed Gotenhafen during the German occupation) served as the operational base for the *Bismarck*.

CHAPTER **6**

PLANNING AND PREPARATION
FOR OPERATION RHINE EXERCISE

O N 2 APRIL 1941, THE GERMAN NAVAL HIGH COMMAND
(Oberkommando der Marine) issued an operational
order that set into motion a series of events leading to the Battle of the
Denmark Strait. The Supreme Commander-in-Chief of the German Navy
(Oberbefehlshaber der Marine) at the time was Grand Admiral (Grossad-
miral) Dr. Erich J.A. Raeder. Admiral Raeder's Chief of the Naval General
Staff and Director of Sea Warfare (Seekriegsleitung) was Vice-Admiral
Otto Schniewind.

Schniewind had commanded a squadron of torpedo boats during
World War I. He also served in the postwar Reichsmarine, where he was
the adjutant to the Minister of War, Otto Gessler, from 1925-1926. In
October 1938, Schniewind became Chief of Staff of the newly formed
Seekriegsleitung, which directed all sea warfare operations. Schniewind's
Chief of Naval Operations was Rear-Admiral Kurt Fricke, who also served
in the German Imperial Navy (Kaiserliche Marine) and Reichsmarine
before his service in the Kriegsmarine of the Third Reich.

Under the German Naval High Command were several regional commands responsible for German naval operations in specific geographical
areas. The two regional commands involved in Operation Rhine Exercise
were Naval Group Command North, which was responsible for all naval
operations in Norwegian waters, and Naval Group Command West, which
was responsible for naval operations in the Atlantic Ocean. Naval Group
Command North was headed by Admiral Rolf Carls, who had his headquarters at Wilhelmshaven, and Naval Group Command West was headed

by Fleet Admiral (Generaladmiral) Alfred Saalwächter, who had his headquarters in Paris.

Also under the Naval High Command were several flag officers in charge of certain types of warships and naval materiel. The most important of these was the Fleet Commander (Flottenchef), who was in charge of all capital ships. At the time, the Fleet Commander was Admiral Günther Lütjens, who had his headquarters in Kiel. Lütjens also began his naval career in the Imperial German Navy, and he continued on in the Reichsmarine and finally in the Kriegmarine. In 1935, he became the Chief of the Officer Personnel Branch on the Naval Staff, and in July 1940, he was chosen to become the Fleet Commander. Early in 1941, Lütjens headed the task force, consisting of the battleships *Gneisenau* and *Scharnhorst,* that sank 19 merchant ships and captured three more under Operation "Berlin."

Previously, the Fleet Commander had also been in charge of cruisers as well as capital ships, but in late 1939, a separate position of Commander-in-Chief Cruisers (Befehlhaber des Kreutzer) was established to take charge of all cruisers in the Kriegsmarine. Admiral Hubert Schmundt served in that capacity from August 1940 to October 1941. Other flag officers were in charge of destroyers (Rear-Admiral Erich Bey), U-boats (Rear-Admiral Karl Dönitz), torpedo boats (Captain Hans Bütow), and minesweepers (Captain Friedrich Ruge).

There would seem to be overlapping authorities between the Group Commander, who had operational control over naval operations within his geographical area, and the commander of the task force when operating within the area of the Group Command. However, the operational order made it clear that while at sea, the task force commander had responsibility for the operation of the task force. In such an event, the Group Commander could only make suggestions to the task force commander and act in a supporting role.

The primary purpose of the operation was to sink enemy merchant vessels in the North Atlantic, but unlike previous operation orders, escorted convoys would also be attacked where the escorts did not represent an excessive risk. The operation was intended to supplement German U-boat activity in sinking Allied shipping by having a strong surface task force intercept convoys bringing critical supplies to the British Isles and destroying as many ships as possible with their gunfire. The German task force

Bismarck heading for Gotenhafen for training exercises in the Baltic Sea.
Photo courtesy of ThyssenKrupp Marine Systems AG

was to be powerful enough to overcome any defense provided to Allied convoys, including older enemy battleships. At the heart of this task force would be the battleship *Bismarck*, soon to become operationally ready.

Ideally, the task force would also have included the battleship *Tirpitz*, the *Bismarck's* sister ship, but she was still far from becoming ready. Both of the two remaining German battleships were laid up at Brest in occupied France for repairs, the *Gneisenau* having sustained damage from an aerial torpedo while at Brest and the *Scharnhorst* needing extensive engine work. Not wanting to delay the operation until another capital ship became available, the German Naval High Command reluctantly had to settle for the heavy cruiser *Prinz Eugen* to accompany the *Bismarck*. The *Prinz Eugen* was commanded by Captain Helmuth Brinkmann and had an extraordinarily large crew of over 1,500 officers and men.

The selection of the *Prinz Eugen* to accompany the *Bismarck* in this operation instead of another battleship would present two significant problems for the task force commander. First of all, the *Prinz Eugen* did not have the armor protection of a battleship and therefore, she would have to be protected by the *Bismarck* against major caliber gunfire from any enemy force they might encounter. If the *Prinz Eugen* were to become disabled, the *Bismarck* would have to do whatever it could to assist the cruiser, thereby distracting the *Bismarck* from its primary mission of commerce raiding.

Second, the tanks of the *Prinz Eugen* had a maximum capacity of 3,250 tons of fuel oil, giving her an operating range of 6,800 nautical miles compared with the *Bismarck's* range of 8,100 miles. This meant that the *Prinz Eugen* would have to be refueled more frequently than the *Bismarck*, again detracting from the *Bismarck's* primary mission.

In the case of fuel oil, which has a specific weight of 57 lbs. per cubic foot, a cubic meter (35.32 cubic feet) weighs almost exactly 2,000 lbs. In some reference material, the amount of fuel oil is given in terms of cubic meters, and in other references, in tons. Since the amounts are the same for all practical purposes, in this publication the amount of fuel oil is expressed in tons.

The operation was placed under the overall command of the Fleet Commander, Admiral Günther Lütjens, just off his recent success in surface raiding with the *Gneisenau* and *Scharnhorst*. Lütjens took command of the new task force in mid-April 1941, and he put the *Bismarck* through its final paces until the crews were honed to near perfection as a cohesive fighting team. The Germans had hoped that the *Gneisenau* would be able

Prinz Eugen joins *Bismarck* for training exercises in the Baltic Sea.
Photo courtesy of MaritimeQuest

to join the task force at sea once her repairs had been completed, but these hopes were soon dashed when British aircraft scored four bomb hits on the ship in a raid on 10 April, putting her out of service for another nine months.

A number of additional warships were allocated to support the operation, and they were placed under the operational control of Admiral Lütjens. Even submarines, which were normally under the Commander of U-boats, could be directed by Lütjens to support the operation if they were operating in the vicinity of the route that the *Bismarck* and *Prinz Eugen* would take. The operational order emphasized the importance of cooperation between the U-boat arm under Rear-Admiral Karl Dönitz and the surface raiders.

Two scout ships (Spähschiffe), the *Gonzenheim* and *Kota Pinang*, would reconnoiter the operational area in advance of the task force. The *Gonzenheim* was a 4,000-ton vessel built in Sweden as the *Kongsfjord* for the Norwegian-America Line in 1937. She was captured by the Germans during the occupation of Norway in 1940 and converted into a barrier-breaker (Sperrbrecher) before becoming a reconnaissance ship. Two fleet supply ships, including the *Ermland*, were allocated to support the operation, as were several tankers, including the *Friedrich Breme*, the *Esso-Hamburg*, the *Heide*, the *Ill*, the *Lothringen*, the *Spichern*, and the *Weissenburg*.

Upon leaving Gotenhafen and reaching Cape Arkona on the northeastern tip of the island of Rügen, the task force would be protected by *Sperrbrecher 13* and *Sperrbrecher 31* on its further passage to the Great Belt, the primary waterway through the heart of Denmark. Sperrbrechers were converted merchant ships of about 5,000 tons or more displacement that were expendable and were used to clear the way for more important vessels through potentially mined waters by merely sailing ahead of the protected ships. They had reinforced bows to resist the blasts of any mines that they might encounter, and they were filled with buoyant material to help keep them from sinking.

The Fifth Minesweeper Flotilla would then escort the task force through the German-laid Skagerrak minefield, and after that, destroyers (Zerstörer) would take over the escort task around the Norwegian coastline. The destroyer screen would include the *Hans Lody* (Z-10), the *Friedrich Eckoldt* (Z-16), the Z-23, and the Z-24. Destroyers after Z-22 were not given names and were known only by their numerical designation. Air cover would be provided to the task force as directed by Group North and Group West in their respective operational areas.

Timing of the operation was most important to provide the maximum security for the task force. The *Bismarck* and *Prinz Eugen*, with their destroyer escorts, were to pass through the Great Belt at night, and be off Kristiansand at 2030 on the following evening. This would allow them to enter Korsfjord the next morning, or if the weather was favorable, Group North recommended that the task force use the Faeroes-Iceland passage to enter the North Atlantic, staying completely clear of Iceland. As an alternative, the task force could head directly north into the Norwegian Sea and refuel at the tanker *Weissenburg* pre-positioned in that area before going on to the Denmark Strait.

On 25 April, Lütjens was ordered to depart with his squadron on the evening of 28 April and begin the implementation of Operation Rhine Exercise. Before the operation could get started, however, it was delayed for a couple of weeks when a mine exploded near the *Prinz Eugen* while on her way to Kiel, causing considerable damage.

On 5 May 1941, Hitler, accompanied by Field Marshal Wilhelm Keitel, the head of the Supreme Command of the German Armed Forces (Oberkommando der Wehrmacht), and several aides, visited the *Bismarck* on an inspection tour. Conspicuously missing from Hitler's entourage was Grand Admiral Erich Raeder, the Supreme Commander-in-Chief of the German Navy. Hitler's party arrived at the Goteshafen roadstead in the fleet tender *Hela*, and they were met on the deck of the *Bismarck* by Admiral Lütjens. Lütjens escorted the Führer on a tour of the ship where he and his staff explained the functions of the various items of equipment on board.

After the tour of the ship, the senior members of the group sat around a conference table where they discussed the merits of sea warfare using surface warships as commerce raiders. Lütjens then described the overall plan of Operation Rhine Exercise to Hitler, who expressed his concern for the risk involved and the impact of the possible loss of the *Bismarck* on German prestige. Fearing Hitler's disapproval of the operation, Lütjens did not advise him of the impending start of the operation. Upon Hitler's departure, Lütjens rendered the traditional naval salute with his hand up to the brim of his cap while Hitler stretched out his right arm and hand in the Nazi salute.

With the *Bismarck* almost ready to sail, the staff of the Fleet Commander, consisting of 65 officers and men, was transferred from their headquarters at Kiel and embarked on the flagship on 12 May. A further delay, however, was incurred when one of *Bismarck's* two cranes broke down during training and required shipyard-level repairs. Finally, on 16 May, Lütjens reported to the German Naval High Command that *Bismarck* and *Prinz Eugen* would be operationally ready by 18 May. The German Naval High Command approved the implementation of Operation Rhine Exercise as of that date, and Group North ordered Lütjens to enter the Great Belt at nightfall on 19 May.

Left: Admiral Günther Lütjens. *Right*: *Prinz Eugen* Captain Helmut Brinkmann. *Both photos courtesy of Maritime Quest*

The auxiliary vessels allocated to support the operation were dispatched from their ports, if they were not already at sea. The scout ships *Gonzenheim* and *Kota Pinang* set sail on 17-18 May and headed for their assigned stations in the North Atlantic. The tankers *Heide* and *Weissenburg* left France and headed for Arctic waters to support the task force if it chose the Denmark Strait escape route. The tanker *Wollin* was ordered to support the task force at Bergen, Norway if it stopped off at that location. The tankers and supply ships *Belchen*, *Ermland*, *Esso Hamburg*, *Friedrich Breme*, *Lothringen*, and *Spichern* set out for their assigned positions in the Atlantic Ocean.

Sperrbrecher 13 and *Sperrbrecher 31* were alerted to the impending

Hitler and Lindemann (left) reviewing crew of *Bismarck* at Gotenhafen.
Photo courtesy of MaritimeQuest

departure of the *Bismarck* and *Prinz Eugen* and they headed for Rügen where they would pick up the task force and lead it through the western end of the Baltic Sea to the Great Belt. The Fifth Minesweeper Flotilla became prepared to escort the task force through the Skagerrak minefield until the *Bismarck* and *Prinz Eugen* reached the open sea. The destroyers *Friedrich Eckholdt* (Z-16) and Z-23 were already with the task force at Gotenhafen, and the destroyer *Hans Lody* (Z-10) was scheduled to join them at the southern entrance to the Great Belt. The operational order also called for destroyer Z-24 to be part of the escort force; however, that destroyer was not included in the final operational orders.

By the time the *Bismarck* was ready to sail, her complement had increased to over 2,200 men, including the staff of the Fleet Commander, prize crews for merchant ships expected to be captured, midshipmen assigned for training, and war correspondents for reporting on the anticipated exploits of the *Bismarck*. The *Bismarck* had been provisioned for three months at sea, and was to be topped off with fuel oil before beginning the operation.

German heavy cruiser *Prinz Eugen* (1940). *Photo courtesy of MaritimeQuest*

Admiral Lütjens with Captain Brinkmann (to rear) reviewing crew of *Prinz Eugen* at Gotenhafen. *Photo courtesy of MaritimeQuest*

At 1000 on the morning of 18 May, Admiral Lütjens visited the *Prinz Eugen*. After inspecting the ship's company gathered on the quarterdeck of the ship, Lütjens met with Captain Brinkmann and key members of his staff to discuss his final plans for the operation. If weather permitted, i.e., became overcast and made the task force less likely to be observed from the air, the *Bismarck* and *Prinz Eugen* would bypass a stop in Norway and continue on to the Arctic Ocean where they would be refueled by the tanker *Weissenburg*. Lütjens stated that his intention was to seek passage through the Denmark Strait and take advantage of the ice fog and speed of their ships while navigating by their radar.

Additional guidance provided by Lütjens included that Fleet approval would be necessary for the launching of torpedoes and the deployment of onboard aircraft by the *Prinz Eugen* during the operation. Aircraft were not to attack ships, but merely report their presence while remaining undetected if possible. Cruisers and auxiliary cruisers were to be engaged only as necessary, and the lightest ammunition should be used to sink steamers to conserve heavy shells. Camouflage was to be maintained while the ships were in Norwegian waters, and the crew was not to be told of the contemplated passage through the Denmark Strait until the order was given to do so.

The final instruction given by Admiral Lütjens to Captain Brinkmann was that the *Prinz Eugen* should proceed separately to Point Green 3 and there meet up with the *Bismarck* at 1100 on the following day, 19 May. Operation Rhine Exercise was about to get underway.

CHAPTER **7**

EXECUTION OF OPERATION
RHINE EXERCISE

IN THE MIDDLE OF THE DAY ON SUNDAY, 18 MAY 1941, THE
Bismarck pulled away from its wharf at Gotenhafen amid
the strains of the German folk song, "Muss i' denn," played by the Fleet
band on the upper deck. The song is about a villager who must leave his
home and sweetheart behind, and the tune has been used as the traditional
farewell for warships leaving port. The *Bismarck* did not go far before
dropping anchor in the roadstead to complete her provisioning and refueling. The *Bismarck* had nearly topped off its tanks when the refueling hose
ruptured, leaving 200 tons of fuel oil yet to be pumped on board. Since
the *Bismarck's* tanks had a capacity of 8,200 tons of fuel oil, the remaining
time was spent cleaning up the spilled fuel rather than loading the additional 200 tons.

At 0200 on the following morning, the *Bismarck* set sail through the
Bay of Puck and around the narrow Hel Peninsula to the Baltic Sea and
then westward to the island of Rügen. On the way, the *Bismarck* was escorted by the destroyers *Friedrich Eckoldt* (Z-16) and Z-23 of the Sixth
Destroyer Flotilla that was assigned to provide anti-submarine protection
for the task force while in coastal waters.

In the meantime, the *Prinz Eugen* left her pier with the aid of tugs at
1112 and anchored nearby in deeper water to take on clean water for her
boilers. At 1640, she weighed anchor and sailed a short distance out of the
harbor before anchoring again to take on fuel. After filling up to 3,232 tons,
18 tons short of her maximum capacity of 3,250, the *Prinz Eugen* weighed
anchor one last time at 2118 and began her separate voyage through the
Baltic Sea to Rügen, where she would meet up again with the *Bismarck*.

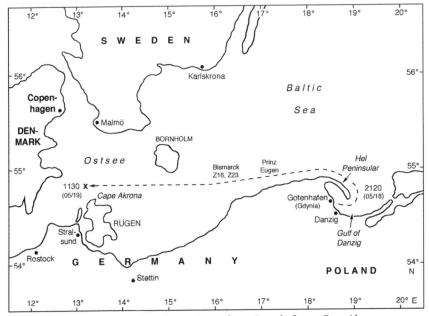

Route of the *Bismarck* and *Prinz Eugen* from Gotenhafen to Cape Akrona.

Route of the German squadron from Rügen to the Great Belt.

At 0800, the *Prinz Eugen* made her first daily report to the Fleet on her fuel status. By then she was down to 3,112 tons (95.8% of capacity). Since the range of the *Prinz Eugen* was significantly less than that of the *Bismarck*, the Fleet staff on the *Bismarck* had to closely monitor the fuel consumption on the cruiser. The *Prinz Eugen* was therefore ordered to report the status of her fuel stores to the Fleet every morning at 0800.

At 1125, the *Prinz Eugen* arrived off Cape Arkona at the northern tip of the island of Rügen where she met up with the *Bismarck* and the two destroyers escorting the flagship. From Cape Arkona, the *Bismarck* and *Prinz Eugen* sailed on together as a unit through the western half of the Baltic Sea to the Great Belt with barrier-breakers *Sperrbrecher 13* and *Sperrbrecher 31* leading the way.

During the day, the task force received a radiogram from Group North reporting that based on aerial reconnaissance, ice formations were normal up to 20° West, but that ice conditions west of that point could not be determined due to poor visibility. Admiral Lütjens had requested that information to determine how close he could come to the Greenland ice cap while transiting the Denmark Strait. Since the Denmark Strait is within range of reconnaissance aircraft operating out of Iceland, it was essential that the task force remain as far west and as long in the dark as possible to avoid being detected.

At 2230, the task force and its escorts reached the Ostsee at the southwestern end of the Baltic, where the destroyer *Hans Lody* (Z-10) joined the group. Commander Alfred Schulze, the commanding officer of the Sixth Destroyer Flotilla, came along on the *Hans Lody* to take personal charge of the escort for the task force. From there, the task force and escorts proceeded up the Great Belt. At 0410, the escorting path clearers, *Sperrbrecher 13* and *Sperrbrecher 31*, broke away in accordance with the operational order after completing their mission without incident.

The task force continued north up the Great Belt, passing Rosnaes on the western coast of the island of Sjaelland (Sealand) at 0448 and reaching the barrier further up on that island at 0616. The capital of Denmark, Copenhagen, is at the opposite (east) end of the island of Sjaelland. At 0800, the *Prinz Eugen* reported to the Fleet that she had 2,924 tons of fuel oil left, which represented 90% of her full load capacity. At 0936, the task force passed the island of Anholt to port, and it soon came across Danish and Swedish fishing boats operating in the Kattegat.

At about 1300, the Swedish aircraft cruiser *Gotland* was seen off to starboard along the coast of Sweden north of the city of Göteborg, and for a while, the cruiser sailed in the same direction as the task force, apparently in an effort to take a longer look at the task force and identify the ships. Having been discovered by the *Gotland*, the Fleet sent a radiogram to Group North reporting that the task force had been observed by a Swedish warship off Marstrand, a small island off the coast of Sweden.

Captain Agren of the *Gotland* immediately reported the sighting of the German task force to Stockholm, where the information was given to the British Naval Attaché in the capital, Captain Henry W. Denham. Captain Denham, in turn, alerted the Admiralty to the sighting of the *Bismarck* and a cruiser in the Kattegat that afternoon, which allowed the British to take necessary precautionary measures to keep the ships under surveillance and to keep them from breaking out into the North Atlantic. Although officially neutral, Sweden sympathized with the Allied cause after the German occupation of its sister Scandinavian countries of Denmark and Norway, and it did everything it could to support the Allied cause covertly.

The task force continued up the Kattegat, and at 1330 it met up with the Fifth Minesweeper Flotilla, which would then escort the task force through the Skagerrak mine field. A half hour later the task force passed through the barrier at Skagen, the northern tip of Denmark and the island of Jylland. Shortly after passing through the barrier, there was a mine alert as the minesweepers ahead of the task force cut loose three mines. The task force then pulled back and took a different path through the area. The task force continued to sail through the Skagerrak, zigzagging on basic course 300° at 17 knots.

At 1717, the task force turned due west on course 270° and headed directly for the opening in the Kristiansand-North barrier, which it passed through from 2111-2200. After clearing the barrier, the task force then continued zigzagging on course 240° until it turned dark. At 2315, the task force turned 46° to starboard on course 286°, and at 0159 on the following morning, it made another turn toward north to course 327° as it rounded the southwestern coast of Norway. At 0245, the ships of the task force were cleared for action in accordance with orders issued by the Fleet commander at 1820 the night before.

As the *Bismarck* and *Prinz Eugen* sailed off the coast of Norway nea Kristiansand early that evening, they were seen by a member of the Nor-

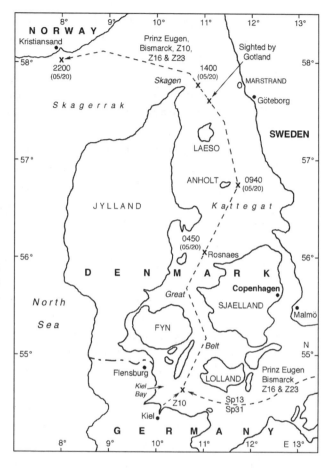

Route of the German
squadron through
the Great Belt.

wegian resistance who happened to be walking near the shoreline at the
time. He could see that the ships in the distance were large German warships, and he promptly passed the news on to other agents. Realizing the
importance of the sighting, the agents immediately sent a message to London with their hidden short-wave radio. By not taking the time to go to
a more remote location for transmitting the message, they risked discovery
of their position by the Germans and put their own lives in danger. The
sighting was welcome news at the Admiralty since they now knew that
the *Bismarck* and her consort were sailing up the coast of Norway.

At 0440, the German squadron turned almost to due north on course
359°, and five minutes later, at 0445, the order to clear the ships for action
was rescinded. At 0645, a radiogram from Group North was received by

the task force advising that a British radio station was ordering all aircraft to be on the alert for two battleships and three destroyers heading north. Four aircraft were sighted in the west at 0706, but they could not be identified.

It was now time for Admiral Lütjens to decide whether to go to Bergen and allow the *Prinz Eugen* and the escorting destroyers to refuel there, or to bypass Norway and head directly for the tanker *Weissenburg* stationed in the Arctic to support the operation. Lütjens determined that the conditions were not favorable to take the latter course of action, so at 0709, he ordered the task force to head for Korsfjord, which would take them to the fjords near Bergen. As usual at 0800, the *Prinz Eugen* reported on her fuel situation to the Fleet, and at the time, her fuel oil was down to 2,547 tons, 78% of capacity.

At 0900, the task force arrived at the entrance to Korsfjord, and the ships picked up a pilot at 0914 to guide them through the fjord and up to Bergen. As soon as the task force entered Korsfjord and was safe from submarine attack, Admiral Lütjens ordered that the camouflage pattern of the German ships be painted over with outboard gray color, which was more suitable for operations in the North Atlantic. This task was begun immediately topside, and it was completed on the hull while the ships were at anchor.

At 1115, Admiral Lütjens advised Captain Brinkmann of his orders for the next two days. It was Lütjens intent to proceed north that very evening, with the *Bismarck* joining the *Prinz Eugen* south of Kalvanes at 2000. Battle stations for anti-aircraft guns (Flak) were to begin at 2200 and for secondary armament at 2300. The state of readiness of the main armament would be determined based on circumstances on the following day. The task force was to steam under Readiness Condition "Two" at 20 knots until 2200, and then increase speed to 27 knots under Readiness Condition "One."

As the German squadron approached Grimstadfjord off to starboard, it began to slow down. The *Bismarck* gradually turned into Grimstadfjord and anchored at the far end of the fjord at about noontime. The *Prinz Eugen* and the three escorting destroyers continued up Hjeltefjord, and they dropped anchor in Kalvanes Bay at 1217. Two merchant vessels were tied up next to the *Prinz Eugen*, one on each side, to provide protection against torpedoes. At 1300, there was an air alarm on the *Bismarck*, but no attack was made on the anchorage. The plane was undoubtedly the

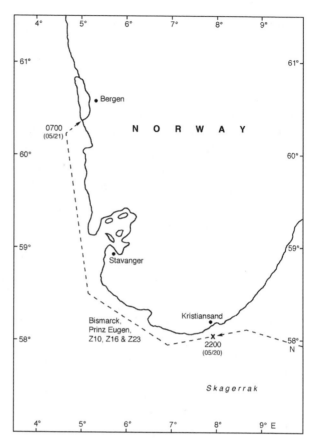

Route of the German squadron to Bergen, Norway.

RAF Spitfire photographic reconnaissance plane that flew over the area about that time in an effort to locate the *Bismarck* and cruiser escort. The sound of the aircraft was heard only for a short period of time, and since no attack occurred, the incident was quickly dismissed.

At 1345, the *Prinz Eugen* began to take on fuel oil from the tanker *Wollin* at the rate of 250 tons an hour. By the time the refueling was completed at 1700 hours, 764 tons of oil had been taken on, giving the ship oil stores of 3,233 tons of fuel oil, 99.5% of capacity. At the same time, the destroyers *Hans Lody* (Z-10), *Friedrich Eckoldt* (Z-16), and Z-23 also refueled from the *Wollin*.

The operational orders did not call for the refueling of the *Bismarck* at Bergen, probably based on the assumption that she would be refueled by the tanker *Weissenburg* in Arctic waters. The tanks of the *Bismarck* were filled with 8,000 tons of fuel oil when she left Gotenhafen, and she consumed about 1,500 tons on the way to Bergen, leaving 6,500 tons of fuel oil still on board. At an average cruising speed of 24 knots, the *Bismarck* would consume 30 tons of fuel oil per hour, so her remaining on board fuel supply would still give her nine days of operation or an operating range of 5,200 nautical miles without refueling.

In contrast, British battleships had a capacity of less than 4,000 tons of fuel oil, including the newest *King George V*-class battleships, which had a capacity of 3,730 tons. Only British battle cruisers had a capacity of more than 4,000 tons of fuel oil, with the *Hood* having a capacity of 4,614 tons and the *Renown*-class having a capacity of between 4,200 and 4,300. This lead to the British policy of always keeping their ships "topped off" on every occasion to refuel.

There were actually four possible routes that Admiral Lütjens could take to break out into the North Atlantic, but the passage between the Orkney Islands and the Shetland Islands and the passage between the Shetland Islands and the Faeroe Islands were ruled out due to their proximity to the British Home Fleet anchorage at Scapa Flow and to British air bases in northern Scotland. That left the passage between the Faeroes and Iceland and the passage through the Denmark Strait between Iceland and Greenland as the only two practical routes that the German squadron could take. The German Naval Group Command West, which was responsible for German naval operations in the Atlantic, favored the passage

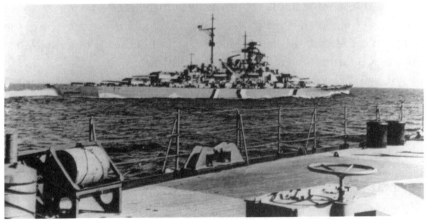

Bismarck en route to Norway. *Photo courtesy of U.S. Naval History and Heritage Command*

Bismarck entering Grimstadfjord near Bergen.
Photo courtesy of U.S. Naval History and Heritage Command

between the Faeroes and Iceland since it was closer, and based on their intelligence, there seemed little risk of being intercepted by the British Home Fleet still thought to be at Scapa Flow.

Admiral Lütjens, however, was not too sure of the safety of that route in view of the task force having been spotted by the Swedish cruiser *Gotland* and a host of Danish and Swedish fishing boats in the Kattegat. He therefore tended to favor the long way around through the Denmark Strait, even though he recognized the dangers of that route. It was a narrow passage between Iceland and the pack ice surrounding Greenland, and its width had been further reduced by a minefield that had been laid off the northwestern coast of Iceland. In the end, however, the decision had been left to him as the operational commander on the scene, and he opted for the Denmark Strait route, which he had used before and was familiar with.

At 1930, the *Prinz Eugen* reported to the Fleet that it was ready to put to sea. The *Bismarck* was already prepared to move out as soon as the *Prinz Eugen* completed her refueling, so she immediately weighed anchor and slowly headed out of Grimstadfjord. The *Bismarck* steamed up Hjeltefjord, where it met up with the *Prinz Eugen* and the escorting destroyers in Kalvanes Bay at about 2000. The ships then continued in single file up Hjeltefjord at a speed of 20 knots until they reached Fedje Island at 2217 where they exited the fjord into the Norwegian Sea. The escorting destroy

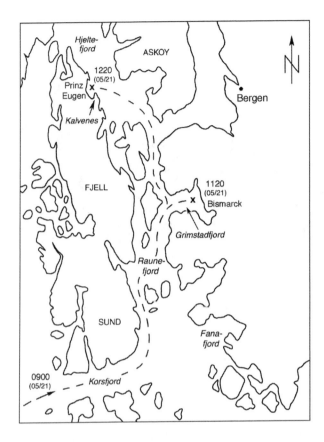

Bismarck and Prinz
Eugen proceed to their
anchorages near
Bergen.

ers then took up their anti-submarine screening positions, and the task
force began to zigzag on general course 290°.

While en route through Hjeltefjord, the task force received a radiogram from Group North at 2038 advising that the radio message of 2004
was probably the basis for the sighting report by radiogram 1737 from
the intelligence service. This latest message was undoubtedly intended as
a warning that the enemy might be aware of the movement of the task
force from spy reports despite negative results from the aerial reconnaissance of the Scapa Flow naval base to determine enemy countermoves.

At 2348, the task force turned due north and proceeded without any
further zigzagging on course 0° at a cruising speed of 24 knots. The destroyers Hans Lody (Z-10), Friedrich Eckoldt (Z-16), and Z-23 were released from their antisubmarine escort duties by the Fleet at 0420, and
they thereupon sailed for the German naval base at Trondheim. At 0800,

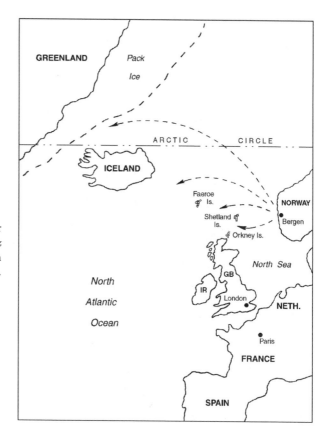

Possible routes for *Bismarck* and *Prinz Eugen* to reach Atlantic Ocean.

the *Prinz Eugen* gave its daily report to the Fleet on its fuel oil situation. At the time, the cruiser still had 2,999 tons (92% of capacity) on board.

At 1053, the task force received another radiogram from Group North and a report from the German Intelligence Service (Beobachtungsdienst or B-Dienst) advising of strong enemy air reconnaissance in the direction of Norway, but too far south to be able to detect the *Bismarck* and *Prinz Eugen* battle group. The message went on to state that the anchorage at Kalvanes Bay was attacked by bombers on the evening of 21 May, but according to other radio messages received, it appears that the progress of the task force had not been detected by the enemy.

At 1203, the German squadron turned 36° to port on course 324°, and at 1215, Admiral Lütjens passed on to Captain Brinkmann his orders for the day. Lütjens' intentions were to proceed through map quadrants AF 1675, 1155 and AE 3313, 2257 from 1200 onward, but if the weather

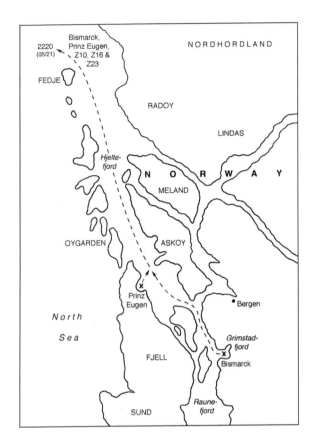

Bismarck and *Prinz Eugen* leave their anchorages near Bergen.

changed, the task force would head directly to the tanker *Weissenburg*. The task force would be on Readiness Condition of Full Combat Alert. Ships would proceed at War Condition "Two" at 24 knots, and at 0400, ships would go to War Condition "One" at 27 knots.

At 1237, there was a submarine and aircraft alert on the *Bismarck* based on a sighting report off the starboard side of the ship. The task force turned to port and began zigzagging for 22 minutes until 1259. At 1307, the alarm ended, but it prompted the order from the Fleet to paint over the aircraft identification markings on the turrets of the *Bismarck* and *Prinz Eugen* and the swastikas on the forecastles and quarterdecks of the two ships. During the day, the *Bismarck* and *Prinz Eugen* spent some time in practicing towing in the event that either ship became disabled.

Group North sent another radiogram to the task force at 1512 in response to Admiral Lütjens' request for information on the extent of the

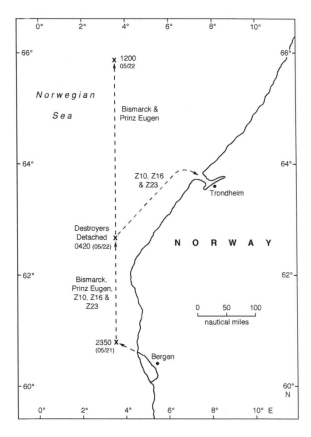

Destroyers are detached as German squadron heads north.

icecap off the coast of Greenland. It merely stated that ice reconnaissance in the area was not possible. This left Admiral Lütjens completely in the dark as to how far west he could go in the Denmark Strait to keep out of range of reconnaissance aircraft operating out of bases in Iceland.

At 1800, the task force turned to course 311°, still steaming at 24 knots. At 1934, a radiogram was received from Group North stating that photo reconnaissance of Scapa Flow was impossible due to the weather, but four heavy units were seen at the base by visual observation. Therefore, it seems that the enemy still did not know the forward progress of the task force.

Ever since leaving Norway, the weather had been overcast, and late in the day it became increasingly hazy. By 1800, it had begun to rain, and by 2116, visibility was down to 300-400 meters and even lower. The German squadron continued to sail at 24 knots, but the *Prinz Eugen* had to follow in the wake of the *Bismarck* and use blinker lights to keep in touch with the flagship. The weather appeared to be favorable for a breakout, and the meteorologists aboard the *Prinz Eugen* believed that it was possible for conditions to hold all the way down to the southern point of Greenland.

At 2309, a radiogram was received from Group North stating that based on air reconnaissance, ice conditions were normal to 20° West, but results further west were still inconclusive due to poor visibility. The message went on to report that one battleship and four heavy cruisers were seen in Plymouth Harbor on 18 May. The massage concluded that this confirmed the assumption that the breakthrough had not yet been detected by the enemy. A skeptical Captain Brinkmann underlined the last part of the message and added a handwritten comment beside the text in the *Prinz Eugen's* war diary: "This really says nothing."

At 2330, the German squadron turned to course 266°, almost due west, and headed for the Denmark Strait. Admiral Lütjens had decided to take advantage of the poor weather conditions and attempt a breakout immediately rather than first refueling at the tanker *Weissenburg*. This would put him at the northern entrance to the Denmark Strait at about 1800, and by hugging the Greenland ice cap, the task force would remain

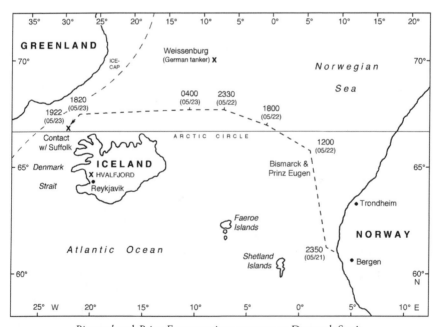

Bismarck and *Prinz Eugen* continue en route to Denmark Strait

as far as possible from reconnaissance aircraft operating out of Iceland. The timing would also place the task force at the nearest point to the British airfields on Iceland during the darkest part of the evening and early morning hours, minimizing the risk of detection from that source. Lütjens hoped that the German squadron would be out of range of the reconnaissance aircraft before turning south into the North Atlantic to begin his commerce raiding operations.

This was a calculated risk for Admiral Lütjens. The fuel situation for the *Prinz Eugen* was not an issue since she topped off her tanks at Bergen, but the *Bismarck* did not. The *Bismarck* left Norway with 6,500 tons of fuel oil in her tanks, and she would consume about 700 tons of fuel oil to reach the Denmark Strait. That still would leave 5,800 tons of fuel oil for her to transit through the Denmark Strait and even begin raiding operations before having to refuel at one of the German tankers pre-positioned in the North Atlantic. At the time, the risk seemed to be small in comparison to the increased risk of being discovered by delaying the breakout by another day.

At 0400 on 23 May, Admiral Lütjens ordered the *Bismarck* and *Prinz Eugen* to increase speed to 27 knots, and at 0404, the task force turned to course 250°. By that time, isolated ice floes were seen, indicating that the task force was nearing the ice cap off the coast of Greenland. The turn to course 250° directed the task force toward the entrance of the Denmark Strait where it would sail as close as possible to the ice cap on its voyage down the passage.

The *Prinz Eugen* gave her daily fuel status report to the Fleet on schedule at 0800, stating that she had 2,466 tons of fuel oil (76% of capacity) on board. At 0958, speed was reduced to 24 knots, and at 1115, Lütjens ordered the task force to go on full combat alert. From 1215-1258, the task force steered along the edge of the icecap, maneuvering around the large ice floes that could damage the hulls of the ships. At 1340, speed was increased again to 27 knots.

At 1403, the task force received a weather report from Group North confirming that the poor weather conditions of overcast skies, rain, and reduced visibility were favorable for the breakthrough to the North Atlantic. At 1420, the task force briefly turned due west to course 270° to come close to the ice cap again. Visibility was variable from 4000-5000 meters at 1500. At 1700, Admiral Lütjens ordered the *Bismarck* and *Prinz*

Bismarck and *Prinz Eugen* practice towing and refueling en route.
Photo courtesy of U.S. Naval History and Heritage Command

Eugen to turn on their magnetic self-protection (Magnetischer Eigen-schutz) degaussing gear, which was intended to neutralize magnetic mines, as they approached the minefield that the British laid off the northwestern coast of Iceland.

At 1811, dark shapes were seen in the distance to starboard, and this resulted in an alarm being given. At 1820, the task force turned to port on course 240°, but two minutes later, at 1822, the dark shapes seen in the distance were identified as icebergs, and the alarm ended. At 1848, the task force turned to course 200° to avoid ice formations as the *Bismarck* and *Prinz Eugen* continued to hug the edge of the Greenland ice cap, zig-zagging around large ice floes. By 1900, the weather had cleared somewhat with improved visibility but still with mist in the distance, and the *Bismarck* and *Prinz Eugen* continued to sail into the Denmark Strait.

CHAPTER 8

PRECAUTIONARY MEASURES
TAKEN BY THE BRITISH

T HE ADMIRALTY WAS ALMOST CERTAIN THAT THE TWO large warships sighted by the Swedish cruiser *Gotland* in the Kattegat were the *Bismarck* in company with a pocket battleship or cruiser. The sighting of the German squadron off Kristiansand confirmed that the *Bismarck* was on the move along the coast of Norway. The Admiralty was aware of the fact that the *Bismarck* was about ready for operational deployment, and they had already taken some precautionary measures to deal with the situation. They were sure that the *Bismarck* would most likely attempt to break out into the North Atlantic through one of the two passages around Iceland.

The Board of the Admiralty was the branch of the British government responsible for naval affairs. It was headed by the First Lord of the Admiralty, a member of Parliament from either the House of Lords or the House of Commons, who was appointed to that position by the Prime Minister. The Admiralty consisted mainly of Sea Lords who were senior admirals in the Royal Navy and Civil Lords who were primarily political figures. At the beginning of World War II, Winston Churchill served as the First Lord of the Admiralty before becoming Prime Minister. He was succeeded at the Admiralty by A.V. Alexander, who served in that position from 1940 until 1945.

The First Sea Lord was in charge of naval operations as well as being the chief of the naval staff and the professional advisor to the government on naval affairs. Admiral of the Fleet Sir Dudley Pound served in that capacity from 1939-1943. Other Sea Lords were responsible for various aspects of the naval establishment, such as personnel (Second Sea Lord), ships and equipment (Third Sea Lord), supplies and transportation (Fourth Sea Lord), naval aviation (Fifth Sea Lord), etc. The Royal Navy was composed of the Home Fleet, various worldwide geographical naval commands, and special task forces, such as Force H, which covered the western Mediterranean and was based at Gibraltar. The Home Fleet operated in British territorial waters and was based at Scapa Flow in the Orkney Islands off the northern coast of Scotland. It was commanded by Admiral Sir John Tovey from 1940 to 1942.

After the invasion of Denmark in April 1940, British forces occupied the Faeroe (Faroe) Islands between the Shetland Islands and Iceland, and then Iceland itself in May 1940, as preemptive measures to keep those territories from falling into German hands. Since Iceland was near the main convoy routes between Halifax and the British Isles, Great Britain established a major naval base at Hvalfjord just north of the capital at Reykjavik. Great Britain also established refueling stations at Reydarfjord and Seydisfjord on the east coast of Iceland for its warships assigned to escort convoys across the North Atlantic. A refueling station for British warships was also established at Skaalefjord in the Faeroe Islands.

Recognizing that the Denmark Strait would be one of the primary passages that would be used by German raiders and supply ships, the British laid several minefields off the northwestern coast of Iceland. This reduced the navigable width of the channel to just a few miles, which could be covered more easily by their warship patrols. German intelligence was aware of the existence of these minefields, but they also knew that the fields did not extend all the way to the fringe of the icepack off the coast of Greenland. This left a narrow channel that was relatively safe for German ships to transit.

The Admiralty had already alerted the First Cruiser Squadron, then on patrol duty in the Denmark Strait, to the possibility of a breakout by the *Bismarck* through that passage. The First Cruiser Squadron was established in January 1941 and placed under the command of Rear-Admiral William F. Wake-Walker, who had just commanded Force K of the South Atlantic Command. Force K consisted of the aircraft carrier *Formidable* and the sister heavy cruisers *Dorsetshire* and *Norfolk* (the flagship). The *Norfolk* and the *Formidable* left the South Atlantic Command on 18 December 1940 and set sail for Scapa Flow while the *Dorsetshire* sailed on to Freetown, South Africa.

Shortly after its arrival at Scapa Flow, Force K was dissolved. The *Norfolk* remained Wake-Walker's flagship, and she was soon joined by the heavy cruiser *Suffolk*, which was then undergoing refit at Greenock Royal Naval Base, to form the First Cruiser Squadron. After a series of assignments at sea and on the Admiralty staff, Wade-Walker achieved flag rank in January 1939, and he was soon assigned as Rear-Admiral commanding the 12th Cruiser Squadron. He was later placed in charge of all vessels involved in the British evacuation of Dunkirk in May 1940. From June to December 1940, Wake-Walker was commander of the First Mine Laying Squadron, which established a mine barrier along the east coast of the British Isles, and in January 1941, he assumed command of the First Cruiser Squadron.

The *Norfolk* and *Suffolk* were both County-class cruisers, but of different types. The *Norfolk* was of the *Dorsetshire*-class, and she was laid down at the Fairfield Shipyard on 8 July 1927, launched on 12 December 1928, and completed on 30 April 1930. She was 590 feet long, had a beam of 66 feet, and displaced 9,925 tons. Its turbine engines could develop 80,000 SHP and could drive the ship at a maximum speed of 32 knots. The *Norfolk* carried eight 8-inch guns in four double turrets, two forward and two aft, eight 4-inch antiaircraft guns, and eight 21-inch torpedo tubes in two quadruple mounts.

The *Norfolk* was equipped with Type 286 metric target-indicating radar operating on a frequency of 214 MHz and 1,400mm wavelength. The radar had a fixed transmitting aerial (Tx) and a fixed receiving aerial (Rx), which required that the ship itself had to be turned for scanning purposes. The *Norfolk* was commanded by Captain Alfred J.L. Phillips, and she had a complement of 710 officers and men.

The *Suffolk*, on the other hand, was a ship of the *Kent*-class. She was laid down at the Portsmouth Dockyard on 10 September 1924, launched on 16 February 1926, and completed on 31 May 1928. She was 590 feet long, had a beam of 68 feet, and displaced 9,800 tons. Her turbine engines could generate 80,000 SHP achieving 31.5 knots, and her armament, including torpedoes, was similar to the *Norfolk*'s.

The *Suffolk* had recently been equipped with a Type 279 metric air warning radar operating on a frequency of 39.9 Mhz and 7,450mm wavelength. The Type 279 radar had separate transmitting (Tx) and receiving (Rx) aerials, but they rotated in unison, which allowed for the detection of targets to the side, but not directly astern. She also had a Type 284 main armament ranging and shot-spotting radar that operated on a frequency of 600 Mhz and 50cm wavelength. The *Suffolk* was commanded by Captain Robert M. Ellis and had a compliment of 679 officers and men.

While not as large or as modern as the *Prinz Eugen*, the *Norfolk* and *Suffolk* were otherwise generally comparable to the German heavy cruiser, especially with respect to armament. The *Suffolk* had been on station at the northern end of the Denmark Strait for several days, and she was running low on fuel. The *Norfolk*, then in the process of refueling at Hvalfjord, was ordered to relieve the *Suffolk* so that she too could be refueled and made ready for extended operations.

On the offhand chance that the German ships would use the passage between the Faeroe Islands and Iceland in their attempt to break out into the North Atlantic, the two light cruisers *Birmingham* and *Manchester*, formerly of the 18th Cruiser Squadron commanded by Vice-Admiral Lancelot E. Holland, were ordered to patrol the Faeroes-Iceland passage. On 19 May, both ships left their base at Scapa Flow and took station in the waters between the Faeroes and Iceland to begin their patrol of that possible breakout route for the *Bismarck*. The *Birmingham* and *Manchester* were modern cruisers of the Town-class, or *Southampton*-class, that were built in the late 1930's. They both were 592 feet long, had a beam of 62 feet, and carried twelve 6-inch guns in four triple turrets, two forward and two aft, eight 4-inch antiaircraft guns, and six 21-inch torpedo tubes in two triple mounts.

The *Birmingham* was laid down at the Devonport Dockyard on 18 July 1935, launched on 1 September 1936, and completed on 18 November 1937. She displaced 9,100 tons and had turbine engines that developed 75,000 SHP and could drive the ship at a maximum speed of 32 knots. The *Birmingham* was commanded by Captain Alexander C.G. Madden and had a compliment of 700 officers and men. The *Manchester* was laid down at the Hawthorne Leslie Shipyard on 18 March 1936, launched on 12 April 1937, and completed on 4 August 1938. She displaced 9,400 tons and had a power plant that developed 82,500 SHP and could drive the ship at a maximum speed of 32.5 knots. The *Manchester* was commanded by Captain H.A. Packer, and like the *Birmingham*, she also had a compliment of 700 officers and men.

The light cruiser *Arethusa* was ordered to remain at Hvalfjord and await further orders when the situation became more defined. The *Arethusa* was a smaller cruiser that was laid down at Chatham Dockyard on 23 January 1933, launched on 6 March 1934, and completed on 23 May 1935. She was 506 feet long, had a beam of 51 feet, and displaced 5,450 tons. The *Arethusa* was powered by turbine engines that generated 64,000 SHP and could drive her at a maximum speed of 32 knots. She carried six 6-inch guns in three twin mounts, two forward and one aft, eight 4-inch anti-aircraft guns, and six 21-inch torpedo tubes in two triple mounts. The *Arethusa* was commanded by Captain A.C. Chapman and had a compliment of 450 officers and men.

Admiral Sir John C. Tovey, Commander-in-Chief of the British Home Fleet stationed at Scapa Flow, was authorized to use all of the naval assets at his disposal to prevent the breakout of the *Bismarck* into the North Atlantic. This included the battleships *King George V* and *Prince of Wales*, the battle cruisers *Hood* and *Repulse*, the aircraft carrier *Victorious*, and several cruisers and destroyers. While actually not part of the Home Fleet, the *Repulse* and *Victorious* happened to be in the area, and they were therefore placed under Admiral Tovey's operational control for the time being.

During World War I, Tovey commanded three different destroyers, and he participated in the battle of Dogger Bank and the battle of Jutland. Between wars, Tovey continued to be involved with destroyers as a flotilla commander, and early in World War II he served as the commander of cruiser and destroyer forces in the Mediterranean in actions against the Italian Navy. Tovey was appointed Commander-in-Chief of the Home Fleet in November 1940.

It now became the task of Admiral Tovey to deploy the naval resources under his command to stop the *Bismarck* at all costs. Tackling the *Bismarck* on a one-for-one basis seemed to be out of the question. The *Bismarck* was the ultimate product of German naval technology, and recent training had undoubtedly brought her crew up to near perfection in performance. Tovey's flagship, the *King George V*, was the only ship in the Royal Navy that had anything like an even chance to stand up to the *Bismarck* alone by virtue of her modern construction and crew experience.

The *King George V* had a standard displacement of 36,700 tons and full load displacement of 42,100 tons. She had an overall length of 745 feet, a beam of 103 feet, and a full load draught of 33 feet. The *King George V* had four sets of Parsons turbines that could generate 110,000 SHP and

HMS *Hood* anchored at Scapa Flow. *Photo courtesy of MaritimeQuest*

drive the ship at her maximum speed of 28.0 knots, and she had a maximum range of 6,000 miles at a speed of 15 knots. She had a catapult across the main deck amidships, and carried two seaplanes in hangers.

The *King George V* carried ten 14-inch guns in one quadruple turret and one double turret forward and one quadruple turret aft. Each Mk VII 14-inch gun had a barrel 52.5 feet (45 calibers) long, and with a muzzle velocity of 2,475 ft/sec, could fire a 1,590-lb. projectile over 35,000 yards at its maximum elevation of 40°. The *King George V* also had a secondary armament of sixteen Mk I 5.25-inch high angle/low angle guns in eight dual mounts, four on each side of the ship, and 32 quick-firing two-pounder Mk VI pom-pom antiaircraft guns in four octuple mounts, two on each side of the ship.

The *King George V* had two main armament fire control stations, the forward station being located just abaft the bridge structure and the after station being located on the after superstructure just before the after "Y" turret. Each station was equipped with a Mk VII director and a 15-foot rangefinder. For her secondary armament of sixteen 5.25-inch guns and antiaircraft guns, the *King George V* had four HACS Mk IV directors, two mounted side-by-side on a support structure aft of the bridge and main armament director and the other two mounted on the after superstructure on either side of the main (rear) mast. This arrangement was intended so that each director could cover a quadrant of the surrounding area with four 5.25-inch guns in two turrets within each quadrant.

British battleship HMS *Prince of Wales* (1941). *Photo courtesy of U.S. National Archives*

Each of *King George V*'s HACS directors was also equipped with a 15-foot rangefinder. In addition, each of her two quadruple 14-inch gun turrets, "A" forward and "Y" aft, was equipped with a 41-foot rangefinder, and her forward double 14-inch gun turret "B" was equipped with a 30-foot rangefinder. The major components of the main and secondary armament systems were stabilized to improve performance. The *King George V* was commanded by Captain W.R. Patterson and had a crew of 1,640 officers and men.

The *Prince of Wales*, a sister ship of the *King George V*, had just been commissioned less than two months earlier, on 31 March 1941, and was under the command of Captain John C. Leach. Technical problems with her main armament system had not as yet been corrected, and at the time she still had contractor personnel on board to assist in that effort. While many members of her crew had been drawn from other ships and had considerable experience in performing their tasks, others came directly from basic seamen's training programs or were recent graduates of naval technical schools. They were individually qualified to perform their tasks, but there was little opportunity for them to train together as a team and function as a cohesive unit.

The *Hood* had the next best chance of challenging the *Bismarck* by herself. She was comparable to the *Bismarck* in size, armament, and speed, and her crew was well trained and experienced. The *Hood*, however, was of World War I vintage, and despite several refits during the intervening years, she was still not up to the standards of a modern warship. Her greatest deficiency was the lack of adequate armor protection, especially her horizontal (deck) armor. This made the *Hood* especially vulnerable to plunging fire, which could penetrate into her vitals at longer ranges.

The *Hood* was built by the John Brown Shipyard at Clydebank near Glasgow, Scotland, and she was completed in 1920. She was commanded by Captain R. Kerr and had a complement of 1,421 officers and men. The *Hood* had a standard displacement of 42,500 tons and a full-load displacement of 48,400 tons. She had an overall length of 860 feet and a beam of 104 feet. Her four sets of turbines could develop 144,000 SHP. The maximum speed of the *Hood* had originally been 32 knots, but she could only do 29.5 knots after her retrofit in 1939. Although earlier equipped with a catapult and float planes, she no longer carried any aircraft since the mid-1930's due to design limitations.

The *Hood's* main armament consisted of eight 15-inch guns in four double turrets, two forward and two aft. Each Mk I 15-inch gun barrel was 52.5 feet (42-calibers) long, and with a muzzle velocity of 2,450 ft/sec, it could shoot a 1,920-lb. AP projectile 29,000 yards at a maximum elevation of 30°. The *Hood* also carried fourteen 4-inch guns, eight in four double mounts and six in single mounts, and a number of smaller anti-aircraft guns.

The *Hood* had two main armament fire control stations. The primary station was located directly over the conning tower in the forward part of the ship, and it was equipped with a fire control director and 30-foot rangefinder. The second station was located on the foretop, and it was also equipped with a director, but only a 15-foot rangefinder. Each of the *Hood's* four main armament gun turrets was also equipped with a 30-foot rangefinder for independent firing if necessary. For directing antiaircraft fire, the *Hood* had three Mk III HACS directors, each of which was equipped with a 15-foot rangefinder.

The *Repulse* was certainly no match for the *Bismarck*. She was also of World War I vintage, having been built at John Brown Shipyard in 1916, and even though she had been modernized in 1933 to increase her secondary armament and improve her armor protection, she did not have the firepower to match that of the *Bismarck*. The *Repulse* was 794 feet long, had a beam of 90 feet, and had a standard displacement of 32,700 tons and a full-load displacement of 37,500 tons. She had turbine engines that developed 120,000 SHP and a maximum speed of 31 knots. The *Repulse* carried six 15-inch guns in three double turrets, two forward and one aft, eight 4-inch guns in single mounts, and eight 4-inch antiaircraft guns. She was commanded by Captain W.C. Tennant and had a crew of 1,181 officers and men.

The *Victorious* could be of help under circumstances that permitted air operations and the launching of aerial torpedoes. She was 753 feet long, had a beam of 96 feet, and had a standard displacement of 26,000 tons. The *Victorious* was powered by turbine engines that could develop 110,000 SHP and drive the ship up to her maximum speed of 32 knots. She could carry as many as 72 aircraft, and she was then the home of No. 820 Fleet Air Arm Squadron and No. 825 Fleet Air Arm Squadron equipped with Fairey Swordfish I torpedo-bombers, and No. 800Z Fleet Air Arm Squadron equipped with Fairey Fulmer fighter aircraft. The *Victorious* was commanded by Captain H.C. Bovell, and she carried a crew of 1,392 officers and men.

The *Bismarck* alone presented a daunting challenge to the British Admiralty. From the information released by the Germans, and intelligence gathered by their own agents, the British realized that the *Bismarck* was superior, at least in some respects, than anything that the British had. While Britain tried to adhere to the terms of naval treaties limiting the size of capital ships to 35,000 tons, there were indications that the construction of the *Bismarck* was not being subjected to that restriction. The *Bismarck's* armament was announced to be eight 15-inch guns, the same as on most British battleships, but the *Bismarck* was likely to be faster and have heavier armor protection than the new British *King George V*-class battleships.

Then there was the matter of *Bismarck's* consort, most likely a heavy cruiser of the *Admiral Hipper*-class and probably the *Prinz Eugen*, the latest ship of that class. While her rapid-firing 8-inch guns would not be likely to inflict any mortal damage to a capital ship, they could cause some damage to communications equipment, fire control sights, and other critical equipment in lightly armored sections of a ship. She therefore could provide a significant contribution to the battle and tip the outcome in favor of the *Bismarck* in an otherwise equal situation.

Admiral Tovey concluded that this was clearly a situation where two capital ships operating in conjunction with each another would be needed to get the job done. He therefore divided his naval resources into two task forces. The battle cruiser *Hood* was teamed with the new, but not fully

Prince of Wales en route to Iceland as seen from *Hood. Drawing by the author*

operational, battleship *Prince of Wales* to form one task force. This was placed under the command of Vice-Admiral Lancelot E. Holland, who flew his flag on the *Hood*. As a precautionary measure, Admiral Holland was ordered to proceed immediately from Scapa Flow to the British naval base at Hvalfjord in Iceland, where he was to refuel his ships and await further developments.

Admiral Holland began his service in the Royal Navy as a gunnery instructor during World War I. Between wars, he commanded the Second Battle Squadron of the Atlantic Fleet, and early in World War II, he commanded the Seventh Cruiser Squadron operating in the Mediterranean. He was then assigned as commander of the Battlecruiser Squadron of the Home Fleet, which consisted of the battle cruisers *Hood, Repulse,* and *Renown,* before being appointed as the task force commander with the *Hood* as his flagship.

Since its own aircraft was unserviceable, the *Prince of Wales* took on board a Walrus seaplane flown in from the Hatston Naval Air Station near Kirkwall, the capital of the Orkney Islands, before departing Scapa Flow. Three civilian workmen from Vickers-Armstrong, the British armaments firm that provided the 14-inch gun systems for the *Prince of Wales*, agreed to remain on board the ship to continue with their work in correcting the problems still being experienced with her main armament system.

Shortly before midnight on 21 May, the *Hood* and *Prince of Wales*, in company with six destroyers, the *Electra, Echo, Anthony, Icarus, Achates,* and *Antelope*, set sail from Scapa Flow. The *Electra* and *Echo* were "E"-class destroyers that were built in 1934. They were 329 feet long, had a beam of 33 feet, and displaced 1,375 tons. Their turbine engines could generate 36,000 SHP and drive the ships at a speed of up to 35.5 knots. They carried four 4.7-inch guns in single mounts and eight 21-inch torpedo tubes in two quadruple mounts. The *Anthony, Icarus, Achates,* and *Antelope* were all "A"-class destroyers that were built in 1930. They were 323 feet long, had a beam of 32 feet, and displaced 1,350 tons. Their turbine engines could develop 34,000 SHP and drive the ships at speeds up to 35 knots. They carried four 4.7-inch guns in single mounts and eight 21-inch torpedo tubes in two quadruple mounts.

After weighing anchor, one by one the ships of the task force slowly headed south toward Hoxa Sound, the main entrance to the anchorage at

Hood en route to Iceland as seen from *Prince of Wales*. *Photo courtesy of MaritimeQuest*

Scapa Flow. As the lead ship approached the narrow opening at Hoxa Gate, tenders swung away the two steel anti-submarine nets that guarded the harbor. These steel nets were installed as a defensive measure after the World War I-vintage battleship, HMS *Royal Oak*, was sunk by the German submarine U-47, commanded by Lieutenant Günther Prien, when the U-boat penetrated the eastern approaches to the harbor on 14 October 1939.

When the task force reached the Pentland Firth at the southern end of the Sound of Hoxa, it turned west and headed for the Atlantic Ocean. As it reached the open waters at the western end of the Pentland Firth, the task force began to spread out and gain speed, with the destroyers taking their position around the *Hood* and *Prince of Wales* to act as an anti-submarine screen for those ships. By 0400 on the morning of 22 May, the task force was heading northwest toward Hvalfjord on a course of 310° and zigzagging at a speed of 20 knots. For the time being, Admiral Tovey would remain at Scapa Flow with the remainder of the Home Fleet pending further word on the *Bismarck*.

CHAPTER **9**

FINAL PREPARATIONS TO
INTERCEPT THE *BISMARCK*

I T WAS NOW URGENT TO LOCATE THE TWO GERMAN SHIPS spotted by the *Gotland* and to keep track of their movements. The Admiralty requested that the Royal Air Force (RAF) Coastal Command undertake reconnaissance flights along the coast of Norway in an attempt to locate and positively identify the reported warships. On the morning of 21 May, two Spitfires of the RAF Photo Reconnaissance Unit (PRU) took off from their base at RAF Wick on the northeastern coast of Scotland to scout the lower portion of the Norwegian coastline, especially its fjord systems which could easily hide the enemy ships. These aircraft were stripped down versions of the famous Spitfire III fighter, but they lacked any armament in favor of increased speed.

The low-winged Supermarine Spitfire III was 30 feet long, had a wingspan of 37 feet and weighed about 6,000 lbs. It was powered by a single 12-cylinder, liquid-cooled V-12 Rolls-Royce Merlin XX engine that generated 1,260 hp and could achieve speeds of up to 362 mph. The plane carried 85 gallons of fuel in a tank behind the pilot and another 133 gallons in two extra 66.5-gallon tanks, one in each wing, which gave it a range of 1,500 miles. The photo reconnaissance (PR) Spitfires had two F.8 and two F.24 cameras mounted in tandem in the fuselage to take overlapping pictures. These Spitfires were painted a light blue color overall to blend in with the sky, and they depended on speed to avoid enemy aircraft. While they had a ceiling of 40,000 feet, they generally operated at an altitude of under 20,000 feet while flying over enemy territory to avoid condensation trails which would reveal their location.

One of the PR Spitfires, piloted by Flying Officer Greenhill, was

RAF photo Spitfire flying over Norwegian fjords. *Drawing by author*

assigned to cover the southern coast of Norway and eastward up to Oslo, while the second aircraft, flown by Pilot Officer Michael "Babe" Suckling, was assigned to cover the southwestern coast of Norway as far north as Bergen. At about 1315, as Suckling was flying north near Bergen, he noticed what appeared to be a cruiser anchored in Grimstadfjord, an inlet off to the east. A short distance further north, he spotted what looked like another cruiser anchored off Kalvenes. He photographed both anchorages, and finding nothing further in the area, he headed back to his base.

When Suckling landed at RAF Wick nearly two hours later, he was met by a technician who immediately removed the cameras from the plane and brought the film to the nearby laboratory for development and printing. A team of photographic interpreters was standing by to go over the prints with magnifying glasses to find any indication of the German warships. One photograph taken over Grimstadfjord showed a large ship surrounded by several much smaller ones. The measurement of its length-to-beam ratio, i.e., 7:1, was consistent with that of a battleship, and the team was now certain that it was the *Bismarck*.

Another photograph, taken a short distance north of Grimstadfjord at

Kalvanes, revealed another large ship, about the size of a cruiser, surrounded by several smaller vessels. That must have been the companion of the *Bismarck* reported by the *Gotland.* The results of the photographic interpretation were then transmitted to the Admiralty, where the Sea Lords would have to make an overall assessment of the situation. There was little doubt that the larger of the two ships photographed in the fjords near Bergen, Norway was the *Bismarck,* and it was highly probable that the other ship was a heavy cruiser of the *Admiral Hipper* class, possibly the *Prinz Eugen.*

After the discovery of the *Bismarck* in Grimstadfjord, RAF Coastal Command was immediately ordered to bomb her anchorage. During the evening of 21 May, six Armstrong Whitworth Whitley bombers of the Coastal Command's No. 612 Squadron stationed at RAF Wick were dispatched to carry out that task. The Whitley Mk. V bomber was a mid-wing aircraft that was 71 feet long, had a wingspan of 84 feet, had an empty weight of 19,300 lbs, and could carry a bomb load of 7,000 lbs. It was powered by two Rolls-Royce Merlin X engines that developed 1,145 hp, and it had a maximum speed of 222 mph and range of 1,650 miles.

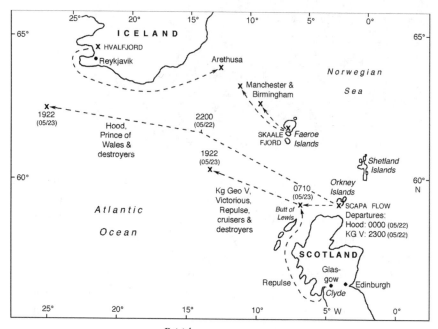

British countermeasures.

Aerial view of *Bismarck* anchored in Grimstadfjord. *Photo courtesy of Maritime Quest*

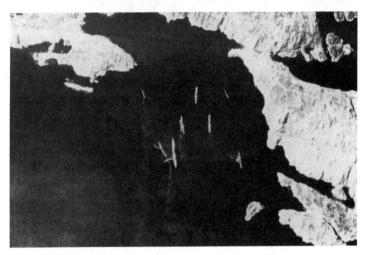

Aerial view of *Prinz Eugen* anchored near Kalvanes. *Photo courtesy of Maritime Quest*

Due to poor visibility, only two of the Whitleys were able to locate the target area, and they dropped their bombs blindly through the low cloud cover without being able to see the results. Continuing bad weather and low visibility prevented any further reconnaissance flights from Coastal Command bases the following day. RAF Bomber Command had been alerted to conduct additional bombing raids over the German ships' anchorages, but they were unable to get any of their aircraft off the ground. It appeared that no further intelligence on the ships would be forthcoming that day until a stroke of fate intervened.

British light cruiser HMS *Arethusa* (1935). *Photo courtesy of MaritimeQuest*

British Town-class light cruiser HMS *Manchester* (1938). *Photo courtesy of MaritimeQuest*

British naval aviation pioneer Captain Henry St. John Fancourt, a veteran of the battle of Jutland, had been given command of the Royal Naval Air Station at Hatston in the Orkney Islands in December 1940. The Hatston Naval Air Station was located about one mile northwest of Kirkwall, the capital of the Orkney Islands, on the Mainland Island, the largest island of the group. After the *Bismarck* and *Prinz Eugen* had been discovered at their anchorages in the Norwegian fjords, Fancourt obtained the release of No. 828 Squadron of Albacore torpedo bombers stationed at Hatston so that they could be redeployed to RAF Sumburgh in the Shetland Islands, where they would be closer to the German ships if they came through the passage between the Faeroe Islands and Iceland.

Fancourt was keeping abreast of efforts by Coastal Command aircraft to determine whether the *Bismarck* was still in Norwegian waters, and realizing the importance of that intelligence to the Allied cause, he was dismayed by the poor prospects of being able to make that determination. He believed that there might be a chance for a single aircraft from Hatston, manned by the most competent personnel available, to reach Bergen and find out if the *Bismarck* was still there.

Before taking any action in the matter, at 1400 Fancourt called in his proposal to his superiors at Coastal Command headquarters, who readily

British battleship HMS *King George V* (1940). *Photo courtesy of MaritimeQuest*

concurred in making the attempt. They of course realized that the mission would be difficult, and it would most likely not yield any results, but the Admiralty was desperate for any intelligence that would enable them to take the further steps necessary to stop the *Bismarck* from breaking out into the Atlantic. It was therefore well worth the risk, and with the approval of Coastal Command, Fancourt began to assemble the crew for the mission.

For the observer, Fancourt chose Commander G.A. Rotherham, a naval aviator with considerable experience in identifying objects at night and in poor visibility from the air. The commander of No. 771 Squadron based at Hatston, Lt. Comdr. Noel E. Goddard, was adamant about being the pilot of the aircraft, and Fancourt agreed to his selection. A radio operator and rear gunner were chosen from a number of volunteers to round out the crew. The aircraft chosen for the mission was a Martin 167 Maryland II light bomber, two of which were available at Hatston at the time.

The Martin 167 Maryland II was a low-wing monoplane that was 47 feet long, had a wingspan of 61 feet, and weighed 60,000 lbs. It was powered by two Pratt & Whitney R-1830-S3C4-G Wasp radial engines that gave it a maximum speed of 215 mph, and it had a range of 2,700 miles. A total of 150 planes of this type were purchased by Great Britain from the United States for the Fleet Air Arm, and it was used mostly for height-finding and target-towing purposes.

The aircraft took off at 1630 and headed for the Norwegian coast. As Goddard flew along the coast, the weather began to break, and by the time he reached the fjords where the *Bismarck* and *Prinz Eugen* had been located, it was clear enough for Rotherham to see that the anchorages were empty. To make sure that the *Bismarck* was truly out of the area, Goddard circled around and flew over Bergen where they encountered heavy anti-aircraft fire. Finding nothing there either, they radioed Coastal Command at 1900 that the *Bismarck* and *Prinz Eugen* were gone. Not satisfied with the radio communication, the Commander-in-Chief of Coastal Command waited until Rotherham had landed at Sumburgh in the Shetland Islands at 1945 to get a firsthand account of the discovery.

Upon receiving confirmation that the *Bismarck* had indeed sailed, Coastal Command passed the information on to the Admiralty, which immediately began to make further adjustments in its forces to counter the renewed threat. Over 24 hours had elapsed since the *Bismarck* and

King George
VI and
Tovey on
HMS *King
George V.*
Photo
courtesy of
Maritime
Quest

Prinz Eugen were last known to be at Bergen, and they could have sailed over 600 miles in that time. The *Hood* and *Prince of Wales* were directed to take station south of Iceland rather than proceed to the British naval base at Hvalfjord, as previously ordered. There they would be in a position to cover the Denmark Strait passage or back up the forces covering the Faeroes-Iceland passage should the *Bismarck* turn up in that area.

The *Suffolk* was ordered to rejoin her flagship, the *Norfolk*, in the Denmark Strait after refueling at Hvalfjord. The light cruiser *Arethusa*, then at Hvalsfjord, was ordered to proceed to the Faeroes-Iceland passage and support the *Birmingham* and *Manchester* on patrol in that passage. The *Birmingham* and *Manchester* were directed to refuel at Skaalefjord, a large inlet on the island of Eysturoy in the Faeroe Islands, and then resume their patrol of the Faeroes-Iceland passage. Skaalefjord was only a short distance away from its capital of Torshavn on the neighboring island of Streymoy.

Admiral Tovey then formed his second task force from the remainder of the Home Fleet that was still at Scapa Flow. This included the battleship *King George V*, the aircraft carrier *Victorious*, four light cruisers of the Second Cruiser Squadron, and six destroyers. The Second Cruiser Squadron was commanded by Rear-Admiral A.T.B. Curteis, and it consisted of his flagship, the *Galatea*, as well as the cruisers *Aurora*, *Kenya*, and *Hermione*. The *Galatea* and *Aurora* were light cruisers of the *Arethusa*-class, which has already been described earlier. The *Galatea* was laid down at the Scotts shipyard on 2 June 1933, launched on 5 August 1934, and completed on 4 August 1935. The *Aurora* was laid down at the Portsmouth Dockyard on 23 July 1935, launched on 20 August 1936, and completed on 12 November 1937.

The *Kenya* was a Crown Colony-class light cruiser of the *Fiji*-class that was laid down at the Stephens shipyard on 18 June 1938, launched on 18 August 1939, and completed on 27 September 1940. She had been assigned to the Tenth Cruiser Squadron at Scapa Flow, but she was released to become part of Admiral Curteis' command for this mission. The *Kenya* was 556 feet long, had a beam of 62 feet, and displaced 8,000 tons. Her turbine engines could produce 72,500 SHP achieving a speed of 33 knots. She carried twelve 6-inch guns in four triple turrets, two forward and two

Admiral Tovey
aboard his flagship
HMS *King George V.*
*Photo courtesy of
Maritime
Quest*

aft, eight 4-inch antiaircraft guns, and six 21-inch torpedo tubes.

The *Hermione* was an antiaircraft cruiser of the *Dido*-class that had just been commissioned on 25 March 1941, and had recently arrived at Scapa Flow to join the Home Fleet. She was laid down at the Stephens shipyard at Glasgow on 6 October 1937 and was launched on 18 May 1939. She was 512 feet long, had a beam of 51 feet, and displaced 5,450 tons. Her turbine engines could generate 62,000 SHP and could drive the ship at a maximum speed of 33 knots. The *Hermione* carried ten 5.25-inch dual-purpose guns in five dual turrets, three forward and two aft, and six 21-inch torpedo tubes in two triple mounts. The *Neptune*, a light cruiser of the *Leander*-class, did not sail with Tovey's task force, but remained at Scapa Flow with a number of destroyers and other vessels of the Home Fleet.

The destroyer force included the destroyers *Inglefield, Intrepid, Punjabi, Nestor, Windsor,* and *Lance.* The flotilla leader *Inglefield* was a destroyer of the "I"-class built in 1937. She was 337 feet long, had a beam of 34 feet, and displaced 1,530 tons. Her turbine engines could develop 38,000 SHP and drive the ship at a maximum speed of 36 knots. She carried five 4.7-inch guns in single mounts and ten 21-inch torpedo tubes in two quintuple mounts. The *Intrepid* was also an "I"-class destroyer built in 1937, but she was only 323 feet long, had a beam of 32 feet, and displaced 1,370 tons.

The *Punjabi* was a Tribal-class destroyer built in 1939. She was 378 feet long, had a beam of 37 feet and displaced 1,870 tons. Her turbine engines could develop 44,000 SHP and achieve a speed of 36 knots. The *Punjabi* carried eight 4.7-inch guns in four dual mounts, two forward and two aft, and four 21-inch torpedo tubes in a single mount. The *Nestor* was a destroyer of the "N"-class that was built in 1941. She was 357 feet long, had a beam of 36 feet, and displaced 1,690 tons. Her turbine engines could develop 40,000 SHP for a maximum 36 knots. The *Nestor* carried six 4.7-inch guns in three dual mounts, two forward and one aft, and ten torpedo tubes in two quintuple mounts.

The *Lance* was an "L"-class destroyer built in 1941. She was 362 feet long, had a beam of 37 feet, and displaced 1,920 tons. Her turbine engines could produce 48,000 SHP and drive the ship at a maximum seed of 36 knots. The *Lance* carried eight 4-inch antiaircraft guns in four dual mounts, two forward and two on raised platforms at the stern, and eight 21-inch torpedo tubes in two quadruple mounts. The *Windsor* was a World War I ship, having been completed in 1918. She was 312 feet long, had a beam of 30 feet, and displaced 1,100 tons. Her turbine engines could generate 27,000 SHP for a top speed of 34 knots. The *Windsor* carried three 4.7-inch guns in single mounts and three torpedo tubes in a single mount.

With his flag on the *King George V,* Admiral Tovey set sail with his task force at 2245 on 22 May. Following the same procedure Admiral Holland's task force had followed on the night before, the ships slowly headed south in a single file through the Sound of Hoxa, passing Hoxa Gate at 2307 and continuing down to the Pentland Firth. There the task force turned west toward the Atlantic Ocean, and upon reaching open waters they began to spread out and speed up. The four cruisers were clustered around the *Victorious* while the destroyers took their positions to the front, sides, and rear of the task force to detect any U-boats that might be lurking along the way. By 0800, the task force was well into the Atlantic Ocean, steering a zigzag pattern on a course of 320° at 18 knots.

The battle cruiser *Repulse,* about to embark on convoy duty, had been recalled from the Firth of Clyde area near Glasgow and ordered to join Admiral Tovey's task force at sea off the Butt of Lewis at the northern tip of the Outer Hebrides of Scotland. There the task force would lie in wait behind the light cruiser screen, ready to pounce on the *Bismarck* should she attempt to come through the Iceland-Faeroes passage, or be prepared to turn westward and support the *Hood-Prince of Wales* task force covering the Denmark Strait. The patrolling cruisers were on full alert, ready to report any sign of the German ships, and the two battle groups were ready to respond to any sighting of the foe.

Everything that could be done in preparation for the expected breakout attempt by the *Bismarck* and her consort had been done. Coverage of the two remaining passages, i.e., Orkneys-Shetlands and Shetlands-Faeroes, was left to the RAF in the unlikely event that the *Bismarck* and *Prinz Eugen* would attempt a breakout so close to the British Isles. In addition to the deployment of the Home Fleet, Force H at Gibraltar had been alerted for possible later support should the *Bismarck* succeed in breaking out. Convoys in the North Atlantic and their naval escorts were also alerted to the possible new danger that they might have to face under those circumstances. Now it became a waiting game until the *Bismarck* could be located.

• PART TWO •

THE BATTLE OF THE
DENMARK STRAIT

British County-class heavy cruiser HMS *Suffolk* (1928). *Photo courtesy of MaritimeQuest*

CHAPTER 10

INITIAL CONTACT BETWEEN
THE OPPOSING FORCES

T HE GERMANS WERE AWARE FROM THEIR INTELLIGENCE
reports that the British had laid minefields off the northwest coast of Iceland, and with the channel already narrowed by the pack
ice off the coast of Greenland, it became a rather risky operation for the
Bismarck and *Prinz Eugen* to negotiate the Denmark Strait. The German
squadron proceeded cautiously down the dangerous channel during the
afternoon of 23 May 1941, with the *Bismarck* and *Prinz Eugen* hugging
the ice cap as they went along. The Germans had to continue making constant turns around large ice floes that could damage the hulls of their ships
while still keeping as close as possible to the ice cap.

Some ten miles to the southwest, the British heavy cruiser *Suffolk* had
just completed the northeast leg of its patrol up the Denmark Strait, and
after hugging the ice cap on the way up, it turned around at 1900 and
sailed close to the edge of the mist on the southwest leg of its patrol route
on course 240°. By sailing close to the mist, the *Suffolk* could quickly take
cover in the fog should the need arise. Since the enemy was expected to
come down from the northeast, the stern watch was increased during the
southwest leg of its patrol to keep the northeast sector under full visual
observation since the *Suffolk's* Type 284 radar had a blind spot in that
direction.

The British minefield off Iceland was established in a definitive pattern
that provided gaps for the transit of friendly vessels, and the *Suffolk* was
careful to be aware of the location of those gaps at all times for possible
escape routes should she suddenly encounter the *Bismarck*. The *Suffolk*
continued on the southwestern leg of her patrol at the relatively slow speed

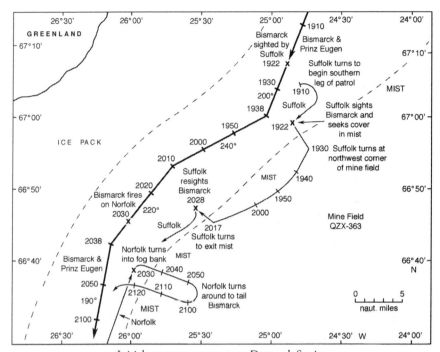

Initial contact at entrance to Denmark Strait.

of 18 knots, while the flagship of the First Cruiser Squadron, the *Norfolk*, was stationed 15 miles further down in the Denmark Strait.

At 1922, a lookout on the stern of the *Suffolk* spotted a dark shape emerging from the mist seven miles off the starboard quarter of the British cruiser, and he immediately gave the alarm. Soon a second shape appeared, and the crew of the *Suffolk* became aware that they had located the *Bismarck* and her heavy cruiser consort. The *Suffolk* quickly gained speed and turned to port into the mist, carefully avoiding the minefield laid in the area. At the same time, her radio operator transmitted a sighting report that was picked up by other Royal Navy ships and the British Admiralty in London.

Radar and hydrophones on the German ships had already detected a ship off their port bow, and a brief visual sighting of the object revealed a ship with a large superstructure and three funnels, most likely a British heavy cruiser. They intercepted the *Suffolk's* sighting report, alerting the Royal Navy of the presence of a German battleship and heavy cruiser in the Denmark Strait, and they realized that they had been discovered.

Admiral Lütjens thereupon sent a message to Group North advising them that the task force had been seen and reported by a British heavy cruiser.

The *Suffolk* waited in its secluded fog-shrouded area until the *Bismarck* and *Prinz Eugen* had passed, and then she moved out to take a shadowing position at the rear of the German squadron. The initial sighting report by the *Suffolk* was followed by a succession of reports from the cruiser that periodically provided information on the position, course, and speed of the *Bismarck* and *Prinz Eugen* as determined from its radar. This allowed the British to begin an accurate plot of the track of the German ships and plan for their interception.

Alerted by the *Suffolk's* initial sighting report, the *Norfolk* raced north to assist her teammate. At 2030, the *Norfolk* suddenly appeared out of the fog about six miles ahead of the *Bismarck*. The German battleship was quick to respond to this new threat and opened up with her forward main battery against the cruiser. The *Norfolk* quickly turned to starboard and headed for cover in the fog as shells from the *Bismarck's* salvos straddled the cruiser or landed in its wake. Fortunately for the cruiser, no hits were scored, but some shell splinters did reach the *Norfolk* without doing any serious damage.

At 2032, the *Norfolk* sent out its own contact report. Like the *Suffolk*,

British County-class heavy cruiser HMS *Norfolk* (1930). *Photo courtesy of MaritimeQuest*

the *Norfolk* also waited until the *Bismarck* and *Prinz Eugen* had passed before coming out and taking a shadowing position to the rear of the German ships. Since the *Suffolk* was already off the starboard quarter of the German squadron, the *Norfolk* stayed off the port quarter of the German ships. The pack ice precluded the Germans from turning to starboard, so the disposition of the British cruisers was ideal for keeping the German squadron under surveillance and reporting its position to other Royal Navy units. The two British heavy cruisers then settled down at a distance of 15-18 miles astern of the *Bismarck* and *Prinz Eugen* and maintained radar contact with them, feeding data on their location, bearing and speed to all concerned.

Admiral Lütjens was very much disturbed that he had been discovered so soon by two British cruisers lurking in the Denmark Strait. He was not sure whether this was just a chance encounter with ships already on patrol

German squadron appearing out of the mist. *Drawing by the author*

Norfolk ducks into a fog bank to avoid fire by *Bismarck*. *Drawing by the author*

in that area, or whether they were sent there specifically to intercept the *Bismarck*. The lack of positive intelligence on the disposition of the Royal Navy was also very frustrating to the German commander.

The blasts from the five salvos fired at the *Norfolk* disabled the forward radar of the *Bismarck*, and Admiral Lütjens ordered the *Prinz Eugen* to take the lead and become the "eyes" for the German squadron. Both ships had been traveling at a speed of 27 knots, and at 2045, the *Bismarck* began to move to port to allow the *Prinz Eugen* to pass the flagship on its starboard side. The *Prinz Eugen* increased her speed to 32 knots, and as soon as she had passed the *Bismarck* and assumed the lead, she reduced her speed to 27 knots again.

The *Norfolk* was fitted with a fixed radar that gave it only limited tracking capability. On the other hand, the *Suffolk* had recently been equipped with a Type 284 radar system that could be rotated, giving her more visibility of targets to the sides as well as to the front, but not to the rear. Admiral Wake-Walker therefore had to rely on the *Suffolk* with its superior radar system to play the key role in tracking the *Bismarck* and *Prinz Eugen*.

As soon as Admiral Holland aboard the *Hood* became aware of the position of the *Bismarck,* he began to finalize his plans for the engagement. Looking at the plot, Holland realized that he was in a very favorable position to settle the issue that very evening. The German squadron was sailing in a southwesterly direction, while Holland's ships were sailing in a northwesterly direction on an intercept course. Admiral Holland was well ahead of the German squadron and could reach the intercept point at about 0200 hours, an hour or so before the Germans could get there.

The British already had a two to one advantage over the German squadron in ships and firepower, and Admiral Holland had ideal conditions whereby he could steam across the path of the oncoming German squadron, giving him twice that advantage over the enemy. With this maneuver, referred to in naval circles as crossing the "T," Holland could place the *Hood* and *Prince of Wales* in a position to block the German squadron and bring their full broadsides to bear on the enemy vessels. On the other hand, the German squadron, coming toward the British blocking force, would be able to use only its forward batteries, and that would give the British force a four to one advantage in heavy firepower over the Germans.

If the *Bismarck* turned sideways, the British would still have a two to one superiority in firepower, and they would be able to divide the fire of the *Bismarck*, making it less effective. If the *Bismarck* turned tail and ran back into the Denmark Strait, the British would have accomplished their primary objective of keeping the *Bismarck* from breaking out into the North Atlantic, and she could be taken care of later. In the meanwhile, the *Suffolk* and *Norfolk*, coming up from the rear, would be in a position to jointly take on the *Prinz Eugen* at two to one odds.

During the remainder of the evening, both forces continued on their convergent courses with the *Suffolk* periodically reporting the position of the German squadron to the Admiralty as well as to Admiral Holland on the *Hood* and Admiral Tovey on *King George V.* The Germans made several attempts during the night to shake their pursuers by course changes, but to no avail. The *Suffolk* picked up every little movement of the German squadron and radioed the information back to the other elements of the Royal Navy.

At about 2200 hours, the *Bismarck*, under cover of a rain squall, doubled back on its course, hoping to catch the British cruisers by surprise, but the enemy was nowhere to be seen. The *Suffolk* had detected the maneuver by its radar, and both cruisers disappeared in the fog as the *Bismarck* approached. The *Bismarck* thereupon returned to its previous course, and the *Suffolk* and *Norfolk* soon caught up to the German ships and resumed their shadowing duties. Admiral Lütjens was now convinced that the British had superior radar and that it was fruitless to try any further maneuvers to break away from their grip on the German ships.

At about midnight, the German ships ran into a snow storm that interfered with the *Suffolk's* radar reception, and contact with the *Bismarck* and *Prinz Eugen* was lost. When contact was not regained within an hour, Admiral Holland decided to turn in a more northerly direction in an attempt to intercept the *Bismarck* should the German squadron turn south while hidden from radar contact. It was a difficult decision for Holland to make, but he could not afford to have the German squadron come down behind him and have free access to the North Atlantic. When contact was still not made by 0200 on the morning of 24 May, Admiral Holland turned in a southwesterly direction, still hoping to cut off the *Bismarck*. At 0246, the *Suffolk* finally regained radar contact with the German squadron and resumed sending out position reports. The *Bismarck* and *Prinz Eugen* had actually maintained their original course all along, and

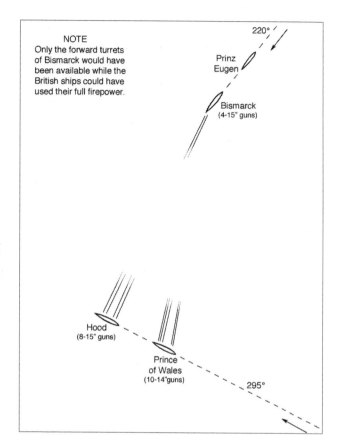

NOTE
Only the forward turrets
of Bismarck would have
been available while the
British ships could have
used their full firepower.

220°

Prinz
Eugen

Bismarck
(4-15" guns)

Holland's plan for
crossing the "T"
on *Bismarck*.

Hood
(8-15" guns)

Prince
of Wales
(10-14"guns)

295°

the maneuver by Admiral Holland turned out to be for naught. Apparently Admiral Lütjens wanted to keep a wide berth between himself and any additional British warships that might approach him from the east. He therefore kept on a course of about 220°, parallel to the coast of Greenland. This gave him limited space to maneuver to the west in the event of an encounter with heavy units of the Royal Navy due to the presence of pack ice off the coast, but it would also take more time for any British ships to reach him.

Admiral Holland was dismayed over this unfortunate turn of events and its consequences. His precautionary move of turning to the north when contact with the *Bismarck* was broken cost him precious time, and more important, the opportunity of being able to cut in front of the *Bismarck* was lost forever. He still had a slight lead over the Germans, but he was no longer far enough ahead of them to execute the blocking maneuver he had hoped for. This reduced his advantage considerably, and it would have a substantial impact on the outcome of the forthcoming battle.

Not wanting to engage in the darkness of night, Admiral Holland at 0321 ordered his task force to turn to course 240° which would allow for the interception of the *Bismarck* as soon as it became light. The *Hood* and *Prince of Wales* increased their speed from 27 to 28 knots at 0353 to ensure they would be able to engage the German squadron at dawn. Their escorting destroyers, however, had difficulty maintaining that speed in the heavy seas of the North Atlantic, so they were allowed to drop off and follow the battle group as best they could. Holland's destroyer escort had been down to four ships, the *Electra*, *Echo*, *Icarus*, and *Achates*, since the *Anthony* and *Antelope* had been detached at 1400 on the previous afternoon to refuel at Hvalfjord. With the remaining four destroyers falling back, the British task force was now without any destroyer escort.

CHAPTER **11**

INTERCEPTION OF THE
GERMAN SQUADRON

A DMIRAL LÜTJENS KNEW OF COURSE THAT HIS POSITION had been radioed to the Admiralty and that all of the available resources of the Royal Navy were being mustered against him. He did not know, however, how little head start he actually had. He was not aware that information on his passage through the Kattegat had been leaked to the British. He was not aware that his ships had been photographed at their anchorages in fjords near Bergen, Norway by an RAF reconnaissance plane, nor that his departure had been detected on the following day. And perhaps most important, Admiral Lütjens did not know of the whereabouts of the Home Fleet.

At 0407, the sensitive hydrophones in the *Prinz Eugen's* listening station began to pick up faint ship noises at a bearing of 286°. Lookouts on both the *Bismarck* and *Prinz Eugen* turned their sights in the direction of the sounds, but there was nothing to be seen on the horizon at that time. It was an hour before dawn, and the sky even to the east was still quite dark. At the time, the British force was still far over the horizon, over 80,000 yards (40 nautical miles) away. The hydrophone operators continued to monitor the noises as they very gradually became louder, and lookouts strained at their sights to get their first glimpses of the new intruders from that direction.

The sky to the east was beginning to lighten up at dawn, and thin plumes of smoke could be seen just over the horizon to the southeast. Lookouts on the *Bismarck* and *Prinz Eugen* kept their eyes glued to the smoke plumes to see if they could identify in any way the source of the smoke. At 0521, the German ships executed a 50° turn to port on course

170° and held that course for eleven minutes until 0532, when they resumed steaming on course 220°. The ships had been hugging the pack ice
along the coast of Greenland, and those turns placed the ships over 8,000
yards (4 nautical miles) further away from the ice pack, giving them more
space to maneuver.

The travel on course 170° also increased the rate of convergence between the two forces to 1,065 yards per minute during that 11-minute
period. Soon after the first turn at 0521, the tops of the thin spar main
masts of ships became visible over the horizon, and by 0532, the entire
masts and even the upper portions of their superstructures could be seen,
identifying the newcomers to be British warships. When the German ships
returned to course 220°, the rate of convergence was reduced to 325 yards
per minute again. The British ships were too far away and not as yet com-

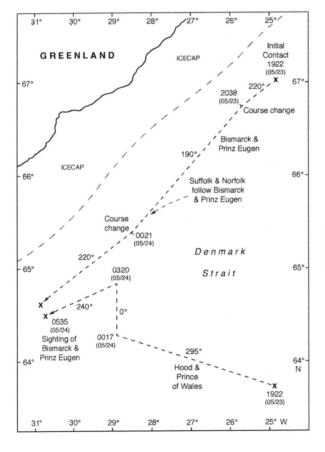

British and German
battle groups sight
each other.

pletely in view to allow them to be positively identified by the lookouts on the *Bismarck* and *Prinz Eugen.*

Lütjens had not received any new intelligence from the German Naval High Command regarding the disposition and movements of British naval units, so he could only speculate as to the nature of the British warships. In all probability, they were two more cruisers called in to reinforce the *Suffolk* and *Norfolk* in their surveillance role, which would make it more difficult for the Germans to shake their pursuers.

The German Naval High Command had earlier advised Admiral Lütjens that the British Home Fleet was still believed to be at its anchorage at Scapa Flow, and he had no reason to believe that any units had left the base since that time. It was therefore difficult for him to conceive that either or both of the two ships sighted might be capital ships, but he could not rule out that possibility. If, however, both ships happened to be older British battleships with a maximum speed of only 25 knots, the German ships could easily outrun them.

Another possibility was that the ships were two battle cruisers. Of the three battle cruisers in the Royal Navy, two of them, the *Renown* and the *Repulse,* were smaller ships, displacing only 26,500 tons and carrying only six 15-inch guns, but they had a speed of 29 knots. Together they could give the *Bismarck* some trouble by dividing her fire, but they were old and vulnerable ships and might be easy to put out of action by a modern, more powerful battleship such as the *Bismarck.* The third battle cruiser was of course the mighty *Hood,* which was about the same size and carried equivalent armament to the *Bismarck.* The *Hood,* in company with one of the smaller battle cruisers, could present a more formidable foe, but the *Hood* was also old and vulnerable.

The British had two new battleships, the *King George V* and *Prince of Wales,* each nominally displacing 35,000 tons and carrying ten 14-inch guns. These ships were theoretically comparable to the *Bismarck* and could attain almost the same speed. The *Prince of Wales,* however, was known to be still undergoing contractor fitting out and her crew was not fully trained, so her availability was questionable. That left only the *King George V* as a serious threat to the *Bismarck.* It had been in service for five months, sufficient time to forge her crew into an effective fighting unit and to work out the mechanical problems common to any new ship.

The worst-case scenario, from Admiral Lütjens point of view, would be the *King George V* in concert with the *Hood*. The *King George V* was a modern ship with a well-trained crew. The *Hood* was the mightiest warship in the world during the post World War I era, and she had already seen combat action in World War II. Her crew was battle-hardened and trained to the ultimate degree of proficiency in gunnery after decades of practice. Together, they could make it very hot for the *Bismarck*, and the *Prinz Eugen* would additionally be hard pressed to defend themselves against both British heavy cruisers coming up from the rear.

The two British warships to the southeast appeared to be traveling on a course roughly parallel to that of the German squadron, and they therefore did not yet represent any additional threat over that posed by the two heavy cruisers that had been tailing the Germans. A short time later, however, it was noted that the British ships had turned toward them at full speed, causing an alarm to be finally sounded on the German ships at 0547.

Admiral Lütjens was under standing orders to avoid any conflict with British warships unless necessary to get at Allied merchant ships carrying war materials to the British Isles. When it became apparent from the plot of the British ships just over the horizon that they were on a course to intercept him, Lütjens ordered the *Bismarck*, which was then about 3,000 yards astern of the *Prinz Eugen*, to increase speed to her maximum of 30.0 knots. At that speed, the *Bismarck* would be able to gain on the *Prinz Eugen*, still traveling at 27.0 knots, but only at a rate of 100 yards per minute. With the *Bismarck* being nearly 300 yards long, she could gain only about one ship-length every three minutes.

The gunners and spotters on the German ships looked hard into their sights to pick up any details of the British ships that would aid in their identification, especially as to their type and capabilities. The *Bismarck* had a 10.5-meter (34.5-foot) stereoscopic rangefinder atop its tower battle mast, which was about 110 feet above the level of the sea, and that provided the best possible view of the enemy. Lütjens continued to contemplate the situation he faced and was anxiously awaiting word on the identity of the two new threats so that he could finalize his plan of action against them.

By 0552, the British ships were fully on the horizon as seen from the foretop of the German ships, but they still could not be identified due to their sharp angle of approach. This led some German observers to still believe that the ships were merely two additional cruisers brought on the scene to assist in the surveillance of the German force.

After radar contact with the *Bismarck* had been reestablished by the *Suffolk*, and the position, course, and speed of the German squadron had been determined, the *Hood* and *Prince of Wales* settled down on a course of 240° and speed of 28 knots so as to intercept the *Bismarck* and *Prinz Eugen* as soon as it became light. Although the sky to the west was still very dark, visibility was continuing to improve during the early morning hours of 24 May, and by 0430, it was up to 24,000 yards (12 nautical miles).

As dawn approached on the morning of 24 May, the crews of the *Hood* and *Prince of Wales* were put on full alert. With both opposing forces steaming on convergent courses, it would be only a matter of time before visual contact was made with the German squadron. Lookouts strained at their sights to catch the first glimpse of the Germans, but it was difficult to make anything out against the dark sky just over the horizon to the west. Finally at 0535, lookouts on the upper director stations on the *Hood* and *Prince of Wales* were able to spot something over the horizon at a bearing of 335°, about 5° abaft the starboard beam of the British ships. Soon thereafter, a second suspicious object was sighted, and it became clear that the *Bismarck* and *Prinz Eugen* had both been finally located at a distance of 41,600 yards (20.5 nautical miles).

At that distance, the lookouts on the *Hood* and *Prince of Wales* were unable to determine exactly what they saw, but they knew that it had to be the German ships since nothing else was known to be in the area at the time. Actually, it was the top half of the large tower battle mast of each of the two ships that they had spotted, but in the darkness, they could not as yet clearly distinguish their shape. Even after visibility had increased as the two forces drew closer and closer together, the almost identical shape and size of the two tower battle masts made it impossible to determine which ship was the *Bismarck* based on that comparison alone.

The distance at which the *Bismarck* and *Prinz Eugen* had been sighted was still far beyond the maximum range of the main guns of the British force. The *Hood's* 15-inch guns could reach 30,000 yards at their maximum elevation of 30°, and the *Prince of Wales'* 14-inch guns could reach 36,000 yards at their maximum elevation of 40°, but the maximum range for effective naval gunfire was considered to be 25,000 yards. Beyond that range, the probability of scoring a hit was highly questionable and most likely just a waste of ammunition due to the normal dispersion of the projectiles from a salvo.

Admiral Holland still had a slight lead over the German squadron, sufficient to ensure that he could intercept the *Bismarck,* but he would no longer be able to put his ships directly in the path of the approaching German squadron as he had earlier hoped. The British task force had since been steaming on a course of 240° (west by southwest), while the German squadron was on a course of 220° (almost directly southwest), placing the two forces at a 20° angle of convergence. At that angle, the rate of convergence was about 325 yards per minute. This meant that the British force would not be within effective firing range of 25,000 yards for another 50 minutes if both forces maintained their present courses and speeds.

Since Admiral Holland did have a slight lead over the German ships, he could take advantage of the situation and bring the issue to a head sooner. At 0537, he ordered the British force to execute a 40° turn to starboard, which put it on a new course of 280°. This turn increased the rate of convergence to 930 yards per minute and would put the *Bismarck* within effective firing range in 17 minutes, or by 0554. The German ships would then be at a bearing of about 50° off the starboard bow, which would still give the *Hood* and *Prince of Wales* enough angle to bring their after turrets to bear.

By 0549, the range had closed to 30,000 yards, but the *Hood's* gunners could still not distinguish between the two German ships against the dark sky in the background. Realizing the importance of opening fire on the *Bismarck* first, Holland ordered his squadron to make another 20° turn to starboard on a new course of 300°, further toward the enemy. On that new course, the angle of convergence was increased to 80° and the rate of convergence was then nearly 1,200 yards per minute. Holland hoped that his gunners, trained to detect configuration differences between the *Bismarck* and *Prinz Eugen,* would soon be able to positively identify the two ships. Pending confirmation to the contrary, the *Hood's* gunners were assuming that the *Bismarck* was in the lead of the German squadron since it seemed more likely that the flagship would lead the squadron into battle.

The German ships had earlier been at a bearing of 50° off the starboard bow of the British ships, but after the British force made its last turn, the Germans were then at a bearing of only 30° off the bow of the

British ships. This no longer made it possible for the rear turrets of the British ships to swing forward enough to bear on the enemy. With a total traverse arc of 270°, the after turrets could only turn 135° forward in either direction from their normal aft position. This meant that the British could engage the enemy with only their forward turrets, reducing their firepower by almost half under those circumstances. At the new convergence rate of 1,200 yards per minute, the range would be down to the magic figure of 25,000 yards in just three minutes.

At 0549, the *Prince of Wales,* in compliance with a flag order from the *Hood,* also began to execute a 20° turn to starboard to course 300°, even though such a turn would also have "wooded" the after "Y" turret of that ship. That left only the forward turrets, i.e., the four guns of "A" turret and the two guns of "B" turret, available to fire on the *Bismarck*. From his somewhat higher vantage point on the *Prince of Wales,* Lt. Comdr. Colin McMullen, the first gunnery officer of the ship, could see a good part of the hulls of the German ships above the horizon. McMullen could then positively identify the right-hand ship as being the *Bismarck,* primarily due to its longer hull, and despite the dark sky above the horizon behind the enemy ships. After having positively identified the second ship as being the *Bismarck,* the gunners on the *Prince of Wales* tracked that ship to determine the range and lead angle for firing their guns.

CHAPTER **12**

THE BRITISH OPEN FIRE

THE TWO OPPOSING FORCES CONTINUED TO CONVERGE on each other, the Germans anxious to advance into the North Atlantic to attack Allied shipping, and the British equally determined to prevent them. The Germans had an excellent view of the British ships silhouetted against the light sky on the eastern horizon, but they still had difficulty in identifying them due to their sharp angle of approach. On the other hand, the German ships were still not fully visible on the horizon, and they were difficult to distinguish from one another against the darkest part of the sky in the west. Acting on the first sighting report from the *Suffolk*, and being unaware that the *Bismarck* and *Prinz Eugen* had switched positions during the night, the gunners on the *Hood* had been tracking the foremost ship in the belief that it was the *Bismarck*.

After several minutes of tracking the left-hand ship as more of it became visible on the horizon, the *Hood's* gunners were able to determine the speed and course of the target and work out a basic firing solution for their guns, considering the time of flight for the shells, the corresponding lead angle, and the projected distance to the target upon impact. However, even to the point of opening fire, it was still impossible to distinguish between the two German ships due to the dark sky in the background and the fact that their hulls were still below the horizon. This led the *Hood's* gunners to continue to erroneously assume that their target was the *Bismarck*.

In addition to the handicap of being able to use only half of his available firepower, Admiral Holland had now placed his ships in the precarious position of sailing on a diagonal course across the enemy's line of fire. This exposed his ships to the greatest probability of a hit from each salvo that straddled them. Since the fall of shot would be elongated along the line of fire, more projectiles from each salvo would have a chance of hitting the ship. On the other hand, if he had headed directly for the *Bismarck* to minimize the target area of the *Hood* and *Prince of Wales*, the *Bismarck* might have been able to pull ahead of the British task force. So under the circumstances, it was a "no win" situation for Admiral Holland.

At a range of 25,000 yards, the gun tubes on *Hood* would have been raised to an elevation of 22°. The elevation of the guns would then have to be continuously adjusted to compensate for the rolling and pitching of the ship up to the time of firing, thus ensuring accurate gun-laying regardless of the attitude of the ship. The gunners would then have to make necessary azimuth adjustments based upon the projected position of the enemy in relation to that of the *Hood*.

With the *Hood's* rear turrets "wooded" by the angle of approach, only the four guns in her two forward turrets were initially available to fire. Of even greater importance, however, was the fact that the *Hood's* gunners were concentrating on the wrong target since the lead ship was actually the *Prinz Eugen* and not the *Bismarck* as they had thought. The initial objective of any naval battle is to reduce the enemy's capability of inflicting damage to your own force as quickly as possible, so it is always prudent to concentrate your fire on the strongest enemy unit first.

With a forward freeboard of only 25 feet, the *Hood* was considered to

HMS *Hood* opens fire on German squadron. *Drawing by the author*

Shells from HMS *Hood* landing near the *Prinz Eugen*.
Photo NH-69723 courtesy of U.S. Naval History and Heritage Command

be a "wet" ship, subject to waves crashing over the forecastle in even moderate seas. Spray from the waves interfered with range-finding from her two forward turrets, each of which was equipped with a rangefinder having a 30-foot base. However, her main fire control director, located above the armored conning tower in the forward part of the superstructure, was also equipped with a 30-foot rangefinder, and this provided adequate range-finding capability. This director was supplemented by the aloft fire control director in the fore fire control top which was equipped with a 15-foot rangefinder.

At 0532:00, the range was almost down to 25,000 yards and Admiral Holland had to make a decision as to which of the German ships to take under fire, even though his gunners were still unable to positively identify which ship was the *Bismarck*. Admiral Holland finally gave the order to open fire on the lead ship, and a signal was sent to the *Prince of Wales* to engage the left-hand ship at a bearing of 337° and range of 25,000 yards.

At 0552:30, the four 15-inch gun tubes in the forward turrets of the *Hood* belched fire and smoke as they hurled armor-piercing projectiles weighing nearly a ton toward the foe. At the range of 25,000 yards, it would take about 50 seconds for the shells to reach their target, but since her guns could be reloaded in only 35 seconds, a second salvo was fired at 0553:05. This second salvo was fired at a shorter range to bracket the target and allow the gunners to acquire the correct range more quickly.

The gunners waited until the telltale splashes indicated the fall of the shots from the first two salvos and then made appropriate azimuth and elevation corrections. The *Hood's* first two salvos landed short of the target, and after making the necessary adjustments, the gunners fired another two salvos, 35 seconds apart, beginning at 0554:10. Fire was again directed at the lead ship, still believing it to be the *Bismarck*. Admiral Holland was anxious to inflict as much damage as he could on the battleship before she could reply with her own guns, but his error in continuing to fire at the wrong target was allowing the *Bismarck* to escape possible damage from the *Hood's* 15-inch guns.

After the *Hood* had fired its fourth salvo at 0554:45, a portion of the hulls of the German ships could finally be seen over the horizon, and it then became evident that the right-hand ship was the *Bismarck* by virtue of her longer hull. When advised that the *Hood* had been firing on the wrong ship, Admiral Holland immediately ordered his task force to switch targets. He then ordered the British task force to make a 20° turn to port, returning it to its earlier course of 280° and allowing the rear turrets of his ships to again bear on the enemy. When the British ships initially opened fire, the German squadron was 30° off their starboard bow at a bearing of 337°. The maximum forward travel of their after turrets was 45° off her starboard beam. The 20° turn ordered at 0555 placed the German squadron 50° off the starboard bow of the *Hood* and opened the arcs of her after turrets, but only barely with 5° to spare.

When the *Hood* settled down on her new course, her gunners revised their firing solution to account for the change in targets and the different rate of closure between the *Hood* and the *Bismarck* resulting from the turn. However, switching targets and adjusting to the turn at 0555 threw off the *Hood's* gunnery at a critical time during the engagement, and her gunners had to start almost from the beginning. The *Hood* fired her next two salvos at the *Bismarck* at 0555:45 and 0556:20, respectively, but still without scoring any hits. The *Hood's* last 20° turn to port did not quite allow her rear turrets to bear on the enemy, and she continued to be limited to using only her forward turrets, which greatly reduced the probability of her achieving a hit.

Shortly after the *Hood* fired her sixth salvo at 0556:20, an 8-inch shell from *Prinz Eugen's* second salvo hit the battle cruiser's upper deck and started a fire among the ready antiaircraft ammunition stored in lockers near the guns. The ammunition consisted of rounds for the twin 4-inch antiaircraft guns mounted on that deck as well as unrifled projectiles (UPs) intended for defense against enemy planes. While not a disastrous hit, it was nevertheless serious enough to cause some concern and distraction aboard the *Hood*.

The *Hood* fired her seventh and eighth salvos at 0557:20 and 0557:55, respectively, and although the salvo patterns appeared to be getting closer, the *Hood* was still unable to score a hit on the *Bismarck*. The *Hood* tried again with another group of two salvos at 0558:50 and 0559:25, but without success. With the *Bismarck* traveling at a slightly higher speed than the British task force, and on a course almost perpendicular to the line of sight from the British ships, the bearing of the target was gradually changing. By 0559, the German squadron was at a bearing of 330°, effectively eliminating the 5° leeway in turret travel and putting the after turrets of the British ships close to their maximum degree of rotation.

Since the after turrets of the British ships were at the end of their forward traverse limits, the ships had to make another turn to port to ensure that they could bear on the enemy. After the *Hood* fired her 10th salvo at 0559:25, Admiral Holland ordered his force to make another 20° turn to port on a new course of 260°. This turn, when fully executed, would have put the German ships at about 65° off the starboard bow of the British. With a 45° forward limit of traverse for the after turrets of the *Hood*, the additional turn would give the after turrets complete freedom to make further azimuth corrections.

Like the *Hood*, the *Prince of Wales* was also a "wet" ship due to her relatively low forward freeboard, and this allowed waves to break over her forecastle, even in

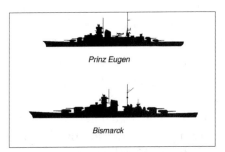

Prinz Eugen

Bismarck

Prinz Eugen

Bismarck

Above: Silhouettes of German ships against light background. *Below:* Same silhouettes against dark background

moderate seas. The longest base, and therefore the most accurate, range-finders on the *Prince of Wales* were incorporated at the rear of her two quadruple 14-inch gun turrets, the most forward "A" turret and the after "Y" turret. Spray from the waves precluded the use of the rangefinder in "A" turret and "Y" turret was wooded, depriving the *Prince of Wales* the use of her longest base and most accurate rangefinders.

The upper forward "B" turret was equipped with a 30-foot range-finder, but it also was rendered inoperative due to spray. That left only the relatively small and less accurate 15-foot rangefinders in the forward and after main armament fire control directors to determine the range to the *Bismarck*. The forward main armament fire control director was located behind and above the bridge of the *Prince of Wales*, and therefore it was not affected by the spray that precluded the use of the forward turret rangefinders.

The *Prince of Wales* was also equipped with two Type 284 radar sets located on the forward and after main armament fire control directors. These radar sets could also determine distances fairly accurately, but only up to 24,000 yards for surface targets. While ineffective at the beginning of the battle, these sets provided ranges that were integrated with data from other rangefinders to come up with firing solutions at ranges below 24,000 yards. The *Prince of Wales* was also equipped with four Type 285 radar sets for use with her 5.25-inch gun fire control directors and four Type 282 radar sets for use with her pom-pom guns.

The initial flag signal from the *Hood* to open fire on the left-hand ship caused some consternation aboard the *Prince of Wales*. McMullen had already identified the righthand (rear) ship as being the *Bismarck* and worked out a firing solution on that basis. After conferring again with McMullen, Captain Leach decided to ignore the order from the flagship and take the word of his own chief gunnery officer as to the identification of the German ships.

At 0553:00, 30 seconds after the flagship opened fire, the 14-inch guns of the forward turrets of the *Prince of Wales* let loose their projectiles, weighing about 1,600 pounds each, at the *Bismarck* at a range of 26,500 yards. The gunners of the *Prince of Wales* fired their salvos in groups of two to avoid having to wait for the fall of shot from the first salvo in the group before firing the next salvo. At the initial range of 26,500 yards, the time of flight of the *Prince of Wales'* shells would have been 48 seconds whereas the recycle time for her guns was 35 seconds. The second salvo was fired at 0553:35 at a range of 26,000 yards.

Both initial salvos by the *Prince of Wales* were "over," apparently as a result of gunners on the *Prince of Wales* wanting to get the range to the *Bismarck* by firing successive down ladders. After the *Prince of Wales* fired her first salvo, A-1 gun, the left gun in forward quadruple turret "A", went out of action due to mechanical difficulties, leaving only three guns in that turret operational.

At 0554:35, the *Prince of Wales* fired her third salvo at a range of 24,375 yards, and at 0555:10, she fired her fourth salvo at a range of 23,600 yards. These salvos were fired as another "down ladder" to get closer to the *Bismarck*, but both of them were still "over." The times of flight for those salvos were now a little over 40 seconds. The gun crew in turret A was finally able to correct the problem with the A-1 gun in time for the fourth salvo, but then it broke down again and remained out of action throughout the remainder of the battle.

When the gunners on the *Hood* realized their error of firing on the *Prinz Eugen* instead of the *Bismarck*, a flag order was given to "shift to the right-hand target," which of course the *Prince of Wales* was already complying with. This resolved the "sticky" situation created when Captain Leach decided to ignore the order from the flagship to fire on the lefthand target.

The *Prince of Wales* then fired two more salvos, her fifth at 0556:05 at 22,000 yards and her sixth at 0556:40 at 21,000 yards, in a further down ladder. The times of flight for those salvos were by then under 40 seconds. While the fifth salvo was still over, the sixth salvo finally achieved a straddle on the *Bismarck*, but no hits were observed. At 0557:35, the *Prince of Wales* fired her seventh salvo at a range of 20,000 yards, and at 0558:10, she fired her eighth at a range of 19,800 yards, but both of these salvos were "over." These salvos were still fired with only the forward turrets of the *Prince of Wales*, but she was finally able to bring her after quadruple "Y" turret to bear on the target in time for her ninth salvo.

At 0559:55, the *Prince of Wales* fired her ninth salvo at 18,000 yards, and at 0559:30, she fired her tenth at 17,000 yards as a regaining down ladder. The times of flight for the shells at that range were now just under 30 seconds. The ninth salvo was another straddle, but again, no hits were observed, and the tenth salvo was seen to be short. After firing her tenth salvo, the *Prince of Wales* began to execute a further 20° turn to port on course 260° in compliance with the signal from the *Hood*. This additional turn was necessary since the changing geometry of the battle arena brought the after turrets of the British ships to the end of their forward traverse limits again, and they could no longer bear on the enemy.

At about 05 59:20, the starboard secondary battery of the *Prince of Wales* opened fire on the *Bismarck* at a range of 18,000 yards. These 5.25-inch multipurpose guns in double mountings had a maximum rate of fire of 8 rounds per minute, and while they would not be able to inflict any mortal damage on a battleship, they could damage optical, communications, and other light equipment on the enemy ship. These guns, however, would soon be out of action as a result of damage done to their directors by hits from the *Bismarck*.

During the first six minutes of the battle, the *Prince of Wales* had the luxury of firing at the *Bismarck* completely unopposed and without receiving any counter-fire from the German squadron, which was concentrating its attention on the *Hood*. This was about to change when at 0558 the *Prinz Eugen* was ordered to switch targets to the rear ship, thought to be the *King George V*, and the *Prince of Wales* soon came under fire from the German cruiser.

CHAPTER **13**

THE LOSS OF HMS *HOOD*

H UGE COLUMNS OF WATER ERUPTED IN THE VICINITY OF the *Prinz Eugen* as the 15-inch projectiles fired by the *Hood* exploded nearby in the sea. A half a minute later, the *Bismarck* had a similar experience as shells from the *Prince of Wales* arrived in her area. If there was any doubt before as to the type of British ships involved, there was none any longer in the minds of the *Bismarck*'s gunners. Only the big guns of capital ships could have produced the blasts seen as the British opened fire on the German squadron and created the gigantic waterspouts caused by their shells exploding in the sea. The angle of approach by the British force still made it difficult to see any distinguishing features of the British ships, and therefore they still could not yet be positively identified.

Admiral Lütjens was surprised to see that the *Prinz Eugen* was also coming under fire from the British ships, but not nearly as much as the crew of the *Prinz Eugen* itself. An element of fear had to come over those aboard the cruiser with the realization that a single hit by a major caliber shell could easily wreak havoc on their relatively thinly armored ship. A 15-inch shell is about seven times more powerful than an 8-inch shell based on their relative weights (i.e., 1,900 pounds versus 270 pounds). The *Prinz Eugen*'s crew naturally assumed that the *Bismarck* would be the primary target of any British capital ships and that they might have to take on one or both of the enemy cruisers following the German squadron, but they did not expect to take fire from enemy capital ships.

Admiral Lütjens realized that he had a real fight on his hands and that he could no longer evade the issue. The range was down to 23,500 yards and the British ships were at a bearing of 70° off the port bows of the German ships, just 20° forward of their port beams. Lütjens finally gave permission to open fire on the British force. The Germans had gained the tactical advantage of being able to employ their full firepower while the British ships were initially limited to their forward turrets only, depriving them of their two to one superiority in firepower.

The *Prinz Eugen* had been traveling on a steady course of 220° since 0532, and her gunners had been tracking the lead ship for over 20 minutes. Although he had not been given any specific instructions from the flagship, Captain Brinkmann naturally assumed that the *Prinz Eugen*, being the lead ship of the German squadron, would take on the lead ship in the enemy column as commanders had done since the time of ships-of-the-line. The *Prinz Eugen's* gunners had been working on a firing solution as they went along, and they were therefore able to detect the last 20° turn to starboard by the lead ship at 0549 and make the necessary corrections before opening fire.

When permission was finally given to open fire, the *Prinz Eugen* fired a full salvo at 0555:00. With her fast-firing 8-inch guns, the *Prinz Eugen* could discharge as many as three to four salvos per minute, and she began a blistering attack on the lead ship in the British force, i.e., the *Hood*. Her guns had a muzzle velocity of over 3,000 feet per second, and her 23cm (8-inch) projectiles, each weighing 270 lbs., could cause some damage to lightly armored sections of even enemy capital ships.

Believing at first that the oncoming British warships were cruisers, the first gunnery officer of the *Prinz Eugen*, Paulus Jasper, decided to use high-explosive shells rather than armor-piercing ones, since they were more effective against lightly armored targets. This choice of ammunition was carried out for the entire period of the battle, but it did have the advantage of distinguishing the detonation of those shells from the armor-piercing shells used by the *Bismarck*.

At the time the *Prinz Eugen* opened fire, the range was down to 22,200 yards, and it would take 38 seconds for the results of her first salvo to become known. Not being certain that the splashes seen in the distance were from *Prinz Eugen's* shells, Jasper fired a second full salvo, which straddled the target and scored a hit on the upper deck of the *Hood*. The hit started a fire that remained visible to the German squadron for the next few minutes.

It was now the *Bismarck's* turn to get into the action. The *Bismarck* was directly astern of the *Prinz Eugen* at the time, but when the *Prinz Eugen* came under fire from the *Hood*, Captain Lindemann altered course to 215° which was 5° to port of the *Prinz Eugen's* course of 220°. With the *Bismarck* traveling at her full speed of 30 knots and *Prinz Eugen* continuing to travel at a speed of 27 knots, the *Bismarck* would eventually pass the *Prinz Eugen* off the cruiser's port beam. The *Bismarck* would then come between the *Prinz Eugen* and *Prince of Wales* and thereby place the *Prinz Eugen* on the lee side to protect the cruiser from heavy British gunfire as prescribed by German naval operating procedures.

The last turn to port by the British ships at 0555:00 put them at a more broadside inclination from the line of sight from the German squadron, and the gunners on the *Bismarck* were finally able to positively identify (erroneously) the enemy ships from their features as being the *Hood* and *King George V*, the worst-case scenario in their minds. The Germans thought that since the *Prince of Wales* had just been commissioned and did not have the time to weld its crew into a cohesive fighting unit, they did not consider the possibility that they would be facing the *Prince of Wales* instead of the *King George V*. The *Hood* was always the foe in war games played by the Kriegsmarine, and the *Bismarck's* gunnery crew was anxious to try out the tactics developed during those war games.

Admiral Lütjens was perplexed by the sudden appearance of what he believed to be the two most powerful ships in the Royal Navy and which were thought to be still at Scapa Flow. Not only had he been let down by his own intelligence service, but he at last realized that the British had been fully aware of his sortie all along and that this was not merely a chance encounter. The enemy knew exactly where he was, but Admiral Lütjens had absolutely no idea of the disposition of British forces that he knew would be directed to intercept him and keep him from accomplishing his mission.

When the *Bismarck's* gunners finally worked out the initial firing solution, considering the time of flight for her shells, the lead angle, and the corresponding range and azimuth, the *Bismarck* opened fire with a full salvo from her eight 15-inch guns on the lead ship shortly after 0555:30. At the time, the *Bismarck* was still 1,500 yards astern of the *Prinz Eugen*, and the range was down to 21,100 yards. With the *Bismarck's* guns having a muzzle velocity of 2,700 feet per second, her 1,760-pound armor-piercing projectiles would reach their target in 32 seconds.

The splashes from the *Bismarck's* first salvo landed ahead of the *Hood* and slightly short, and her gunners made the necessary adjustments in the azimuth and elevation of the guns before she fired again. Her second salvo was fired at 0557:00 at a range of 20,100 yards, and there was another wait of 30 seconds before the telltale splashes would reveal where it had landed and what further corrections might be necessary. The second salvo by the *Bismarck* also went wide of the target, but by then the gunners on the *Bismarck* realized that the British ships had probably made a turn to port from their previous course.

When the new course and speed of the *Hood* had been determined from successive sightings, the *Bismarck's* gunners worked out new range and azimuth settings for their guns. They then fired their third salvo at the *Hood* at 0558:00 at a range of 19,000 yards. After a 28-second wait, they could see the splashes of their shells erupt around the *Hood*. Again no hits, but they were able to straddle the target.

After her second salvo, the *Prinz Eugen* began a rapid-fire attack against the *Hood*, firing at a rate of one salvo every 25 seconds, but she scored no further hits. When the *Bismarck* achieved a straddle on the *Hood* with her third salvo, Admiral Lütjens knew that it was just a matter of time before the *Bismarck* would begin scoring hits on the British battle cruiser. Having the range on the *Hood*, and not wanting to leave the *Prince of Wales* unattended, Lütjens ordered the *Prinz Eugen* to shift target to the *Prince of Wales*. By that time, the *Bismarck* had probably received at least one if not two hits from the *Prince of Wales*, and coming under fire from the *Prinz Eugen* could possibly interfere with the gunnery of the British battleship sufficiently to make it more difficult for her to score any more hits on the *Bismarck*.

After firing her sixth salvo at the *Hood* at 0557:40, the gunners on the *Prinz Eugen* turned their sights toward the *Prince of Wales*. It took about a minute to make the necessary changes in elevation and azimuth, and at 0558:40, the *Prinz Eugen* begin firing at the British battleship. With this new arrangement, the lines of fire from the German ships would be crossing each other instead of being parallel or converging on one ship. The lead ship of the German squadron would now be firing at the rear ship in the British column while the rear ship in the German squadron would continue to fire at the lead ship of the British.

In addition to taking on the *Prince of Wales*, the *Prinz Eugen* was

Bismarck opens fire on HMS *Hood* (0555).
Photo NH-69722 courtesy of U.S. Naval History and Heritage Command

Bismarck moves up on port side of *Prinz Eugen*.
Photo NH-69729 courtesy of U.S. Naval History and Heritage Command

ordered by Admiral Lütjens to keep the British cruisers *Norfolk* and *Suffolk*, still trailing the German force, under observation and to prevent any unexpected incursion from that direction. At the time, the *Norfolk* and *Suffolk* were still over 10 nautical miles (20,000 yards) astern of the *Prinz Eugen*, and therefore they really posed no threat to the German squadron. At almost zero inclination, the *Bismarck* and *Prinz Eugen* could not even be distinguished from one another at that distance.

Having found the range, the *Bismarck's* first gunnery officer, Lt. Comdr. Adalbert Schneider, ordered the firing of three more salvos in rapid succession at the *Hood.* These salvos were 25 seconds apart, beginning at 0559:10 and at an initial range of 17,800 yards. After the fourth salvo, each additional one was then fired at a slightly reduced elevation with the hope that the *Hood* would sail into the impact area of each salvo as the range between the opposing forces continued to drop. The *Bismarck* fired her fifth salvo at 0559:35 at 17,300 yards, and it had a flight time of 25 seconds.

The first of three rapid-fire salvos (the fourth in total count) fired by the *Bismarck* straddled the *Hood* but without scoring any hits. The fifth salvo, however, landed with devastating effect at 0600:00, just as the *Hood* was still executing her second 20° turn to port onto course 260°. Most of the shells from that salvo fell harmlessly into the sea, but one projectile plunged into the stern of the ship in the area below her after turrets. The shell penetrated the *Hood's* armored side and exploded in one of her after magazines, causing the ammunition stored therein to blow up. British experts believe that the smaller magazine with ammunition for the secondary armament of 4-inch guns may have exploded first, and that this ignited the ammunition for the *Hood's* 15-inch guns in the main magazines.

A large sheet of flame was seen to shoot skyward near the mainmast of the *Hood,* and this was followed by a tremendous explosion in the after section of the ship. The *Hood* had been dealt a mortal blow when tons of cordite propellant stored in her magazines detonated. In the maelstrom created by exploding powder, high explosive shells could also be seen rapidly detonating. The force of the explosion literally tore the ship apart with debris consisting of shattered structural members, equipment, and even human remains raining down on the ship and the surrounding sea. A huge cloud of brown and yellowish smoke boiled skyward above the remains of *Hood,* marking the end of her long and illustrious career.

Hood is hit in stern end of ship and blows up. *Drawing by the author*

Hood blowing up as seen from *Prinz Eugen*.
Photo NH-69724 courtesy of U.S. Naval History and Heritage Command

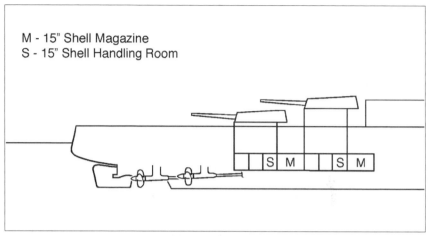

M - 15" Shell Magazine
S - 15" Shell Handling Room

Location of aft magazines and shell rooms on *Hood.*

Shells from *Bismarck's* sixth salvo land in front of *Hood.*
Photo NH-69731 courtesy of U.S. Naval History and Heritage Command

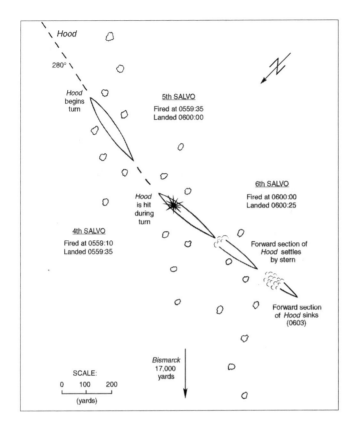

Bismarck's fourth, fifth and sixth salvos fired at *Hood.*

The *Bismarck* fired its sixth salvo at the *Hood* at 0600:00, just before her gunners realized that the battle cruiser had blown up, but it was a wasted salvo since the fifth one had already done the job. The sixth salvo landed in front of the huge smoke cloud enveloping the *Hood,* and it can be readily seen in one of the photographs taken from the *Prinz Eugen* during the battle.

The officers and crewmen on the bridge of the *Hood* were so concentrated on the ongoing action against the *Bismarck* that they scarcely noticed what had happened to their own ship. They felt the jolt when the ship was hit, but they had no idea at first that the after section of the ship had been blown away and that the *Hood* was in imminent danger of sinking. The helmsman first noticed that he had lost steering control of the ship, and then the rest of the bridge crew finally realized that there was something dreadfully wrong. They began to sense that the ship was slowing down and taking a gradual list to port. A look outside by one of the crewmembers revealed the stern obscured by smoke and confirmed the fact the *Hood* was indeed sinking by the stern.

The blown off aft section of the *Hood* quickly slowed down as its ragged broad surface, acting as a brake, pushed against the sea and rapidly filled with water. It gradually tilted forward as the water gushed in, lifting the stern end completely out of the water and exposing the ship's screws and rudder underneath. Within a minute, the stern slipped beneath the sea, taking all within it to a watery grave.

The momentum of the forward section of the *Hood*, however, caused it to surge ahead, but without the push from her screws, that section also began to slow down and take on water more rapidly through its shattered after end. As the after part of the ship became heavier, it caused the front end to begin lifting out of the water. Crew members who were on the bridge, in adjacent areas, in gun positions or other locations on deck, or

Aft end of *Hood* breaks away and sinks rapidly. *Drawing by the author*

Forward end of *Hood* takes on water from broken rear end. *Drawing by the author*

otherwise had access to avenues of escape, began to scramble for survival as the ship took on a greater list and sank deeper into the water.

As the *Hood* continued to sink downward by the stern, its forward section became almost upright out of the water, causing some to liken it to a church steeple. Observers saw what appeared to be the guns in the *Hood's* forward turrets fire one more salvo aimlessly into the air as the forward section of the ship continued to sink. After the *Hood* had fired her tenth salvo at 0559:25, her guns were probably reloaded and ready to fire by 0600:00 when she was mortally stricken. It may have been possible for the firing circuits to be short-circuited by the seawater gushing into the forward section of the ship, causing the guns to fire spontaneously.

However, the forward section of the *Hood* was later found to be separated from the rest of the hull on the ocean floor, leading to speculation that there may have been a secondary explosion in that part of the ship. Such an explosion with its resultant smoke could have been mistaken for the Hood firing one last salvo as she was sinking. The issue is still open to speculation.

Bow of Hood rises as stern end continues to sink.
Drawing by the author

Finally the sea closed over the bow of the *Hood* about three minutes after she had been struck, taking hundreds more of her crew in their steel tomb to the ocean floor. For a few moments, the sea seemed to boil as the air trapped in the sinking ship continued to bubble its way to the surface. All that remained on the surface after the bow disappeared were pieces of floating debris, patches of fuel oil, a couple of Carley rafts, and a few survivors.

There was little time to abandon ship once it became certain that the *Hood* was going to sink, however several crewmen were able to clear the ship before she went under. Admiral Holland and Captain Kerr apparently made no effort to escape and went down with their ship in true naval tradition. Eventually, only three crewman survived the sinking of the *Hood*. Thus ended the illustrious career of the most revered ship in the Royal Navy and one of the most renowned fighting ships in all of naval history.

Admiral Wake-Walker, who saw the *Hood* blow up from his position on the bridge of the *Norfolk*, immediately radioed the news to the Admiralty and to Admiral Tovey on *King George V*, which was still sailing on a westerly course to intercept the *Bismarck*. The news was initially received in disbelief: How could the pride of the Royal Navy be so quickly destroyed? But then reality set in, and now the entire weight of British resources would be devoted to avenge the *Hood* and sink the *Bismarck*.

The destruction of the *Hood* was reminiscent of the loss of three British battle cruisers during the battle of Jutland in World War I. The battle cruiser concept was the brainchild of Sir John Fisher, who as First Sea Lord of the British Admiralty before the war had a number of these ships built. Fisher believed that the thicker armor of battleships could be sacrificed for the greater speed of cruisers to enable heavy firepower to be brought into play more quickly during a naval battle.

The battle cruiser concept was discredited by the Battle of Jutland, and it was eventually replaced by the concept of the fast battleship, which offered a better balance between armament, armor protection, and speed. During World War II, the United States built two ships classified as battle cruisers—the *Alaska* and *Guam*—to counter Japanese cruisers and German pocket battleships, but these ships were not cost effective, and were scrapped after the war. Another ship of that class, the *Hawaii*, was launched, but never completed, and three more were authorized, but never even laid down as their programs were cancelled.

CHAPTER 14

HMS *PRINCE OF WALES* FIGHTS ALONE

WHEN THE *HOOD* BLEW UP, THE *PRINCE OF WALES* WAS also still turning to port, and if she had completed this turn, it would have put the ship directly in line with the sinking *Hood*. To avoid the wreckage of the *Hood*, Captain Leach ordered a hard turn to starboard. After the *Prince of Wales* had turned sufficiently to ensure that she could clear the *Hood*, Leach had the ship straightened out again. The *Prince of Wales* soon came abreast of the stricken *Hood* engulfed in a cloud of smoke. Through the smoke, Captain Leach could see part of the *Hood's* stern still sticking out of the water, but sinking rapidly. The forward section of the *Hood* had some remaining forward momentum, but it had taken a list to port and was settling rapidly at the stern.

The maneuver to avoid the wreck of the *Hood* turned the *Prince of Wales* toward the *Bismarck* and again "wooded" her after "Y" turret, keeping it from bearing on the enemy. As soon as the ship settled down and her forward guns could be retrained on the *Bismarck*, the *Prince of Wales* fired her 11th salvo at the German battleship with the remaining five operable guns

Hood explodes in path of turning *Prince of Wales. Drawing by the author*

of her forward turrets. This salvo was fired at 0600:45 at a range of 17,100 yards with a flight time of 27 seconds, but the salvo fell short. After firing her 11th salvo, the *Prince of Wales* turned hard to port to a new course that would enable her rear turret to train again on the enemy and allow her to resume firing full broadsides at the *Bismarck*.

At 0601:30, after the *Prince of Wales* had circled around the sinking remains of the *Hood* and settled down on her new course, she fired her 12th salvo at the *Bismarck* at a range of 17,100 yards. By that time, the *Prince of Wales* had regained the use of her after "Y" turret, but she had also lost the use of another forward gun due to mechanical difficulties. The A-3 gun of the forward quadruple turret temporarily went out of action after the 11th salvo, reducing that turret to only two operational guns. The total firepower of the *Prince of Wales* was now reduced by 20% with two of her ten 14-inch guns out of service.

The crews of the *Bismarck* and *Prinz Eugen* were at first struck with awe when the *Hood* blew up, and then they were overcome with elation. They had just destroyed the pride of the Royal Navy without receiving any significant damage in return. This was a truly remarkable feat, and it tended to confirm their earlier belief in the invincibility of the *Bismarck*. The Germans, however, soon came to their senses and realized that they were still facing a dangerous foe that could yet inflict grievous damage to their squadron and thwart their mission.

The *Bismarck's* gunners then turned their attention to the *Prince of Wales*. She was now at about the same range that the *Hood* had been when she was hit and just two degrees to the left. The *Bismarck* fired her first salvo at the British battleship at 0600:40, and by that time, the range was down to 16,200 yards and the flight time of her shells was 24 seconds. The gunners on the *Bismarck* did not detect the hard turn to starboard made by the *Prince of Wales* after the *Hood* had blown up, and they used the same lead angle as they did for the *Hood*, causing their first salvo to land harmlessly to the right of the target. After making the necessary correction in azimuth, the *Bismarck's* gunners fired their second salvo at the *Prince of Wales* at 0601:10 at a range of 15,700 yards.

A few seconds after the *Prince of Wales* fired her 12th salvo at 0601:30, a heavy hit was felt on the starboard side of the ship. *Bismarck's* second salvo had landed in line with the *Prince of Wales*, but just short of the target. One shell from that salvo, however, struck the *Prince of Wales* some

Bismarck fires on *Prince of Wales.*
Photo NH-69730 courtesy of U.S. Naval History and Heritage Command

25 feet under the waterline amidships. The partially spent shell pierced the hull plating of the *Prince of Wales* and continued another 12 feet within the hull before being stopped by an armored bulkhead, but without exploding. Having been an armored-piercing (AP) shell, it had not hit anything solid enough to set off the fuse. The hit, however, did cause some flooding and loss of fuel oil, which slightly affected the speed of the ship.

Since the shell did not explode, the gunners on the *Bismarck* were unaware of the hit on the *Prince of Wales*, knowing only that the salvo fell somewhat short of the target. After increasing the range to compensate for the short fall of the previous salvo, the *Bismarck* fired her third salvo at the *Prince of Wales* at 0601:40. That salvo flew mostly above the target, but two shells from that salvo, possibly fired from the same turret, struck the forward upper works of the *Prince of Wales* at about 0602.

One of those shells passed diagonally through the compass platform, an enclosed structure directly above the bridge from which Captain Leach was controlling the ship. At the time, the compass platform was also manned by the navigating officer and a number of ratings who performed mostly communications functions. The shell killed or wounded all at that station except Captain Leach and the Chief Yeoman of Signals. It also damaged or destroyed much of the equipment within the compass plat-

Bismarck off port beam of *Prinz Eugen.*
Photo BA-1401 courtesy of German Bundesarchiv; photographer, Lagemann

form. The armor-piercing shell continued though the port searchlight control position and the splinter shield surrounding that position without exploding.

A second shell from *Bismarck's* third salvo struck the support structure for the *Prince of Wales'* forward port and starboard high-angle (HA) 5.25-inch gun directors, severing the electrical leads to the forward port director and causing the forward starboard director to jam. The shell entered the large rounded opening in the front of the support structure and above the captain's sea cabin in the upper bridge house. It then traveled diagonally through the support structure and exited on the port side without exploding. The shell distorted the support structure and caused some other damage in the vicinity.

The 5.25-inch guns on the starboard side of the *Prince of Wales* had opened fire just a couple of minutes earlier when the range had come down to 18,600 yards. The guns had gotten off only three salvos before the director support structure was hit. Fire control for all the 5.25-inch guns was then switched to the rear pair of directors, but soon they were adversely affected by the other hit on the *Prince of Wales*. The limited fire by the *Prince of Wales'* secondary battery of sixteen 5.25-inch guns had no effect on the battle.

On the bridge of the *Prince of Wales*, the staff could hear the terrible sound of a heavy shell hitting the compass platform above, and soon, blood began to trickle down the voice tube by which orders were passed down from above. A party was immediately dispatched to the compass platform to determine what had happened, and when they arrived, they saw that it was in shambles. After surveying the scene, they gave first aid to the wounded navigating officer and assisted Captain Leach, who was momentarily dazed by the event, back down to the bridge, where he again took command of the ship.

Besides the physical damage done, the hit on the compass platform partially disrupted the command and control of the *Prince of Wales*, but not its firing. McMullen continued to maintain a constant rate of fire on the *Bismarck* from his station in the forward main armament director located between the compass platform and the support structure for the forward secondary armament directors, both of which were hit by shells from the *Bismarck*. Since those shells sliced through those structures without exploding, McMullen was totally unaware of those hits and was completely free to concentrate his efforts on hitting the *Bismarck*.

During the moments that Captain Leach was temporarily incapacitated, the *Bismarck* fired several more salvos at the *Prince of Wales* and scored one additional hit. The 15-inch shell first struck the starboard crane, knocking it out of service, and it then exploded on the boat deck abaft the ship's rear funnel. That hit did extensive splinter damage to nearby compartments and killed and wounded a number of personnel. Several boats were destroyed, and the Walrus aircraft on the catapult between the two funnels was so severely damaged by shell fragments that it had to be jettisoned overboard. The after port 5.25-inch gun director was also hit by shell fragments, putting it out of action and further curtailing fire by the secondary 5.25-inch gun battery.

At 0559:30, when the range came down to 18,000 yards, the secondary battery of the *Bismarck*, consisting of six 150mm (5.9-inch) guns in three double turrets on the port side of the ship, also began firing at the British. First gunnery officer Paulus Jasper on the *Prinz Eugen* reported seeing strikes by the secondary guns of the *Bismarck* on the *Prince of Wales*, which he also had under fire at the time. When the *Prince of Wales* was later inspected in a British dockyard, it was difficult to determine whether any of the hits scored on the ship were actually from 5.9-inch projectiles

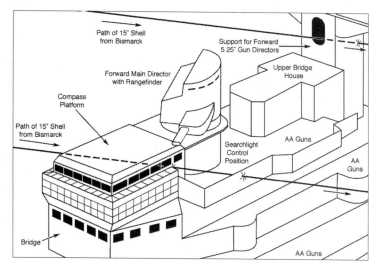

Hit on compass platform of *Prince of Wales.*

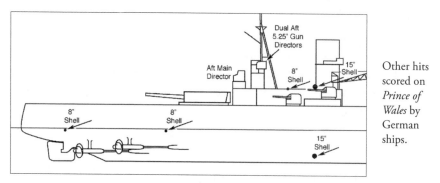

Other hits scored on *Prince of Wales* by German ships.

from the *Bismarck's* secondary battery as opposed to 8-inch shells from the *Prinz Eugen.*

Having been directed to fire on the *Prince of Wales* in compliance with an earlier order from Admiral Lütjens to switch targets to that ship, the *Prinz Eugen* was soon locked in on the target. The *Prinz Eugen* fired her first full salvo against the *Prince of Wales* at 0558:40 at a range of 18,400 yards. The shells from that salvo landed 30 seconds later, and at 0559:10, the *Prinz Eugen* fired a ranging group to straddle the target. When that was achieved, rapid-fire commenced with the *Prinz Eugen's* guns firing a salvo about every 25 seconds. Over the entire course of the battle, the *Prinz Eugen* fired an average of one salvo every 27-28 seconds.

The turns made by the *Prince of Wales* to get around the wreckage of the *Hood* momentarily threw off the gunnery of the *Prinz Eugen,* but as the *Prince of Wales* settled down on its new course, the gunners on the German cruiser finally regained the proper range and bearing to the target. In a matter of a minute or two, the *Prinz Eugen* began scoring hits on the *Prince of Wales*, adding to the damage done by the *Bismarck*.

One 8-inch shell from the *Prinz Eugen* penetrated the boat deck to the rear of the aft funnel of the *Prince of Wales*, destroying one of the boats on deck in the process. The shell continued through several compartments, beginning with the compartment containing the ammunition hoist for the nearby 5.25-inch gun mounts. The shell finally came to rest on the port side of the ship without exploding, and it was immediately thrown overboard by the crew.

The *Prinz Eugen* scored two more hits on the *Prince of Wales*, both of which were in the after section of the ship, and in both of these cases, the shells did explode, causing some damage. One shell entered the hull at about the waterline and just abaft the armored bulkhead, and the blast damaged several cabins in the area and caused the flooding of some middle deck compartments. The second hit was also at the waterline near the stern end of the ship. The shell exploded upon penetrating the hull near the steering gear compartment, and it also destroyed some cabins and caused additional flooding.

Prince of Wales continues to fire at *Bismarck*. *Drawing by the author*

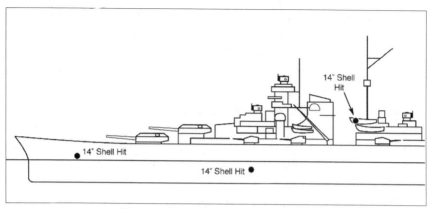

Hits scored on *Bismarck* by *Prince of Wales*.

In view of both latter hits occurring at about the same level, and the proximity of the two hits to one another, it is quite possible that these two hits were achieved by the same salvo, and even from two guns in the same turret. Salvos of multiple rounds generally have a dispersion factor of about one-degree or one-percent, e.g., 200 yards dispersion at a range of 20,000 yards.

Despite the hits and near misses scored by the German ships, the *Prince of Wales* continued to fire at the *Bismarck*. Her 12th salvo was still short, but her 13th salvo, fired at 0602:20 at a range of 16,500 yards, produced another straddle on the *Bismarck*. As with the two earlier straddles, no hits were observed by the spotters on the *Prince of Wales*. The *Prince of Wales'* 14th salvo, fired at 0602:55 at a range of 16,300 yards, however, was over.

At the onset of the battle, preparations were begun on the *Prinz Eugen* to launch a torpedo attack against the British ships should they come within range. The standard German 21-inch, type G7a (T1) torpedo used by the *Prinz Eugen* had a maximum range of 14,000 meters (15,300 yards), nearly eight nautical miles, at a speed of 30 knots. At that range and speed, it would have taken the torpedo a full 15 minutes to reach its target. However, with the *Bismarck* closing in on the port side of the *Prinz Eugen*, it was no longer possible for the cruiser to launch any torpedoes in the direction of the enemy since they would have cut directly across the path of the oncoming *Bismarck*. Captain Brinkmann made no mention in the *Prinz Eugen's* war diary of any intent to launch a torpedo attack against the *Prince of Wales*.

Captain Brinkmann realized that with the *Bismarck* continuing to come up on the port side of his ship, and with fire from the *Prince of Wales* often coming over the *Bismarck*, his ship might be in danger of being hit by one of those "overs." Since the *Prinz Eugen* would soon be in the line of fire from the *Prince of Wales*, at 0603:00 Brinkmann ordered his ship to make a series of turns to starboard that would increase the separation between the *Bismarck* and *Prinz Eugen*, making the cruiser less vulnerable to being hit. The maneuver also placed the *Prinz Eugen* on the lee side of the *Bismarck* sooner, giving her greater protection from fire by the *Prince of Wales*.

Captain Brinkmann would later explain his action as being necessitated by the sound of torpedoes believed to have been launched by the *Hood* before she blew up, but the *Hood* was actually too far away at the time to have launched any torpedoes, and the *Prince of Wales* was not even equipped with torpedo tubes. This maneuver, however, put the *Prince of Wales* out of range for the *Prinz Eugen* to fire her own torpedoes, and Brinkmann would later be criticized by his superiors for the failure of the *Prinz Eugen* to also use its torpedo armament against the British battleship.

The *Prince of Wales* fired her 15th and 16th salvos in a zigzag pattern, the first at 0603:45 at a range of 15,000 yards and the second at 0604:20 at a range of 15,100 yards, but both of those salvos fell short. With the Germans continuing to direct accurate fire against the *Prince of Wales* and the British ship seemingly unable to inflict any serious damage on the *Bismarck*, it was soon coming to the time when a decision had to be made regarding the continuation of this unequal struggle.

CHAPTER 15

THE END OF THE BATTLE

AFTER RETURNING FROM THE WRECKED COMPASS PLATform to the bridge below, Captain Leach, who was visibly shaken up by his experience, took stock of the situation. By that time, the *Prince of Wales* had already received four hits by 15-inch shells from the *Bismarck*, as well as three 8-inch shells scored by the *Prinz Eugen*. Difficulties were still being experienced with the main armament system of the *Prince of Wales,* and with two guns completely out of action, it was difficult to keep up effective fire. The damage done to the ship, while not critical in itself, obviously had an adverse impact on the execution of further combat operations by the crew.

In the exchange of gunfire between the two opposing forces, the *Prince of Wales* was definitely getting the worst of it with little if any damage having been inflicted on the enemy. With the *Prince of Wales* now coming under rapid fire from both German ships, the shell splashes of rounds that landed short in front of their ship were coming with such frequency that it became difficult for the gun crews of the British battleship to even spot their own fall of shot.

Believing that further engagement by the *Prince of Wales* could possibly result in more serious damage and even the loss of his ship, without being able to stop or seriously damage the *Bismarck*, Captain Leach ordered the *Prince of Wales* to withdraw from the arena. It was a difficult decision to make, but he felt that he had no other choice. He knew that there were other ships on the way to intercept the *Bismarck,* and he considered it foolhardy to risk a valuable asset of the Royal Navy for the very remote possibility of inflicting some damage to his opponent.

The *Prince of Wales* had actually scored three hits on the *Bismarck*, but

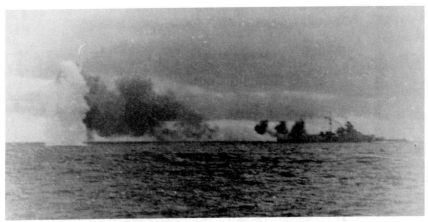

Bismarck continues to fire at *Prince of Wales*.
Photo NH-69728 courtesy of U.S. Naval History and Heritage Command

Shell from *Prince of Wales* lands near *Bismarck*.
Photo BA-1501 courtesy of German Bundesarchiv; photographer, Lagemann

none of them could be discerned by its crew amid the splashes of other shells hitting the water around the target. Some historians later speculated that the hits were probably scored when the *Prince of Wales* reported straddling the *Bismarck* with her 6th, 9th and 13th salvos. While this of course is feasible, there is also the possibility that the *Bismarck* may have received at least one hit by a salvo that was just short of the target. It is therefore impossible to establish the timing of the hits on the *Bismarck* with any degree of certainty.

At about 0605, Captain Leach ordered the *Prince of Wales* to execute a sharp turn to port on a course of 160° while producing a smoke screen to cover his withdrawal. During this turn, the *Prince of Wales* fired her 17th and 18th salvos at the *Bismarck*. The 17th salvo was fired at 0605:15 at a range of 14,100 yards, and the 18th was fired at 0605:50, also at the same range. Both salvos were ragged as the ship was under full wheel and tilting heavily at the time, but they were definitely short since it was later determined that the true range was actually 14,500 yards.

When the *Prince of Wales* completed its turn to course 160°, its forward main armament fire control director became "wooded" and the *Bismarck* could no longer be observed. The turn placed the course of the *Prince of Wales* almost perpendicular to the course of the German squadron, and the line of sight from the forward main director was thereby blocked by the support structure for the forward 5.25-inch gun directors. As a result, fire control was switched over to the after main armament fire control director. Unfortunately, however, the smoke created by the *Prince of Wales'* own smoke screen also obscured visibility from the after main armament fire control director of the ship. This in effect prevented the firing of any of the main armament guns of the *Prince of Wales* under central control.

The gunnery officer in charge of the after "Y" turret was able to see the *Bismarck* under the smoke, so he took it upon himself to fire four rounds from that turret under local control. He fired two one-round salvos between 0607 and 0608, the splashes of which were captured on two of the still photographs and on the movie film taken of the *Bismarck* from the *Prinz Eugen* during the last two minutes of the battle. A two-round salvo was probably fired after that since the *Prinz Eugen's* war diary had an entry at 0621 stating that the "*King George V*" fired shortly again, but that the impacts were outside of the area of the ship.

The *Prinz Eugen* continued to fire at the *Prince of Wales* during the sharp turns to starboard begun at 0603, but after the last turn was completed at 0607, the bow of the *Bismarck* became visible in the sights of Paulus Jasper, the first gunnery officer on the *Prinz Eugen*, which were trained on the *Prince of Wales*. It was apparent that the *Bismarck* was gradually coming between the *Prinz Eugen* and the British ship to protect the cruiser, and the order was soon given not to fire over the *Bismarck*. Right after that, the order was given to cease fire, and as soon as the *Prinz Eugen* fired her 28th and final salvo, she ceased fire at 0609:00.

With the *Prince of Wales* partially obscured by smoke, the *Bismarck* reduced her fire to groups of turrets, forward and after, and finally down to individual turrets, causing a "ripple" effect as seen from the *Prince of Wales*. After the *Prince of Wales* had turned to course 160°, she was almost perpendicular to the course of the *Bismarck*, and difficult to discern in the smoke cloud that she generated. At about 0606, the *Bismarck* fired a split salvo 10 seconds apart with her forward group of turrets at a range of 15,100 yards, and this was followed 40 seconds later with another split salvo from her after group of turrets at a range of 15,700 yards.

At about 0607, the *Bismarck* fired a split salvo with her forward group of turrets, and 25 seconds later she fired another split salvo with the same forward group. The range had now increased to 16,100 yards for the first salvo and 16,300 yards for the second. The *Bismarck* then fired a salvo from her after group of turrets, and after waiting for the results of that salvo to become known, she fired a ranging salvo from three of her four main armament turrets. The first turret to fire was a forward one, and this was followed by one rear turret and then the second rear turret.

With the target becoming more obscure with the increasing range and smoke, further expenditure of ammunition became unwarranted, and Admiral Lütjens decided to call off the action. Immediately after the *Bis-*

Bismarck is illuminated by flash from its own guns.
Photo NH-69726 courtesy of U.S. Naval History and Heritage Command

marck fired one last salvo from her forward turrets at the departing *Prince of Wales*, the order was given to cease fire at about 0610. At the same time, Lütjens ordered the *Prinz Eugen* to again take the lead of the German squadron, and the cruiser immediately began to increase her speed from 27.0 to 32.5 knots. The *Prinz Eugen* maintained that speed from 0610 to 0620, but once she had passed the *Bismarck* and attained a comfortable lead over the flagship, the *Prinz Eugen* cut back her speed to 30.5 knots.

The Germans were somewhat surprised to see the *Prince of Wales* turn away from the action and retire behind a smoke screen in such a short period of time. They knew that both the *Prinz Eugen* and the *Bismarck* had probably scored hits, but they had no idea of how seriously the ship was damaged. There was some sentiment expressed by Captain Lindemann and other officers aboard the *Bismarck* that they should pursue the *Prince of Wales* and "finish her off," but that of course was out of the question. Admiral Lütjens realized that to pursue the *Prince of Wales* would be contrary to his standing orders from the German Naval High Command to avoid any engagement with enemy naval units whenever possible.

While the *Prince of Wales* was undoubtedly damaged, there seemed to be little impact on her firepower, and she was therefore still capable of inflicting serious damage on the *Bismarck*. Lütjens also had to consider

Bismarck fires final salvo at retreating *Prince of Wales*.
Photo NH-69727 courtesy of U.S. Naval History and Heritage Command

32° 10'
32° 00'
31° 50'
31° 40'
31° 30'
170°
0532
0535
Bismarck &
Prinz Eugen
63° 30'
63° 30'
220°
0553
Prinz
Eugen
215°
41,600
yards
0605
25,000
yards
63° 20'
63° 20'
14,500
yards
Bismarck
Prince of Wales
opens fire on
Bismarck
British ships
sight German
squadron
0535
Prince
of Wales
retreats
0605
0559
Hood
blows up
0600
280°
0553
Turn
0555
300°
Prince
of Wales
240°
Turn
0549
280°
Turn
0537
Hood
160°
63° 10'
63° 10'
Prince
of Wales
32° 10'
32° 00'
31° 50'
31° 40'
31° 30'

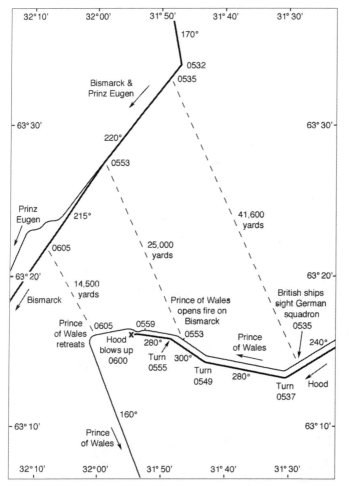

Overall map of the battle of the Denmark Strait.

that pursuit of the enemy battleship could lead the German squadron closer to other British naval units that were undoubtedly on their way to intercept the Germans. Furthermore, it was still believed that the retreating British battleship was actually the more experienced *King George V* and therefore would probably not be that easy to "finish off."

The German ships had no sooner ceased fire with their main armament when there was an enemy aircraft alert caused by the sudden appearance of a Sunderland flying boat in the vicinity. Realizing that the Sunderland could carry bombs, primarily for use against German U-boats, both ships opened fire on the aircraft, which thereupon headed for cloud cover. Antiaircraft fire continued for the next few minutes whenever the Sunderland came into view, but a cease-fire was ordered at 0620 when the aircraft settled down and maintained a surveillance position astern of the German squadron out of range of their antiaircraft fire.

The *Prinz Eugen's* cameraman Lagemann took one last battle photograph of the *Bismarck* shortly after 0610. It showed the battleship just after it fired its last salvo at the *Prince of Wales* and while the smoke cloud from her firing was still prominent. A second or two later, the movie cameraman ceased filming the action, thus ending photographic coverage of the battle.

Paul Schmalenbach, the second gunnery officer on the *Prinz Eugen*, observed the battle from his post at the main antiaircraft action station, and he acknowledged in his report included in the *Prinz Eugen's* war diary that he turned his sights to look at the *Bismarck* several times during the latter phase of the battle. With the *Bismarck* coming up on the port side of the *Prinz Eugen*, all he would have had to do was turn his sights a few degrees to the left to see the flagship, and he could easily risk this small digression before returning his full attention to the target. After the war, Schmalenbach wrote an article on the *Prinz Eugen* that included a diagram showing the *Bismarck* on the port side of the *Prinz Eugen* from 0600 until after 0609.

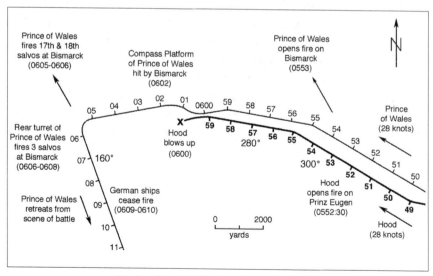

Tracks of the British ships during the battle.

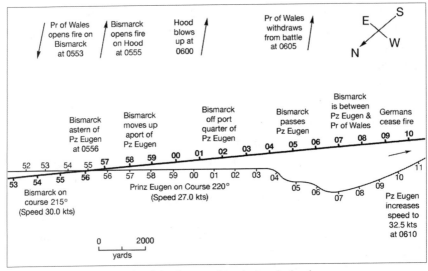

Tracks of the German ships during the battle.

The *Bismarck* fired six salvos against the *Hood* and twelve salvos at the *Prince of Wales*, although toward the end, they were not full salvos. The *Prinz Eugen* fired a total of 28 salvos during the battle, six directed at the *Hood* and 22 at the *Prince of Wales*. On the British side, it was estimated that the *Hood* fired ten salvos during the battle, the initial four at the *Prinz Eugen* and the remaining six at the *Bismarck*. Her salvos were mostly 4-gun salvos fired from her forward turrets, and therefore she consumed a limited amount of 15-inch shells before she was stricken. The *Prince of Wales* fired a total of 18 salvos under the control of her forward main armament director and three more salvos totaling four rounds from her "Y" turret under local control. She was also initially limited to her forward turrets and was further handicapped by the breakdown of at least two of her forward 14-inch guns.

CHAPTER **16**

BRITISH HEAVY CRUISER OPERATIONS DURING THE BATTLE

A S DAWN ON THE MORNING OF 24 MAY APPROACHED, there was much apprehension aboard the ships of the First Cruiser Squadron with the knowledge that a great sea battle was about to take place in front of them. At 0537, the cruisers received the message from the *Prince of Wales* stating that it had sighted the *Bismarck*, and this was followed at 0543 with *Hood's* sighting report. At the time, the British cruisers were 15 miles (30,000 yards) astern of the German squadron and following it at a speed of 29 knots.

Until then, the First Cruiser Squadron was operating independently under Admiralty orders, but once the *Hood* and *Prince of Wales* came on the scene, the unit fell under the operating control of Admiral Holland as the senior commander in the area over Rear-Admiral Wake-Walker. Holland devoted his full attention to coming to grips with the *Bismarck*, and he therefore issued no orders to Wake-Walker regarding the role of the cruisers in the forthcoming battle. As a result, the First Cruiser Squadron continued its assigned task of tailing the German squadron and reporting on its activities.

At 0553, the *Suffolk* reported heavy gun flashes bearing 185° with the *Bismarck* firing to port half a minute later, and at 0556:30, the *Suffolk* reported that the *Prinz Eugen* had opened fire to port. Actually, the *Hood* opened fire at 0552:30, followed by the *Prince of Wales* at 0553:00, and the German ships did not open fire until 0555:00. The *Suffolk* then reported at 0559 that the *Hood* had blown up, but the *Prince of Wales* reported the time as being 0600. In many cases, times given in reports are based on after-the-fact reconstructions of events that took place, and therefore they could be off by a minute or more.

When the *Hood* sank, taking down Admiral Holland with her, Rear Admiral Wake-Walker then became the senior officer on the scene, and therefore the *Prince of Wales* came under his command. When Captain Leach advised him of his intention to break off the action with the *Bismarck*, Wake-Walker had no alternative but to concur in that decision since he had no detailed knowledge of the condition of the *Prince of Wales* or any other circumstances bearing on the matter. Wake-Walker, however, did intend to find out as soon as possible whether the *Prince of Wales* was still able to support the ongoing operations against the *Bismarck*.

At 0605, the *Suffolk* reported that it had set a course and speed to keep on the starboard quarter of the German squadron. At 0612, she reported that the fighting had ceased, except for some AA fire from the *Bismarck* that was being directed at a Sunderland flying boat circling the area. The report went on to state that three hits from heavy ships' fire were observed on the *Bismarck* during the action, but gave no specific information regarding those hits.

At 0616, the Type 284 ranging radar on the *Suffolk* was indicating a range of 19,000 yards while trained on the *Prinz Eugen*, causing its crew to believe that the *Prinz Eugen* had turned and was now closing on them. At 0619, the *Suffolk* opened fire in the direction of the *Prinz Eugen*, using range data from its Type 284 radar. By 0623, the ranges started decreasing rapidly, and a minute later, it was down to 12,400 yards. Realizing that there was something wrong, the *Suffolk* ceased fire after firing six salvoes toward the *Prinz Eugen*. It was later deduced that the radar had actually been ranging on the Sunderland flying boat that had been flying over the area at the time.

The *Suffolk* continued tracking the German squadron on a course of 210° and at a distance of 18 miles (31,700 yards) with the *Norfolk* off to the port side of her. Shortly after 0630, the *Norfolk* came close to the point where the *Hood* went down, but she could not stop to pick up any survivors. It was far too important for the cruisers to maintain contact with the German squadron and lead heavy units of the Royal Navy to intercept the *Bismarck*. Wake-Walker ordered the destroyers that were originally part of the *Hood* and *Prince of Wales* task force, but were left behind in rough seas, to pick up *Hood* survivors as the ships came upon the scene.

By 0630, the *Prince of Wales* had turned around and sailed on a course of 250° to join the First Cruiser Squadron. Captain Leach transmitted a detailed report on the damage sustained by the *Prince of Wales* to Admiral Wake-Walker, who then considered the *Prince of Wales* to still be a valuable asset to the squadron in a supporting role. At 0707, Wake-Walker ordered the Prince of Wales to follow the squadron on course 210° at a speed of 26 knots.

As more information on the Battle of the Denmark Strait later became available, there was some criticism of Admiral Holland for failing to take full advantage of the firepower of the two heavy cruisers on the scene in his battle against the *Bismarck* and the *Prinz Eugen*, pointing out the significant contribution of the *Prinz Eugen* toward the outcome of the battle. Such criticism fails to take into account the unfavorable circumstances that Admiral Holland was faced with as a result of the *Suffolk* losing contact with the German squadron for nearly three hours on the morning of the battle.

Upon arriving at the scene of the battle, Holland had only a slight advantage in distance over the German squadron, necessitating that he approach at an acute angle that prevented the after turrets of his own ships from bearing on the enemy. He gradually swung around with two 20° turns to port to open the arcs on the after turrets of the *Hood* and *Prince of Wales*, but by that time it was too late. Before either ship could complete its last turn, the *Hood* was fatally hit by a shell from the *Bismarck*, leaving the *Prince of Wales* alone to face the combined firepower of the *Bismarck* and *Prinz Eugen*.

The Germans had the speed advantage over the British ships with the *Bismarck* being able to do 30.0 knots and the *Prinz Eugen* 32.5 knots, versus 29.0 knots for the *Prince of Wales* and 29.5 for the *Hood*. Anything other than an immediate assault on the German squadron would have allowed the *Bismarck* and *Prinz Eugen* to gradually pull away from the *Hood* and *Prince of Wales*. There was just no time at all for Holland to assemble his forces into a more effective fighting unit before taking on the *Bismarck* and *Prinz Eugen*.

The primary responsibility of the First Cruiser Squadron was to maintain contact with the German squadron and radio its position, course and speed to the Admiralty and other units of the Royal Navy closing in on the enemy force. This could only be done from the rear, and at a safe distance to avoid coming under fire from the *Bismarck* should she suddenly reverse course, as she had done once before during the night. Even if the *Norfolk* and *Suffolk* had increased their speed to 32 knots at the beginning of the battle, the most that they could gain on the *Bismarck* was 70 yards per minute, and it would have taken them over an hour from 15 miles away to even come within effective gun range of the German ships.

While Admiral Holland could be faulted for some of the decisions that he made, which was easy to do with the benefit of 20/20 hindsight, there appears to have been little opportunity for the effective use of the two heavy cruisers during the battle under the circumstances.

CHAPTER **17**

EXPLOITS OF THE RAF COASTAL
COMMAND DURING THE BATTLE

THE BRUNT OF THE EFFORTS TO STOP THE *BISMARCK* FELL
on the Royal Navy; however, significant contributions
were made by the RAF Coastal Command in support of those operations.
The Coastal Command was established in 1936, and its primary mission
in World War II was aerial reconnaissance and anti-submarine warfare. It
was also involved in commerce raiding of German transport ships, air-sea
rescue operations, and weather observation.

On 15 April 1941, operational control of the Coastal Command was
assigned to the Admiralty in view of the latter's primary role in conducting
sea warfare in the Atlantic. This allowed the Admiralty to issue direct
orders to Coastal Command units in critical situations while the Royal Air
Force continued to manage personnel, equipment and logistics matters
for those units. At the time of the *Bismarck* operation, Coastal Command
was commanded by Air Marshal Sir Frederick Bowhill, and its headquarters was at Northwood, a western suburb of London. The headquarters
was physically located in the adjacent settlement of Eastbury in the county
of Hertfortshire, but it was served by the Northwood Post Office in the
Hillington District.

As previously mentioned, a specially-equipped Spitfire from the Photo
Reconnaissance Unit of Coastal Command based at RAF Wick, Scotland
photographed the *Bismarck* and *Prinz Eugen* at their respective anchorages
in the fjords near Bergen, Norway on 21 May. On the following morning,
a flight of Coastal Command bombers attempted to bomb the anchorages,
but only two planes were able to reach their objective due to the poor visibility. They dropped their bombs blindly over the target area without

being able to determine the results of their efforts. Subsequent reconnaissance flights during the day by Coastal Command aircraft were also hampered by bad weather and low visibility, and it was not until early evening that it could be confirmed that the German ships had sailed.

Since the Denmark Strait was one of the most likely routes for the German squadron to take to reach the Atlantic, Coastal Command ordered No. 98 Squadron, based at RAF Kaldadarnes on the southwestern coast of Iceland, to patrol the Denmark Strait on a continuous basis. No. 98 Squadron was equipped with Fairey Battle I aircraft for this purpose, and at dawn on 23 May, the first Battle took off, followed later by two additional planes in sequence. The first Battle ran into rainy weather and poor visibility, causing it to abandon its patrol, and the two others had to return to base for the same reason a short time later.

The Fairey Battle I was an all-metal, three-man, low-wing light bomber powered by a single 1,030-hp Merlin engine mounted in its nose. The aircraft was 52 feet long, had a wingspan of 54 feet, and weighted 10,800 lbs. The Battle was armed with a single starboard wing-mounted 0.303 cal. machine gun and a Vickers K-gun that could be fired from the rear cockpit. It carried a bomb load of 1,000 lbs that was stowed internally within its wings, and it had an operating range of 1,000 miles. The first Battle entered service with the Royal Air Force in 1937, and production continued until 1941.

When Coastal Command received word that the *Bismarck* and *Prinz Eugen* had been sighted by the heavy cruisers *Suffolk* and *Norfolk* patrolling the northern entrance to the Denmark Strait at 1922 on 23 May, it immediately ordered No. 269 Squadron, also based at RAF Kaldadarnes, to reconnoiter the area. Flight Lt. Devitt took off in his Lockheed Hudson L/269 at 2118, but after flying over the area for a couple of hours and seeing nothing in the darkness below, he returned to his base, landing at 0205 on the following morning.

Hudson G/269, piloted by Flying Officer A.J. Pinhorn, took off from Kaldadarnes at 0200, just before Hudson L/269 landed, to take up the patrol of the Denmark Strait, and it arrived at the scene of the battle just as the *Hood* blew up. It remained in the area for a short while before returning to its base at 0835. One additional Hudson from No. 269 Squadron, D/269 piloted by Sgt. Grieg, participated in the effort to assist the British naval task force in its battle with the *Bismarck*. It took off at

0505, but the pilot was never able to see the German ships, and he returned to base at 1117.

The Lockheed Hudson III was an American-built light bomber and reconnaissance aircraft adapted from the design of the Lockheed 14 Super Electra commercial airliner to meet RAF specifications. The low-wing, twin-tail aircraft was 44 feet long, had a wingspan of 65 feet, and weighed 17,500 lbs fully loaded. It was powered by two 1,200-hp Wright Cyclone 9-cylinder radial engines. It carried two 0.303 cal. machine guns in the nose and two 0.303 cal. machine guns in a dorsal turret, and it had a payload of 750-lbs in bombs or depth charges. The plane had a maximum speed of 255 mph and a combat range of 2,160 miles.

In addition to the landplanes based at Kaldadarnes, a Short Sunderland long-range flying boat, currently under the operational control of No. 100 Wing at the RAF Flying Boat Base, Reykjavik, Iceland, was added to the resources being devoted to stop the *Bismarck*. The Sunderland Z/201 was assigned to No. 201 Squadron based at RAF Sullom Voe in the Shetland Islands north of Scotland, but on 12 May 1941, this aircraft was redeployed to Reykjavik to add to the capabilities of No. 100 Wing to fulfill its long-range reconnaissance mission. A couple of months earlier, on 19 March, RAF Area Headquarters, Iceland was established over No. 30 Wing (landplanes) and No. 100 Wing (flying boats).

At 2035 on 23 May, Sunderland Z/201, commanded by Flight Lieutenant R.J. Vaughn, took off from the Flying Boat Base at Reykjavik and headed for the Denmark Strait to locate the *Bismarck*. He arrived at the scene at about 0555 and first spotted a County-class heavy cruiser, probably the *Norfolk*, which would have been closer to the approaching aircraft than the *Suffolk*, steaming at a speed of 28 knots on course 240°. Further ahead, Lt. Vaughn could see gunfire being exchanged between two lines of ships traveling on parallel courses at about 12 miles (24,000 yards) apart. The leading ship in the left column, i.e., the *Hood*, was seen to be on fire but still able to fire her main armament guns. The identity of the ships could not yet be determined at the time.

The Sunderland then headed over the starboard column of ships, and the second ship in line, i.e., the *Bismarck*, was seen to be smoking and trailing oil. The *Bismarck* had indeed been hit by the *Prince of Wales* and was losing oil, but the smoke most likely came from the *Bismarck's* funnel since there was no fire on board the ship. While approaching the German formation, Lt. Vaughn saw an explosion on the foremost ship in the port column of ships that had been on fire, witnessing the doom of the *Hood* at 0600. At about the same time, the Sunderland came under antiaircraft fire from the German ships and had to seek cloud cover.

When the Sunderland emerged from its cloud cover a couple of minutes later, only the tip of the *Hood's* bow was still above water. That would have been about 0603 since later testimony at the Admiralty inquiry into the sinking of the *Hood* indicated that the *Hood* sank in three minutes. The second ship in the port column, i.e., the *Prince of Wales*, was then seen to fire a salvo at the *Bismarck*, which came close but scored no hits. Soon after that, the ship reversed course, laying a smoke screen to cover its withdrawal. This observation is consistent with the *Prince of Wales* retiring from the scene of battle at 0605, as described earlier. Lt. Vaughn reported that the battle lasted for ten minutes after he arrived on the scene, further establishing 0605 as the time when the *Prince of Wales* turned away from the engagement.

Lt. Vaughn then witnessed the *Bismarck* and *Prinz Eugen* continue to fire at the *Prince of Wales* as the latter sailed away, but no further hits were scored. The Sunderland kept going in and out of cloud cover to avoid enemy antiaircraft fire, but still keeping the enemy squadron under observation. Upon emerging again from clouds, the Sunderland flew over the area where the *Hood* had gone down and saw that the sea was covered with debris and a large oil slick from the sunken ship. A Carley raft could be seen amid the floating remains of the *Hood*, but no survivors were visible from the aircraft.

Sunderland Z/201 remained on the scene for about another three hours, cruising just out of range of the antiaircraft guns of the German squadron and keeping the British warships below continuously informed of its course and speed. The aircraft then headed back to its base, landing at the RAF Flying Boat Base Reykjavik at 1003 after being airborne for over 13-1/2 hours.

The design of the RAF Short Sunderland high-wing flying boat was based generally on the famous "C"-class Empire flying boats produced by the Short Brothers aircraft company of Rochester, England for commercial use. The Sunderland Mk.1 was 85 feet long, had a 110-foot wingspan, and weighed 50,100 lbs. It was powered by four Bristol Pegasus XXII 1,010-hp 9-cylinder engines, had a top speed of 210 mph, cruising speed of 178 mph, and a normal range of 1,780 miles. The aircraft had a payload of 2,000 lbs in bombs, mines, or depth charges, and carried two 0.303 cal. machine guns in a nose turret, four 0.303 cal. machine guns in a tail turret, and one 0.303 cal. machine gun on either side of the fuselage aft of the wing.

Three Hudson bombers of No. 269 Squadron stationed at Kaldadarnes also participated in the search for the *Bismarck* during the early morning hours of 24 May. Hudson G/269 took off at 0200 and arrived at the scene at 0354. Its crew was able to see the *Hood* blow up in the distance, but little else, and it returned to base at 0835. Hudson D/269 took off at 0505 and was airborne until 1117, but its crew was not able to see the enemy ships at all due to the poor visibility below. Hudson M/269 followed Hudson D/269, taking off one minute later than D/269 at 0506, and it remained airborne for over six hours. Its crew was able to see the British cruisers on the scene, but the capital ships could not be identified and it returned to base at 1140.

The task of shadowing the *Bismarck* was taken over by Catalina flying boat L/240 of RAF No. 240 Squadron. No. 240 Squadron was based at RAF Killadeas on Lower Lough Erne in Northern Ireland, but Catalina L/240 was currently deployed to RAF Flying Boat Base Reykjavik to enhance its long-range reconnaissance capabilities, as was Sunderland Z/201.

Catalina L/240 took off from Reykjavik at 0708 and headed west to the last reported position of the *Bismarck*. The Catalina L/240 sighted the Bismarck at 1232, and also keeping out of range of German antiaircraft guns, it continued to relay information on the course and speed of the German squadron to surface units. The aircraft maintained contact with the German squadron until 1440, but then it developed a problem with one of its two engines and had to return to its base.

"Catalina" was the name given by the Royal Air Force to the American-built Consolidated PBY-5 flying boat used by the U.S. Navy and sold to Great Britain under the wartime "Lend-Lease" Program. The U.S. Navy later officially adopted the name "Catalina" for its own PBY-5 aircraft. The Catalina was a high-wing aircraft with its wing raised above the fuselage by a large pylon structure and further supported by struts to keep it well above the water. Its outer wing floats were uniquely retractable, folding outwards to become the wing tips.

The Catalina I was 64 feet long, had a wingspan of 104 feet, empty weight of 17,500-lbs, and a full load weight of 34,000 lbs. It was powered by two Pratt & Whitney R-1830-82 1,200-hp radial engines that were mounted in the leading edge of its wing. The aircraft had a top speed of 190 mph, cruising speed of 115 mph, and a range of over 2,500 miles. It was armed with two 0.303 cal. machine guns in its nose turret, one 0.50 cal. machine gun in each of its waist blister gun positions, and one 0.303 cal. machine gun in the lower part of the tail, and it could carry a 4,000-lb load of bombs or depth charges.

The RAF Coastal Command continued to participate in the *Bismarck* operation and was destined to soon play a vital role in the eventual destruction of the German battleship.

• PART THREE •

EVENTS SUBSEQUENT
TO THE BATTLE

Prinz Eugen passes *Bismarck* after the battle.
Photo courtesy of U.S. Naval History and Heritage Command

CHAPTER 18

BRITISH FORCES REGROUP TO PURSUE THE *BISMARCK*

WHEN THE *HOOD* WAS LOST, REAR-ADMIRAL WAKE-Walker automatically became the senior commander on the scene by virtue of his rank over Captain Leach, but not having been directly involved in the action against the German squadron, he wisely left the decision-making on further conduct of the battle to Captain Leach. When Captain Leach decided to have the *Prince of Wales* break off the action with the *Bismarck*, Admiral Wake-Walker concurred in that decision, but he was determined to find out whether the *Prince of Wales* could still contribute to the overall effort being made to stop the *Bismarck*.

The *Prince of Wales* continued to retire at full speed on course 160° until she was out of range of the *Bismarck's* guns. She then began to slow down, and at about 0630 she turned to port, circled around, and then proceeded on course 250° toward the *Norfolk*. During this time, Captain Leach further assessed the damage to his ship and sent out a report to Admiral Wake-Walker and the Admiralty, stating that "A" and "B" turrets were in action, but only two guns in "Y" turret were ready. He further reported that about 400 tons of water had entered the ship, mainly abaft the after bulkhead, and that the compartment above the steering compartment was flooded, but that the steering gear was in action. Captain Leach concluded with the assertion that the estimated best speed of the *Prince of Wales* was 27 knots.

Based upon Captain Leach's damage assessment, Admiral Wake-Walker believed that the *Prince of Wales*, despite the damage it sustained, would still be a valuable asset to his squadron. The *Prince of Wales* remained a potent fighting machine that might yet be needed to help destroy the *Bis-*

marck in conjunction with other units of the Royal Navy en route to intercept her. At 0633, Wake-Walker advised Captain Leach of his intention to continue maintaining contact with the German squadron to keep it under surveillance with the assistance of the *Prince of Wales*.

Admiral Wake-Walker then turned to other pressing matters, the most urgent of which was the rescue of the *Hood's* survivors. His flagship, the *Norfolk,* passed close to the area where the *Hood* had gone down, but there was nothing that he could do about it at the time. There was the more urgent need to keep the *Bismarck* under surveillance and direct other units of the Royal Navy to intercept the German squadron and end its threat to Allied shipping. At 0637, Wake-Walker radioed the destroyers that had been escorting the *Hood* and *Prince of Wales* before they were detached by Admiral Holland due to rough seas and ordered them to perform the task of rescuing the *Hood* survivors.

It took the remaining four destroyers, the *Electra, Echo, Icarus,* and *Achates,* over an hour to reach the position where the *Hood* had gone down, arriving on the scene at 0745. The sea was covered by an assortment of floating debris and patches of oil, and amid the flotsam, the *Electra* could find only three survivors out of the *Hood's* complement of 1,421

Prinz Eugen again takes the lead of the German squadron.
Photo courtesy of U.S. Naval History and Heritage Command

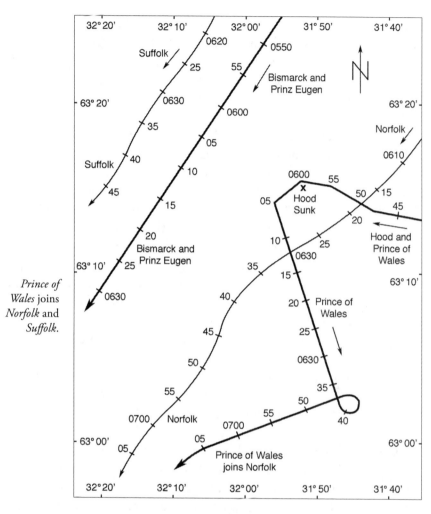

officers and men. Two of the survivors were swimming, while the third
was in a Carley raft. Midshipman W.J. Dundas was on duty as midshipman of the watch on the upper bridge of the *Hood* during the action. Sea-
man R.E. Tilburn was on the boat deck when the *Hood* was fatally stricken,
and Ordinary Signalman A.E. Briggs was on the compass platform at the
time. All would later give testimony at the Admiralty inquest into the loss
of HMS *Hood*.

The destroyers continued to search the area for over an hour, but finding no more survivors, they finally had to abandon their efforts at 0900.
The destroyers set sail for Hvalfjord, the British naval base in Iceland,

where they arrived at 2000 that evening. There the *Electra* dropped off the three *Hood* survivors for medical treatment. With the *Anthony* and *Antelope* already at Hvalfjord, having been detached earlier to refuel, all of the six destroyers of Admiral Holland's original screening force were now reunited at Hvalfjord, and they remained at the base pending further instructions.

At 0707, Wake-Walker ordered the *Prince of Wales* to follow his flagship at best speed, giving the *Norfolk's* course as 210° and speed as 26 knots. A half hour later, at 0737, the *Prince of Wales* was ordered to maintain a position ten miles astern of the *Norfolk* and be prepared to engage the enemy if the *Bismarck* reversed course to attack the cruisers. Course and speed were to be adjusted as necessary to maintain that position.

Engineers and damage control parties on the *Prince of Wales* quickly took stock of the damage that the ship had sustained. Debris was promptly removed, repairs within the scope of the crew were undertaken, and the *Prince of Wales* was soon made as ship-shape as possible. The civilian contractor workmen on board continued working on the main armament system, which had still given the gun crews trouble throughout the engagement. They finally succeeded in restoring, at least temporarily, the full firepower of the ship with the two defective guns of "Y" turret having been made ready to fire at 0720. The command and control of the ship was resumed on the compass platform and the *Prince of Wales* was again operationally ready for further action.

On the *Bismarck*, the chief engineering officer, Lt. Comdr. Walter Lehmann, and his staff began making a detailed assessment of the damage done to the ship as a result of the three hits scored by the *Prince of Wales*. One of those hits was relatively minor and caused only superficial damage. The shell struck one of the boats stored on the upper deck, but it did not explode, continuing on until it hit the water on the far side of the ship. Another shell struck the port side of the ship below the armor belt under the forward secondary 150mm gun turret, flooding the forward port generator room and power station and damaging the bulkheads near two of the boiler rooms. Power was eventually lost completely in the flooded power station, but the *Bismarck* had sufficient redundant power to keep all of its essential combat equipment operating.

The third hit, however, was far more serious. The shell struck just above the waterline in the forward part of the hull, but well within the area covered by the bow wave, allowing water to gush into the hull with every wave that the *Bismarck* plowed through. Water cascaded into the hull, especially through the large five-foot exit hole on the starboard side of the ship, and this caused the flooding of several compartments.

Temporary repairs to the damaged hull were made during the battle, but more permanent repairs were begun after the action. Although attempts were made to seal the holes and pump out the water, they were not completely successful. Nearly 2,000 tons of water remained in the flooded compartments of the ship, and this caused the *Bismarck* to be down at the bow by three degrees and take on a list of nine degrees to port. Water pressure against the forward bulkheads created by the forward motion of the ship caused the top speed of the *Bismarck* to be limited to 28 knots to keep the bulkheads from collapsing.

The same hit also affected the fuel supply of the *Bismarck*. At least one of the fuel storage tanks in the hull was ruptured, causing the loss of some of the *Bismarck's* precious fuel reserves and leaving a conspicuous trail of oil coming from the ship. With the forward pumping station flooded, it became impossible to transfer fuel oil from the forward fuel storage tank to the ready use fuel tanks near the boilers. This left 1,000 tons of fuel oil, one eighth of her storage capacity, unavailable for use by the *Bismarck*.

After considering all of his options, including a return to Norway, as some of his staff suggested, Admiral Lütjens decided to go to the French port of St. Nazaire, the closest port under German control with a dry-dock of sufficient size to accommodate the *Bismarck*. St. Nazaire had the huge Normandie Drydock at the Penhoët Shipyard that had serviced the 83,500-ton French liner *Normandie*. Going first to St. Nazaire had other advantages. Repairs would not take long since the damage was not extensive. At St. Nazaire, the *Bismarck* could link up with the battleships *Gneisenau* and *Scharnhorst,* now nearby at Brest, and form a more powerful battle group than with just the *Prinz Eugen*. That would restore the Operation "Rhine Exercise" closer to its original concept.

Admiral Lütjens had also decided to detach the *Prinz Eugen* to proceed with raiding operations on her own. It was thought that the *Prinz Eugen* might be able to do some damage to Allied shipping as well as keep the Royal Navy occupied until the new battle group could be formed. With the *Prinz Eugen* again leading the German squadron, this put her in a good position to be detached when the time came. At 0810, Lütjens radioed Naval Group Command North of his intentions to detach *Prinz Eugen* and then go to St. Nazaire.

In view of continued concern about the oil trail being left by the leaking fuel tanks of the *Bismarck*, which made it easier for the British to track the German squadron, the *Prinz Eugen* was ordered to fall back and disperse the oil trail behind the German flagship. At 1010, the *Prinz Eugen* reduced her speed to 16 knots for 20 minutes until she fell behind the flagship. The *Prinz Eugen* then resumed a speed of 26 knots and remained astern of the *Bismarck* for half an hour in an effort to break up the *Bismarck's* oil trail. At 1100, the *Prinz Eugen* resumed her position in the van of the German squadron.

After learning of the loss of the *Hood* and the retreat of the *Prince of Wales*, the Admiralty took stock of the situation and began to mobilize additional resources of the Royal Navy to assist in the destruction of the *Bismarck*. Admiral Tovey was positioned to intercept the German squadron with his task force, consisting of the battleship *King George V*, battle cruiser *Repulse*, and aircraft carrier *Victorious*, but that might not be enough to get the job done in view of the speed and firepower of the *Bismarck*.

Force H, stationed at Gibraltar and under the command of Vice-Admiral Sir James F. Somerville, was the most potent unit available, and that task force was ordered to proceed north to intercept the *Bismarck*. Force H consisted of the aircraft carrier *Ark Royal*, battle cruiser *Renown*, light cruiser *Sheffield*, and destroyers *Faulknor*, *Foresight*, *Forester*, *Foxhound*, *Fury*, and *Hesperus*. The *Ark Royal* had an overall length of 800 feet, beam of 95 feet, and displaced 22,000 tons. She had geared turbines, which developed 102,000 SHP, and her three shafts could drive the ship at a speed of over 30 knots. The *Ark Royal* was defended by sixteen 4.5-inch antiaircraft guns and a host of smaller antiaircraft guns, and she carried 72 aircraft. She was commanded by Captain L.E. Maund, and she had a crew of 1,575 officers and men.

The *Renown* was a sister ship of the battle cruiser *Repulse* and had the identical features as described earlier for the *Repulse*. The *Sheffield* was a Town-class light cruiser of the *Southampton*-class and had the same features as described earlier for the *Birmingham*. The *Faulknor*, *Foresight*, *Forester*, *Foxhound*, and *Fury* were "F"-class destroyers that were built in 1935 and which displaced 1,400 tons, carried four 4.7-inch quick-firing guns and eight 21-inch torpedo tubes, and had a speed of 36 knots. The

Destroyer HMS *Electra* picks up *Hood* survivors. *Drawing by the author*

Hesperus was an "H"-class destroyer built in 1940 which displaced 1,340 tons, also carried four 4.7-inch guns and eight 21-inch torpedo tubes, and also had a speed of 36 knots.

The battleship *Rodney*, which was escorting the troop transport *Britannic* from the Clyde to Boston, was ordered to leave her charge and head for the *Bismarck*. Leaving the destroyer HMS *Eskimo* behind to guard the *Britannic*, the *Rodney*, in company with the destroyers *Mashona, Somali,* and *Tartar,* set sail on a course to intercept the *Bismarck*. The *Rodney* was one of two battleships built after World War I as replacements for older battleships to round out Great Britain's quota of 15 capital ships allowed under the Washington Naval Treaty of 1922.

The *Rodney* was a truncated version of a larger ship planned for the Royal Navy, but which had to be scaled-down due to the 35,000-ton limit imposed by the Washington Naval Treaty on new capital ship construction. She turned out to be 690 feet long, had a beam of 106 feet, and displaced 33,900 tons. The *Rodney* was powered by turbine engines, which generated 45,000 SHP, and her two shafts could drive her at a maximum speed of 21 knots. Due to her truncated design, she carried all of her main armament of nine 16-inch guns in three triple turrets on the forecastle of the ship, with the center turret above the forward and rear turrets of the group. The *Rodney* also carried twelve 6-inch guns in three double turrets on either side of the ship, six 4.7-inch antiaircraft guns, and two 24.5-inch underwater torpedo tubes. The *Rodney* was commanded by Captain Frederick H.G. Dalrymple-Hamilton and had a compliment of 1,314 officers and men.

The British battleship *Ramillies*, then escorting a convoy at sea, was also directed to converge on the *Bismarck*, her place to be taken by her sister ship, the *Revenge*, which was at the eastern end of the convoy route at Halifax, Canada. These ships, both of the *Royal Sovereign*-class, were 580 feet long, had a beam of 89 feet, and displaced 29,150 tons. They were powered by turbine engines that generated 40,000 SHP, and their four screws could drive them at speeds up to 21.5 knots. The ships carried eight 15-inch guns in four double turrets, two forward and two aft, the standard for nearly all British battleships of World War I vintage still in service, twelve 6-inch guns,

British destroyer HMS *Electra* (1934).
Photo courtesy of MaritimeQuest

a host of antiaircraft guns, and four 21-inch submerged torpedo tubes.

The morning had been overcast, but by noon, the weather had deteriorated with rain and fog engulfing the area. This turn in the weather was welcome news to Admiral Lütjens since those conditions would be more favorable for any attempt to detach the *Prinz Eugen* and then for the *Bismarck* to make good her escape when the time came.

At noon, operational control of Rhine Exercise was transferred from the German Naval Group Command North to the Naval Group Command West. Naval Group Command North, which was commanded by Fleet Admiral Rolf Carls and had its headquarters at Wilhelmshaven, had been responsible for the movements of the German squadron while in Norwegian and Arctic waters, but when they entered the Atlantic, they came under the geographical jurisdiction of Naval Group Command West, which was commanded by Fleet Admiral Alfred Saalwächter with his headquarters in Paris.

The *Norfolk* and *Suffolk* continued their role of shadowing the German squadron, but now with the firepower of the *Prince of Wales* supporting them, they had less to fear from any attempt by the Germans to engage them in action. During the morning of 24 May, the three-ship task force under Rear-Admiral Wake-Walker continued to maintain contact with the German squadron, which was still steaming in a southwesterly direction. At 1300, the German ships turned due south on course 180°, and this course change was immediately reported by the *Suffolk*.

Admiral Tovey was quite pleased with the report that the German squadron had turned south since that would bring the *Bismarck* closer to an intercept point with his task force. He still had another eight hours to sail before the *Bismarck* would come within range of *Victorious'* aircraft and another few hours more before his ships could engage, but there now would be more light available to conduct operations against the German squadron as a result of that turn. Tovey decided to take advantage of the situation by ordering the *Victorious* to head directly for a point that would allow for a torpedo attack on the *Bismarck* that same evening while he continued on to an intercept point for a surface engagement.

At about 1500, the *Victorious* detached herself from Tovey's task force and headed for the plotted point that would put her at a distance of 100 miles from the *Bismarck* where she could launch an attack with her Swordfish torpedo bombers. The *Victorious* was escorted on her mission by four light cruisers of the Second Cruiser Squadron commanded by Rear-Admiral A.T.B. Curteis, who was placed in overall command of the force. The cruisers were his flagship, the *Galatea*, as well as the *Aurora*, *Kenya*, and *Hemione*.

The *Suffolk* continued to report the enemy's position, course, and speed periodically throughout the rest of the afternoon. Due to the radio silence maintained by Tovey's task force, Wake-Walker had no idea when the flagship of the Home Fleet would be in a position to engage the *Bismarck*. Captain Leach, having been part of the Home Fleet at Scapa Flow, could make an educated guess based on his knowledge of Tovey's intentions, but he could not be sure of the time that the interception would take place. All that Wake-Walker could do was keep Tovey informed of *Bismarck's* movements until that time came.

Catalina flying boat G/210, which had taken over surveillance of the German squadron from Hudson M/269 at about 1430, continued to shadow the *Bismarck* and *Prinz Eugen* from a safe distance astern of the enemy ships for another two hours before it developed engine trouble and had to leave the scene at 1640 and return to its base at Reykjavik.

CHAPTER 19

CONTACT LOST WITH *PRINZ EUGEN* AND THE *BISMARCK*

A T 1420, ADMIRAL LÜTJENS SIGNALED CAPTAIN BRINK-mann of his plan for the detachment of the *Prinz Eugen*. At the appropriate time, the *Bismarck* would turn to the west during a rain squall to draw away their pursuers. Upon receiving the code word "Hood," the *Prinz Eugen* was to maintain course and speed for three hours after separation from the *Bismarck*. Upon successful detachment, the *Prinz Eugen* was directed to refuel from either *Belchen* or *Lothringen*, German tankers deployed in advance to support Rhine Exercise, before beginning commerce raiding operations on her own.

During the late afternoon of 24 May, the weather remained poor, and Admiral Lütjens decided that this might be a good time to detach the *Prinz Eugen*. At 1540, just after the German squadron had entered another rain squall, the *Bismarck* signaled the *Prinz Eugen* to execute "Hood." The *Bismarck* turned west as planned, but soon ran out of the rain squall and was immediately spotted by one of her pursuers. The *Bismarck* quickly turned around and reestablished contact with the *Prinz Eugen* in the failed attempt to detach the cruiser. It was not until two and a half hours later that another attempt was made to detach the *Prinz Eugen*.

At 1814, while both ships were in a fog bank, the order to execute "Hood" was signaled to the *Prinz Eugen* for the second time. As before, the *Bismarck* turned to starboard and headed west for some distance, but then she headed north toward her pursuers. At 1840, the *Bismarck* emerged from the fogbank, and seeing the *Suffolk*, she immediately opened fire on the cruiser at a range of 20,000 yards. The *Suffolk* took evasive action and generated smoke before returning fire. The *Suffolk* fired a total of nine salvos at the *Bismarck* during the short engagement, one of which was seen to straddle the German battleship, but no hits were observed.

The *Prince of Wales*, some six miles to the rear of the *Suffolk*, also saw the *Bismarck* emerge from the fog, and she opened up with her 14-inch guns on the enemy ship. The *Prince of Wales* fired twelve salvos at the *Bismarck* at a range of 30,000 yards, well beyond the 25,000-yard range considered to be the maximum for effective fire, and not surprisingly, scored no hits. At that range, the *Prince of Wales* was an obscure target for the *Bismarck*, so after firing a few salvos at the *Suffolk*, the German battleship turned away and headed south again. The *Prince of Wales* ordered a cease-fire at 1900, but during the brief exchange of gunfire, two guns in her "A" turret had temporarily broken down again.

The *Prinz Eugen* had increased her speed from 26.0 knots to 31.0 knots by 1920, and she continued on her southerly course as directed by the flagship. She was soon beyond the radar range of the British force, and after making good her escape, she reduced her speed to 29.0 knots at 2100 and headed for a rendezvous with one of the German tankers positioned to support the operation.

With the *Prinz Eugen* now safely detached, Admiral Lütjens sent a short message to the German Directorate of Sea Warfare at 1914 advising them of the recent action with the *Prince of Wales* and that the *Prinz Eugen* had been released to refuel. He also stated that the enemy remained in contact with the *Bismarck*. Just before sending that message, Lütjens received a message from Naval Command Group West concurring in his decision to head for St. Nazaire and advising that preparations were being made to receive the *Bismarck* at that port. They also suggested that if the *Bismarck* broke away, it should make a long detour on the way to port, possibly hoping that the British force could be lured across a line of U-boats that was then being deployed for that purpose.

Admiral Lütjens responded at 2056 that it would be unlikely for the *Bismarck* to shake off its pursuers in view of the long-range radar that the British possessed. He added that due to his critical fuel situation, the *Bismarck* would have to head straight for St. Nazaire. While the damage done to the *Bismarck* had been reported to higher authority, this was the first time that the *Bismarck's* fuel situation was reported as being critical as a result of that damage. It obviously resulted in a sobering reassessment of the situation by the German Naval High Command.

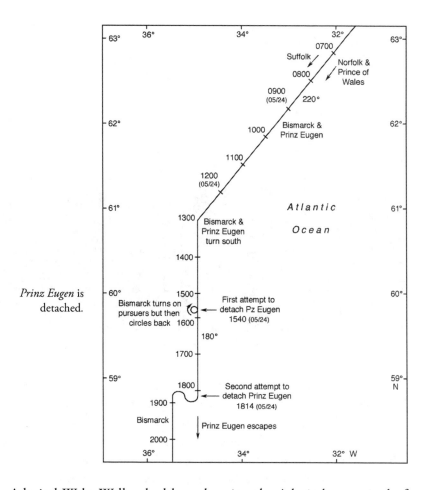

Admiral Wake-Walker had been keeping the Admiralty apprised of the ongoing chase throughout the day. Based on that information, the Admiralty was orchestrating the convergence of all available British naval forces in the region toward the interception of the German squadron. The remainder of the Home Fleet under Admiral Tovey was now steaming in a southwesterly direction to intercept the *Bismarck*. The crews of the battleship *King George V*, the battle cruiser *Repulse*, and the aircraft carrier *Victorious* were all anxious to meet up with the *Bismarck* and avenge the *Hood*.

After the German squadron turned south at 1300, it placed them on a course that would enable Admiral Curties' detached task force to intercept them at about 2100. The situation was changed, however, when the

Bismarck turns on pursuers while *Prinz Eugen* escapes. *Drawing by the author*

Bismarck turned to the west at 1814 to allow the *Prinz Eugen* to be detached. That placed the *Bismarck* further away from the anticipated intercept point, and thereby the interception would be delayed by at least an hour.

At about 2200, while it was still light, Admiral Curteis' task force came within aircraft range of the *Bismarck*, and he ordered an air strike from the *Victorious* in an effort to disable the *Bismarck*, or at least slow her down. At 2208, after the *Victorious* had turned into the wind, nine Swordfish I torpedo bombers of No. 825 Squadron, under the command of Lt. Comdr. Eugene Esmonde, took off from the carrier to launch a torpedo attack. Two of the six Fulmer aircraft of No. 800Z Squadron were launched at the same time to assist the attack force reach the target and to observe the results of the air strike.

The Fairey Swordfish I was a biplane that had fabric-covered metal-frame fuselage and wings, and fixed landing gear. Its wings were foldable to facilitate stowage on an aircraft carrier, and it was equipped with an arresting hook for carrier landings. The Swordfish was 36 feet long, had a wingspan of 45 feet, and had a maximum take-off weight of 9,250 lbs. It was powered by a single 690 hp. Bristol Pegasus IIIM3 air-cooled radial

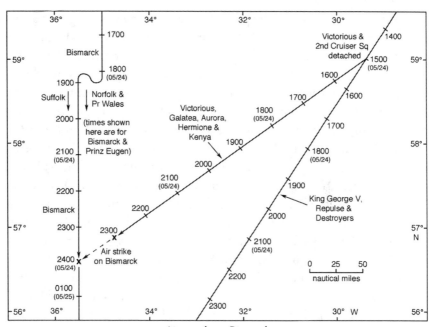

Air attack on *Bismarck.*

engine that gave it a maximum speed of 139 mph.

The Swordfish had a fixed 0.303 cal. Vickers machine gun that fired forward between the propeller blades, and a flexible-mounted 0.303 cal. machine gun in the rear cockpit. It normally carried one 18-inch torpedo between its fixed landing gear wheels, but it could carry a 1,500 lb. bomb load instead. The British 18-inch aerial torpedo weighed 1,610 lbs, and it was considerably smaller than the standard 21-inch torpedoes carried on submarines and surface ships, but they still could inflict serious damage, even to a battleship, if they struck outside the armored belt of the vessel.

The Fairey Fulmer was a two-seater, low-wing, carrier-based fighter. It was 40 feet long, had a wingspan of 46 feet, and weighed 9,800 lbs. The Fulmer was powered by a 1,080-hp Rolls Royce Merlin VIII liquid-cooled engine that gave it a maximum speed of 280 mph. Like the Spitfire land-based fighter, the Fulmer carried eight 0.303 cal. wing-mounted machine guns. It also had foldable wings and an arresting gear for carrier operations.

The torpedo bombers arrived at the scene at around midnight and they immediately began their attack. When one Swordfish came down out of the clouds, however, the pilot observed a strange-looking ship ahead of him and he withheld dropping his torpedo. It turned out to be the U.S. Coast Guard cutter *Modoc*, which was on patrol in the area. The *Modoc* was a cutter of the *Tampa*-class, 240 feet long, having a beam of 39 feet, and displacing 1,506 tons. She carried two 5-inch deck guns and had a maximum speed of 16 knots. The *Modoc* was built in 1922 by the Union Construction Company in Oakland, California and served on the International Ice Patrol, established after the sinking of the *Titanic*, before being transferred to the U.S. Navy in November 1941. Since then, it had been on the Greenland Patrol rescuing seamen from torpedoed merchant ships.

The pilot went on to locate the *Bismarck* and launch his torpedo at the German battleship, as did the other eight Swordfish aircraft. One hit was scored amidships, but due to the *Bismarck's* heavy side armor protection, no damage was done. All of the Swordfish returned safely to the *Victorious* in spite of the heavy antiaircraft fire directed against them and the ensuing darkness. The two Fulmers, however, ran out of fuel and had to ditch in the sea, but their crews were recovered. Darkness soon set in, precluding any further air strikes that evening.

At 0200, after the torpedo bombers had left the scene, lookouts on the *Suffolk* spotted a ship in the mist some distance away. Believing that it was the *Bismarck*, the cruiser was getting ready to open fire when it disappeared again in the mist. The *Norfolk*, unaware of any other ship in the area, ordered the *Prince of Wales* to fire on the ship as well, but the *Prince of Wales* withheld fire in the belief that it may have been an American Coast Guard cutter. It was another close call for the *Modoc*, which also came close to being hit by shell fragments raining down from anti-aircraft fire from the *Bismarck*.

The *Suffolk* continued to keep the *Bismarck* under radar surveillance and send out periodic position reports on the ship during the evening of 24 May. Fearing that German U-Boats may have been dispatched to attack elements of the Royal Navy engaged in the pursuit of the *Bismarck*, the *Norfolk* and *Suffolk* begin zigzagging, 30° to port for 10 minutes and then 30° to starboard for 10 minutes. While on her port leg, the *Suffolk* would temporarily lose radar contact with the *Bismarck* at a distance over 25,000 yards, but after turning back to starboard, she would soon regain contact. During the night, the crew of the *Bismarck* noted that the British ships were staying to their port quarter (i.e., to the east of the *Bismarck's* track) and that they had begun zigzagging. Admiral Lütjens, suspecting that the *Bismarck* might temporarily be out of radar range of the British ships, decided to take advantage of those maneuvers and try to break away from his pursuers.

In the early morning hours of 25 May, the *Suffolk* was beginning to make another southeastward swing on her zigzag course, which would again put her out of radar contact with the *Bismarck* for a few moments. When the *Suffolk* seemed to be approaching the limit of her southeastward leg, Admiral Lütjens ordered the *Bismarck* to make an immediate turn to starboard and to continue almost due west at high speed away from the British force. The ruse worked, and when the *Suffolk* returned on the southwestern leg of her zigzag course, she still had no contact with the *Bismarck*.

Admiral Lütjens, after breaking free of *Suffolk's* radar, made a wide swing to the north and circled around to the rear of the British task force. Once he had completed the circle, he headed in a southeasterly direction on course 130° toward St. Nazaire on the French Atlantic coast. The *Suffolk* was last in contact with the *Bismarck* at 0306, and when the *Bismarck* did not subsequently reappear on her radar screen as expected, she tried to regain radar contact by speeding in a southwesterly direction, but to

British aircraft carrier HMS *Victorious* (1941). *Photo courtesy of MaritimeQuest*

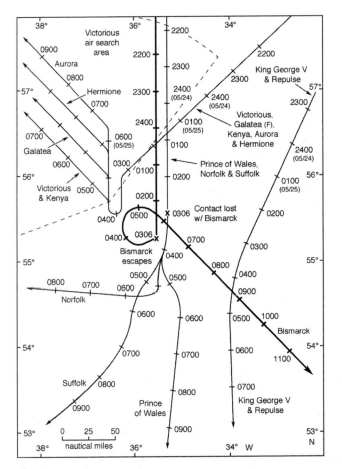

Escape of the
Bismarck.

no avail. When this failed to produce the *Bismarck*, Captain Ellis of the *Suffolk* advised Admiral Wake-Walker at 0401 that contact with the German battleship had been lost.

When Admiral Tovey learned that contact with the *Bismarck* had been lost, he was deeply disappointed. His task force was only a few hours away from being able to intercept the German battleship and he was anxious to avenge the loss of the *Hood* and settle the matter once and for all. Now, instead of preparing for battle, he had to plan a strategy to reacquire the elusive target before he could finally bring the *Bismarck* to bay. As it turned out, the loss of contact with the *Bismarck* at this point in time may have been a blessing in disguise since it avoided a battle that could have resulted in further British casualties and damage to ships of the Royal Navy.

CHAPTER 20

THE FINAL HUNT FOR THE
BISMARCK

W HEN ADVISED OF THE LOSS OF RADAR CONTACT WITH
the *Bismarck*, Admiral Wake-Walker ordered the *Suffolk* to continue searching in a southwesterly direction while he sailed with the *Norfolk* in a more westerly direction in an attempt to regain contact with the enemy battleship. The *Prince of Wales*, having incurred some underwater damage in her fight with the German squadron, could now do only 27 knots. She was therefore more of a handicap than an asset to the First Cruiser Division in its new role of trying to relocate the *Bismarck*, so at 0630, she was released to join Admiral Tovey's battle force where she could add her firepower to that of the *King George V* and *Repulse*.

At 0630, Admiral Tovey ordered Rear-Admiral Curteis to have the *Victorious* conduct an air search in the sector between 280° and 040° and to a depth of 100 miles to try to relocate the *Bismarck*. At 0810, seven Swordfish aircraft took off from the *Victorious* and headed for their assigned search areas. Curteis also had the four light cruisers of his Second Cruiser Squadron conduct a surface sweep in that same general direction. It seemed obvious to all that the *Bismarck* had turned to the west in making its escape, and that is where they concentrated their search efforts. One Swordfish was lost in the search operation, and the others had nothing to report upon returning to the *Victorious*.

Admiral Tovey continued to sail to the southwest in the belief that the *Bismarck* would continue to break out in that direction. By sailing that middle course, Tovey would be in a position to quickly turn to either side should the *Bismarck* be found to the south or to the west of her last reported position. Unbeknown to either side, however, the course of the

Bismarck, after making her circle around Admiral Wake-Walker's task force, cut across the track of Admiral Tovey's task force after it had passed through that same area a short time before.

By now, the *Repulse* was running low on fuel, and at 0906, she was detached to go to Newfoundland for refueling. While en route to Newfoundland, the *Repulse* would continue to search for the *Bismarck* in the far west region. With the *Repulse* having to leave the task force, Admiral Tovey had to take stock of the resources that might be available to him for stopping the *Bismarck*. The *Prince of Wales* was of questionable value in view of her continuing main armament problems and combat damage. Tovey's best hope was for the battleship *Rodney*, with her nine 16-inch guns, to join his task force. The *Rodney* was then 350 miles from the last reported position of the *Bismarck* and heading southwest in an attempt to intercept her. The *Rodney* was now in a favorable position to intercept the *Bismarck* if she was heading for a French port.

The light cruiser *Edinburgh*, like the *Rodney*, was also in a position to cover the southeastern sector of possible escape routes for the *Bismarck*. Another battleship, the *Ramillies*, was about 400 miles south of the last reported position of the *Bismarck* and heading northwest as instructed by the Admiralty, but she was too far away to provide any direct assistance. Likewise, the heavy cruiser *London* was covering the region of the Canary Islands, and it was decided to allow her to remain in that region. Force H, now more urgently needed than before, was speeding northward off the coast of Spain after leaving its convoy as ordered by the Admiralty a few hours earlier.

Although the *Bismarck* had made good its escape, it was still receiving radar signals emanating from British warships, and believing that the British were still in radar contact with the ship, Admiral Lütjens began transmitting to Group West a long and detailed account of the battle with the *Hood* and *Prince of Wales*, including his intent to go to St. Nazaire for repairs, and comments on the effectiveness of British radar. Not having intercepted any further enemy reports on the position of the *Bismarck*, Group West was convinced that contact with the *Bismarck* had been lost, and they therefore advised Lütjens to immediately stop his transmission. But it was too late—British stations had already picked up the transmission and were attempting to triangulate his position by the direction of the signal from each station.

British bases
involved in
hunt for the
Bismarck.

Unfortunately, however, the interceptions were mostly from stations in the British Isles and the direction lines were therefore almost parallel, providing little triangulation to pinpoint the exact location of the elusive battleship. What was certain, however, was that the *Bismarck* was now east of its last reported position rather than west of it. What was uncertain was whether the *Bismarck* was heading northeast toward the North Sea or southeast to a port in German-occupied France or a port in friendly Spain, such as Ferrol on the northwestern coast of the country. Although neutral, Spain's dictator Francisco Franco was still deeply indebted to Germany and Italy for their support during the Spanish Civil War, which ensured his victory.

The interception of Lütjens' message led to a massive change in the direction of the search from west to east, but much of the effort was directed to the northeast, wasting precious time and fuel resources. Being itself unclear as to the exact location of the *Bismarck*, the Admiralty merely passed on the intercept data without clear-cut instructions, leaving it up to the individual commanders to make their own interpretation. Finally, after further review of the data and consultation with additional experts in the field, the Admiralty was now convinced that the *Bismarck* was actually heading southeast to a French port for repairs, and it issued the necessary clarification orders accordingly.

Admiral Tovey passed on the Admiralty instructions to the ships under his command at 1047, and this immediately put several of the ships out of the running due to their location. At 1100, the *Prince of Wales* altered course northward, and at 1500, it turned eastward to course 083°. At 1540, Captain Leach radioed Admiral Tovey that he would remain on that course until 2000, when it would head for Hvalfjord to refuel. At 1730, the *Prince of Wales* crossed paths with the *Norfolk*, which was heading eastward on the assumption that the *Bismarck* was heading toward a French port, and at 2000, she turned toward Hvalfjord.

At 0800 on the following morning, the *Prince of Wales* was met by two light cruisers of the Second Cruiser Squadron, the *Galatea* and the *Aurora*, which immediately took up screening positions for the *Prince of Wales*. Not wanting to leave the *Prince of Wales* unattended, the division commander, Rear-Admiral Curteis, who flew his flag on the *Galatea*, split his command, leaving the *Kenya* and *Hermione* to continue escorting the carrier *Victorious* heading east to refuel while he went to the assistance of the *Prince of Wales*.

At 1620, the *Prince of Wales* and her cruiser escort were joined by three destroyers from Hvalfjord, the *Electra*, *Antelope*, and *Anthony*, to add an anti-submarine screen for the British battleship. These destroyers were all part of Admiral Holland's original destroyer screen, the *Electra*, of course, being the destroyer that brought the *Hood* survivors to that base. The *Antelope* and *Anthony* were the two destroyers that had to be released earlier when they ran low on fuel oil and had to go to Hvalfjord to refuel. The ships arrived at Hvalfjord on the morning of 27 May with the *Prince of Wales* dropping her anchor at 1115.

The RAF Coastal Command participated in the search for the *Bismarck* throughout 25 May, sending out long-range Sunderland and Cata-

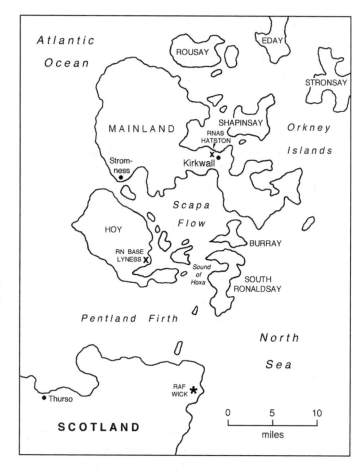

British bases in Orkney Islands.

lina flying boats and Hudson observation planes from various bases around the perimeter of the search area. Aircraft of the Royal Canadian Air Force, operating from their base at Gander, Newfoundland, added their support by covering the western section of the North Atlantic. However, without more positive guidance on the likely locations of the *Bismarck*, none of the aircraft were able to locate the German battleship.

As soon as he learned of the escape of the *Bismarck*, Air Marshal Sir Frederick Bowhill, Commander-in-Chief of RAF Coastal Command, became personally involved in efforts to locate the German battleship. On the morning of 25 May, he met with his staff to develop a definitive search pattern to cover the possible routes of the *Bismarck* based on the latest assessment of the Admiralty of the ship's position, course, and speed. After consultation with the Naval Staff, the plan for a parallel-track search using three Catalina long-range flying boats was approved with minor changes. Two Catalina flying boats took off from their base at Castle Archdale in Northern Ireland at 1350, and these aircraft were followed by the third Catalina at 1400.

RAF Castle Archdale was the most westerly of the bases used by the Coastal Command during World War II, and it was therefore one of the command's most important bases for anti-submarine warfare in view of its proximity to the North Atlantic. By secret agreement with the Irish Republic, British aircraft were allowed to fly over Ireland's Donegal Province to reach the North Atlantic directly instead of having to circle around the province from the north. Although neutral in the war, the Irish had no desire for the Germans to win over Great Britain, and they covertly assisted the British in their war effort against the Axis powers as best they could.

Located on Lower Lough Erne, RAF Castle Archdale was home to No. 209 and No. 240 Squadrons of the Coastal Command, which were equipped with Catalina I flying boats. The base had personnel quarters, canteens, stores, recreation facilities, a control tower, hangers, flying boat pens, a slipway, workshops, and as many as 100 flying boat moorings offshore to accommodate the needs of those squadrons. A separate training base was located at RAF Killadeas, just ten miles down the lake south from RAF Castle Archdale.

The Catalinas were still in the air conducting their sweep when the Admiralty determined that the *Bismarck* was probably on a more southerly course than previous thought and heading for the French coast. As a result, instructions were radioed to the aircraft to alter their search area in accordance with this new guidance, which they immediately complied with, but the new area was covered mostly after dark. During the night, one of the aircraft made contact with the light cruiser *Edinburgh*, and on two occasions, the wakes of ships could be seen in the darkness below, but they could not be identified as friend or foe. The Catalinas returned to RAF Castle Archdale after their sweep, landing between 1030 and noon on the following morning after having spent nearly 24 hours aloft.

During the afternoon of 25 May, workmen aboard the *Bismarck* began construction of a dummy funnel that they planned to erect amidships in an attempt to disguise the ship as a British warship. They hoped that it would fool the British at least from the air in view of renewed British

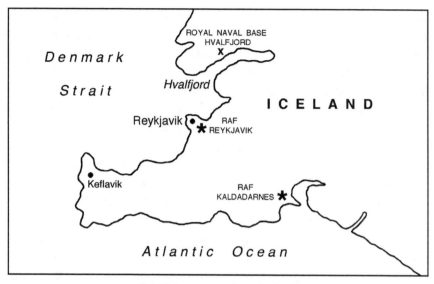

British bases in southwest Iceland.

aerial surveillance expected in the morning. With the loss of much of her fuel reserves as a result of damage inflicted by the *Prince of Wales*, the *Bismarck* was forced to reduce her speed during the day to a more economical 20 knots instead of her maximum sustained speed of 28 knots. A repair crew was subsequently able to open the valves in the flooded forward part of the ship to allow part of the fuel reserves earlier cut off for use by the *Bismarck's* boilers, but this only slightly alleviated the problem caused by the loss of so much of her fuel supply.

Admiral Tovey left Scapa Flow with a screen of four destroyers, but one-by-one they had to be detached to refuel, and the task force was now left without a destroyer screen. At 2230 on 25 May, Tovey requested if the Admiralty could make some destroyers available to provide an anti-submarine defense for his task force. The *Rodney* was expected to join Tovey soon, and she still had three destroyers with her, but their fuel situation was beginning to be of some concern as well. Reluctantly, the Admiralty detached five destroyers of the Fourth Destroyer Flotilla under Captain Philip Vian from troop convoy WS8B en route from Glasgow to the Indian Ocean to provide a screen for the *King George V* and the *Rodney*.

At the time, 2400 on 25 May, the convoy and its destroyer escort was 240 nautical miles southeast of the *King George V*. Vian, flying his flag on

Cossack, was ordered to join the *King George V* with *Sikh* and *Zulu* while *Maori* and the Polish destroyer *Piorun* were to join the *Rodney*. The *Cossack*, *Sikh*, *Zulu*, and *Maori* were all Tribal-class destroyers like the *Punjabi* described earlier. The *Piorun* was originally a British "N"-class destroyer built in 1940 and named the *Narissa*. She was transferred to the Polish Navy in 1940 as a replacement for the Polish destroyer *Grom*, which was lost off the Norwegian coast in May of that year. She was 357 feet long, had a beam of 36 feet, and a standard displacement of 1,690 tons. The *Piorun* was powered by turbine engines that could generate 40,000 SHP and drive the ship at a maximum speed of 36 knots. She carried six 4.7-inch guns in three double mounts, two forward and one aft, and ten 21-inch torpedo tubes in two quintuple mounts.

Vian became famous when he, as the captain of the destroyer *Cossack*, made a daring rescue of British seamen imprisoned on the German supply ship *Altmark* in February 1940. The *Altmark* had supported the raiding operations of the *Admiral Graf Spee* before the pocket battleship was stopped by British warships off Montevideo, Uruguay in December 1939. Returning to Germany with 300 prisoners taken from the ships sunk by the *Admiral Graf Spee*, the *Altmark* was intercepted by British warships off the southern coast of Norway near Stavanger. She turned into a small fjord for protection, but the *Cossack* followed her in. When the *Altmark* became grounded in the fjord, crewmen from the *Cossack* boarded her and forcibly freed the prisoners, who were then returned to England.

During the evening of 25 May, Air Marshal Bowhill contemplated a new search pattern for the following morning. It was finally decided that there would be two crossover patrols beginning at 0930 with the northernmost patrol covering the area between a direct line to Brest and the center of the Bay of Biscay, and the southernmost patrol covering the area between the center of the Bay of Biscay to Cape Finisterre on the northwest corner of the Iberian Peninsula, to include the Spanish port of Ferrol. The depth of the patrols were established based on the projected distances that the *Bismarck* may have traveled at different speeds during the period.

Catalina Z/209 of No. 209 Squadron took off from RAF Castle Archdale at 0300 on the morning of 26 May, and she was followed by Catalina M/240 of No. 240 Squadron a short time later. Catalina Z/209 arrived at the beginning of its search area, the southernmost of the two segments assigned, at 0930,and an hour later, at 1030, its pilot sighted a large war-

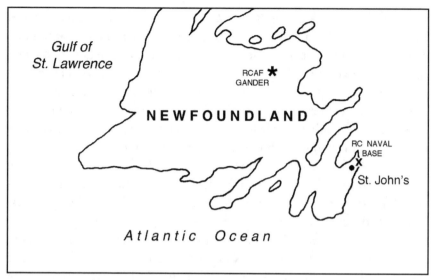

Gulf of St. Lawrence

RCAF ★ GANDER

N E W F O U N D L A N D

RC NAVAL BASE

St. John's

Atlantic Ocean

British bases in Newfoundland, Canada.

ship trailing a white wake some distance away in the sea below. Wanting to make a positive identification of the ship, RAF Flying Officer Dennis Briggs flew the Catalina into cloud cover until near the vessel, and then he dropped down to get a closer look. When the Catalina came out of the clouds, it was met by a hail of antiaircraft fire. The dummy funnel constructed by the crew of the *Bismarck* had not as yet been erected, but in the end, it would have served no useful purpose since by opening fire, the *Bismarck* had immediately revealed her true identity as an enemy warship.

Briggs and his co-pilot, U.S. Navy Ensign Leonard "Tuck" Smith, saw enough of the ship to positively identify it as a battleship, and the radio operator immediately sent out a sighting report to that effect. Ensign Smith was one of 17 U.S. naval aviators who volunteered to go to Great Britain under wartime conditions and train British pilots to fly the Catalina flying boats newly acquired by Great Britain from the United States under the Lend-Lease Act. In return, the U.S. naval aviators received valuable wartime operational experience that would later serve them well when the United States entered the war. As regular co-pilots went on leave, Americans would take their place in the cockpit and co-fly the mission. Ensign Smith was among the nine U.S. pilots sent to RAF Castle Archdale while the remaining eight went to RAF Oban in Scotland.

Catalina Z/209 kept the *Bismarck* under observation at a safe distance, but lost contact for a short while. Since the *Bismarck* kept on the same course and steamed at the same speed, the aircraft soon regained contact with the German ship. When the RAF commander and his American co-pilot of Catalina M/240, the companion aircraft to Z/209 that had been assigned the northernmost sector of the search area, heard the sighting report, they immediately headed for the reported position to assist their teammates in keeping the *Bismarck* under surveillance.

Flying Officer Briggs was anxious to land his Z/209 Catalina before dark since *Bismarck's* anti-aircraft fire had caused some damage to his aircraft. Shell fragments from the flak had punctured the hull in several places, and while the crew aboard the plane tried to plug some of the holes, many were beyond their reach. Catalina M/240 took over the task of maintaining contact with the *Bismarck* while Catalina Z/209 returned to base, and it kept up its surveillance until 1800 when it also had to return to base. By that time, Swordfish aircraft from the *Ark Royal* had also discovered the *Bismarck* and were maintaining constant surveillance over the ship.

Briggs radioed the base of the damage to the aircraft, and preparations were made to accommodate its return to Castle Archdale. The base contacted the local Enniskillen Fire Service, and they were able to provide a portable fire pump that could be brought out to the plane on a barge. Catalina Z/209 landed on Lower Lough Erne at about 2130, and it immediately began to take on water through the holes in its hull. The portable pump arrived none too soon as the plane was already low in the water by that time. The firemen kept the plane afloat for the next two days while base engineers attempted to seal as many holes as possible. On the third day, the Catalina took off, after being pumped as dry as possible, and it then headed for a base in England where more permanent repairs could be made.

In the meantime, Force H, steaming north from Gibraltar, was getting close to the point of intercepting the *Bismarck* if the German battleship was now heading toward Brest or St. Nazaire in accordance with the latest assessment by the Admiralty. Not wanting to be caught by surprise and face an enemy with superior firepower, Admiral Somerville, who flew his flag on the battle cruiser *Renown*, ordered the *Ark Royal* to conduct an air search of the area at dawn on 26 May. The *Renown* was a sister ship of the battle cruiser *Repulse*, which had been part of Admiral Tovey's task force,

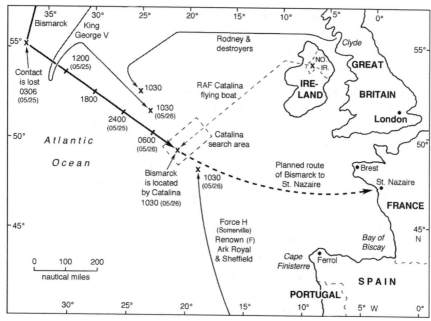

The *Bismarck* is located by RAF Catalina flying boat.

and in view of her vintage, size, and armament, she was certainly no match for the *Bismarck*.

The *Renown* was built by the Fairfield Shipyard on the River Clyde near Glasgow, Scotland in 1916. She was 750 feet long, had a beam of 103 feet, and a standard displacement of 32,000 tons. The *Renown* had turbine engines that produced 120,000 SHP and could drive the ship at speeds up to 32 knots. The *Renown* carried six 15-inch guns in three double turrets, two forward and one aft, but unlike her sister ship, her secondary armament consisted of twenty 4.5-inch antiaircraft guns in ten twin mounts, five on either side of the ship. Also unlike the *Repulse*, the *Renown* did not have any torpedo tubes, but she did carry two Walrus aircraft. The *Renown* was commanded by Captain R.R. McGrigor and had a complement of 1,205 officers and men.

The *Ark Royal* was a one-of-a-kind aircraft carrier that was laid down in September 1935 at the Cammell Laird Shipyard in Birkenhead near Liverpool, England. She was launched in April 1937 and completed in November 1938. She had an overall length of 800 feet, a beam of 95 feet, and standard displacement of 22,000 tons. Her turbine engines could generate 102,000 SHP and drive the ship at a maximum speed of nearly 31 knots. She could carry as many as 72 aircraft of different types, and at the time, she was home to No. 810, No. 818, and No. 820 Fleet Air Arm Squadrons equipped with Fairey Swordfish I torpedo bombers and No. 807 and No. 808 Fleet Air Arm Squadrons equipped with Fairey Fulmer fighter aircraft. Her armament consisted of sixteen 4.5-inch and numerous smaller caliber antiaircraft guns. The *Ark Royal* was commanded by Captain Loben E. Maund and had a complement of 1,575 officers and men.

The third major element of Force H was the *Sheffield*, a light cruiser of the *Southampton*-class that was built by Vickers-Armstrong (Tyne) in 1937. The *Sheffield* was a sister ship of the *Birmingham*, the characteristics of which were described earlier. The ship was commanded by Captain Charles A.A. Larcom, and it had a complement of 700 officers and men.

Early in the evening of 25 May, a strong gale developed, creating high seas and very windy conditions. Force H had to progressively reduce its speed from 25 knots down to 17 knots overnight to avoid damage to its

RAF Catalina Flying boat locates the *Bismarck*. *Drawing by the author*

ships. In the morning, the waves were still over 40 feet high, and the winds across the deck of the *Ark Royal* reached 50 miles an hour, making carrier air operations extremely difficult if not almost impossible. Despite the weather conditions, Somerville was still intent on launching a search effort for the *Bismarck* in the morning if at all possible and regardless of the risks involved.

Somerville had devised a trapezoidal-shaped search zone that was bounded by specific coordinates and had a depth that considered the *Bismarck* traveling at speeds from 21 to 25 knots. The search zone, which was tapered outward toward the Bay of Biscay, was similar in shape to the one being used by the two Catalina flying boats, and it covered the same general area. Despite rough seas and a rain-swept deck, the *Ark Royal* was able to launch the ten Swordfish aircraft of the surveillance force between 0845 and 0900. At about 1100, one of the Swordfish sighted the *Bismarck* and immediately sent back a contact report giving the position of the German battleship at the time. The Swordfish remained on the scene until relieved by another Swordfish, and from then on, Force H took over constant surveillance of the *Bismarck*.

The sight of the Catalina flying boat did not disturb the crew of the *Bismarck* too much since they knew that it was a long-range aircraft and therefore the ship was not in any immediate danger as a result of being sighted by that plane. Their confidence was short-lived, however, when an hour later they spotted a biplane with fixed landing gear, which indicated that a British aircraft carrier was in the vicinity. They then realized that it was just a matter of time before they would come under air attack and possibly also under fire from British surface units. While not knowing the extent of the forces being amassed against them, the Germans were understandably becoming concerned about their chances of survival.

CHAPTER **21**

BISMARCK IS DISABLED

A DMIRAL TOVEY AND THE ADMIRALTY WERE INITIALLY elated by the news that the *Bismarck* had finally been located by the Catalina flying boat, but when they plotted her position, it became abundantly clear that the prospects of stopping her were now very remote. At the time of sighting, the *Bismarck* was still nearly 700 nautical miles from Brest, but the *King George V's* earlier wild goose chase to the northeast, based on the Admiralty's initial assessment of the *Bismarck's* track, now placed the British flagship 135 miles north of the *Bismarck*, a distance too far to gain even if the *Bismarck* continued to steam at 20 knots and the *King George V* raced at full speed. Another deterrent was the fact that the *King George V* herself was running low on fuel, and she would not have been able to proceed at anywhere near full speed.

The battleship *Rodney* was a little closer, 125 miles to the northwest of the German battleship, but she was badly in need of a refit and could not even do 22 knots, so she could not catch up with the *Bismarck* either. The light cruiser *Edinburgh* was within range, but armed with only 6-inch guns, she had little chance of inflicting any serious damage on the *Bismarck*. Captain Vian's destroyer force was heading for Admiral Tovey's task force as ordered when it received word of the *Bismarck's* discovery. Vian immediately turned around, and on his own initiative, headed directly for the last reported position of the *Bismarck* in the belief that his destroyers might be able to play a part in slowing the battleship down.

The plot revealed that only Force H was close enough to engage the *Bismarck*. At 1030, when the *Bismarck* was sighted by Catalina Z/209, Force H was actually ahead of the *Bismarck* and only a short distance away from the path of the oncoming enemy ship. The battle cruiser *Renown* of

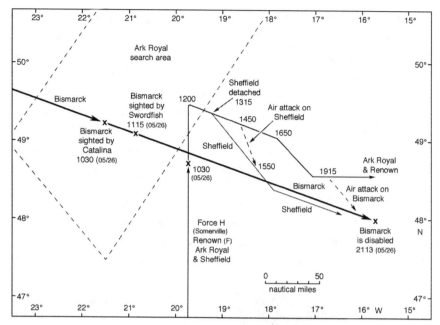

Force H intercepts and disables *Bismarck*.

Force H could have easily closed with the *Bismarck*, but considering her limited firepower and protection, she obviously could not have stopped the *Bismarck* by herself. Admiral Somerville had no intention of using the *Renown* to engage the *Bismarck*, but to ensure that there would no display of foolhardy heroics, the Admiralty sent a message to Somerville specifically prohibiting the employment of the *Renown* except if the *Bismarck* was already engaged by either the *King George V* or the *Rodney*.

The task of slowing down the *Bismarck* obviously fell to the *Ark Royal* since only her torpedo planes had the range and weapons to do the job. By the time a specific plan of action had been decided upon, Force H had already steamed some distance further north before Admiral Somerville turned his ships on a course parallel to that of the *Bismarck* and in the same direction at about noon. Preparations were already underway to launch an air strike against the *Bismarck* as soon as possible. The strike force would consist of fifteen Swordfish torpedo bombers selected from all three Fleet Air Arm Swordfish Squadrons aboard the ship, i.e., No. 810, No.818 and No. 820 Squadrons, and the force would be commanded by Lt. Comdr. James A. Stewart-Moore, the commander of No. 820 Squadron.

The Swordfish torpedo planes of the strike force were fueled, and 18-inch naval aircraft torpedoes were attached to the underside of their fuselages as their crews were being briefed. The torpedoes were armed with new magnetic detonators that were designed to explode in the presence of a strong magnetic field, such as the metallic hull of a ship, so they were set to run at a depth of 30 feet to pass below the hull of the *Bismarck* and there to detonate, blowing a large hole in the unprotected bottom of the ship. Even with a double bottom and extensive compartmentalization, such a hit could cause considerable flooding and at least slow down a ship the size of the *Bismarck*.

In the meantime, Swordfish reconnaissance aircraft were continuing to keep the *Bismarck* under constant surveillance. Admiral Somerville decided, however, it wouldn't hurt to have the *Sheffield*, which was not otherwise engaged, also maintain surveillance of the German battleship

Captain Maund and Admiral Somerville on *Ark Royal*. *Photo courtesy of Maritime Quest*

in the event that air contact was lost due to weather conditions. He therefore signaled the *Sheffield* at 1315 to move out and take station astern of the *Bismarck*, reporting back on her location, course and speed periodically. The *Sheffield's* departure under hazy weather conditions remained unnoticed by the crew of the *Ark Royal*, which was busy at the time preparing for the torpedo strike against the *Bismarck*.

Somerville then sent a message to the Admiralty advising them of his action to have the *Sheffield* also maintain contact with the *Bismarck*, with an information copy to *Ark Royal*. Since the message was not directed to the *Ark Royal*, when the information copy was received in her wireless room, it was not immediately decoded, as directed messages were, but placed aside until all directed messages had been decoded. With the large volume of directed messages coming in at the time, the information copy regarding the dispatch of the *Sheffield* to maintain contact with the *Bismarck* was not acted upon for some time.

In the final briefing before their departure, the crews of the attack aircraft were advised that the *Bismarck* was alone and that they need not worry about any other ship being in the area. At about 1430, the *Ark Royal* turned around 180° and headed into the wind to allow the take-off of the attack force. The seas were heavy with high waves that caused the ship to bob up and down with each swell. Shortly before 1500, the Swordfish began taking off from the pitching flight deck of the *Ark Royal*, and within ten minutes, all 15 aircraft had miraculously gotten into the air, formed up, and then headed south to the last reported position of the *Bismarck*. After all of the planes had left, the *Ark Royal* turned around again and resumed sailing in a southeasterly direction.

By then the decoders in the wireless room of the *Ark Royal* had gotten around to the message in which Somerville advised the Admiralty of the detachment of *Sheffield* to close on the *Bismarck* and keep the German battleship under surveillance from the surface as well as from air. When the signals officer read the message, he instantly recognized its implications and raced to the bridge to show the message to Captain Maund. Without wasting any time, Maund ordered that a message be sent immediately and in the clear to all planes of the attack group to watch out for the *Sheffield*.

For many of the pilots, the message had come too late and they had already begun to attack the *Sheffield*. Having been told that the *Bismarck* was alone in the area, as soon as they saw the dark shape of the *Sheffield* in the distance, they immediately got into position to attack the ship. They would stay in cloud cover until they were sufficiently ahead of the target, and then they would come down out of the clouds and drop their torpedoes at a lead angle in front of the oncoming ship. Torpedoes were not very much faster than the ship itself, so they had to be aimed some distance ahead of the ship to arrive at the same position as the ship in the 40 seconds or so that it would take for the torpedo to reach that point.

On the *Sheffield*, Captain Larcom had received a message that the *Ark Royal* would soon be launching an air attack against the *Bismarck*, so he alerted his antiaircraft crews of the imminent approach of friendly aircraft and to withhold fire. A short time later, the sound of the aircraft could be heard in the distance and some could even be seen from time to time between breaks in the cloud cover. Larcom's joy at seeing the Swordfish on their way to attack the *Bismarck* was soon replaced by the horror of seeing the Swordfish dive out of the clouds and begin attacking his own ship. He ordered full speed and turned toward the planes so that he could at least comb the tracks of any oncoming torpedoes.

Larcom took evasive action as the first torpedo was dropped, but then to his surprise, the second torpedo exploded on contacting the water. Several more torpedoes exploded as they hit the sea, indicating that the magnetic detonators were defective and prone to explode just by impact with the water. By skillful maneuvering, the *Sheffield* avoided being hit by any of the torpedoes that remained intact upon hitting the sea, to the thankful relief of all concerned. Three more aircraft, which had not as yet begun their attack, turned away and headed back to the *Ark Royal*, jettisoning their torpedoes into the sea along the way. This was standard practice since carriers could not afford the risk of a mishap with aircraft landing with live torpedoes.

One-by-one, the pilots of the attack force returned to the *Ark Royal*, dejected at the thought of missing the opportunity to stop the *Bismarck* and horrified by the experience of attacking one of their own ships instead. With the after deck of the *Ark Royal* rising and falling by as much as 50 feet in the heavy seas that continued to persist, landing on the carrier proved to be far more difficult than taking off from it. Timing was of the essence to land just as the stern of the ship began its descent. Most of the planes made it, but in one case, a Swordfish was hit by a rapidly rising deck as it was landing, and the impact virtually destroyed the aircraft.

Force H: HMS *Renown, Ark Royal,* and *Sheffield. Photo courtesy of MaritimeQuest*

Captain Maund tried to console the returning crewmen, and he told them to have something to eat and to get some rest before trying one more time to attack the *Bismarck* before darkness set in. As soon as the planes arrived below deck, they were refueled and rearmed. The magnetic detonators were replaced with regular detonators that would explode on contact with the ship, so the torpedoes had to be set for a shallower depth. Normally, a 20-foot depth would have been called for, but with the high seas running, it was decided to set the torpedoes to run at a depth of only 10 feet to ensure that they would not run under the bow or stern of the *Bismarck* if raised by the sea.

Somerville had no desire to enlighten the Admiralty and the other forces involved in the operation on the fiasco that had just taken place, so he merely advised them that no hits were scored on the *Bismarck*. This was true, but certainly not the entire truth. The message actually caused more concern at the Admiralty than if the entire story had been told to them, leading them to believe that conditions were so bad that none of the Swordfish was able to score a hit on the *Bismarck*. Even the announcement

Squadron of Swordfish aircraft flying over *Ark Royal*. *Photo courtesy of MaritimeQuest*

that another effort would be mounted before nightfall didn't seem very promising if no hits could be scored under conditions that might have been more favorable than under a second attempt, at least with respect to lighting.

The *Sheffield*, which had not as yet reached the *Bismarck* when she was attacked, finally sighted the German battleship at 1740, and she promptly took station about ten miles astern of her foe. From there, the *Sheffield* began shadowing the *Bismarck* and sending out periodic position reports on the enemy. The *Sheffield* was now in a perfect position to give final bearings on the *Bismarck* to the next strike force of Swordfish torpedo bombers so that they could more easily locate the target.

During the day, morale aboard the *Bismarck* had became low, from the fleet commander down to the lowest rating, as the interception of radio traffic clearly indicated that units of the Royal Navy were closing in on them. Admiral Lütjens believed that it was just a matter of time before the *Bismarck* would be surrounded by a far superior force and that the ship would be destroyed. The fuel shortage caused by the *Prince of Wales'* fateful hit required the *Bismarck* to steam at an economical speed of only 20 knots so that she would have sufficient fuel to reach St. Nazaire. Topping off her tanks in Norway or from the tanker *Weissenburg* in the Arctic Ocean would certainly have eased the situation, but that was not done.

The *Bismarck* initially had a supply of 8,000 tons of fuel oil, and she used about 1,000 tons a day, which would enable her to cover nearly 800 miles in one day when traveling at a speed of 28 knots. By the time she stopped at Bergen, Norway, she was down to about 6,500 tons (80% of her capacity), and she used another 2,000 tons before engaging the *Hood* and *Prince of Wales*. Over 1,000 tons of oil became contaminated with sea water or made inaccessible due to the hit scored by the *Prince of Wales*. Had the *Bismarck* been able to travel at 28 knots, she would have already been under the protective cover of the Luftwaffe by that afternoon.

As the day wore on and there still had been no attack, hope was beginning to mount on the *Bismarck*. The *Bismarck* was now also being shadowed by the *Sheffield*, but the crew was surprised that they had not yet come under any air attack. They knew that an aircraft carrier was in the area from the earlier sighting of a Swordfish plane on a scouting mission. Of course, they were unaware of the abortive raid conducted in mid-afternoon against the *Sheffield*, so they had every reason to hope for escape as night approached. In another couple of hours, they would come under the concealing mantle of darkness, and by morning they would be under the protective wings of the Luftwaffe.

On the *Ark Royal*, the pilots had been given their final briefing, and by 1900, the 15 Swordfish were ready on the deck of the carrier. The strike force had been organized into two groups, with three sub-flights of two to three aircraft in each group. The first group was headed by Lt. Comdr. Travenen P. Coode, the commander of No. 818 Squadron, and it consisted of four aircraft from No. 810 Squadron and four aircraft from his own No. 818 Squadron. The second group was headed by Lt. Comdr. Stewart-Moore, and all of the seven aircraft of that group came from his own No. 820 Squadron. Although Lt. Comdr. Mervyn Johnstone, commander of No. 810 Squadron, was involved in the search for the *Bismarck*, he was not among the members of the aircrews that participated in the attack itself.

The Swordfish aircraft began taking off again at 1910, and they at once formed up and headed for the *Bismarck*. This time they knew that the *Sheffield* was in the area, and they used her to get their final bearings to the target. The first planes arrived over the *Sheffield* just before 2000, and they were directed to the *Bismarck* as being twelve miles dead ahead.

At first, the pilots could not locate the *Bismarck* in the rain and low cloud cover, and they had to return to the *Sheffield* to get new bearings on the German battleship. The *Bismarck*, however, did detect the flight of Swordfish in the vicinity, and an air alarm was sounded at 2030. When the aircraft disappeared, the alarm ended, but the antiaircraft crews remained on alert at their stations. The second time around, the Swordfish pilots finally found their quarry at about 2100, and they began their attack. On the *Bismarck*, the air alarm sounded again, and the antiaircraft crews immediately went into action, putting up a heavy defense against the attacking aircraft. The Swordfish pilots, however, were able to break through the defensive fire and press their attacks. One hit was scored amidships on the port side of the *Bismarck* early in the attack, but the torpedo struck the heavily armored side of the ship and did relatively little damage.

Most of the attack force approached the *Bismarck* from the port side of the ship as she steamed across their path. Two sub-flights, however, circled around the *Bismarck* to attack her from her starboard side while she was still occupied with the attacks from her port side. One pilot came out of the cloud cover about two miles off the starboard bow of the *Bismarck* and found himself in a very favorable position to launch a torpedo attack against the ship. He eased up on the throttle and let his plane come down to under 90 knots (100 miles per hour) in speed and just under 100 feet above the level of the sea. At about a mile away, the pilot aimed the nose of the Swordfish toward an imaginary point about two ship lengths ahead of the bow of the *Bismarck* and then released his torpedo. Coming under heavy fire from the *Bismarck*, he immediately swung away from the target and headed back to the *Ark Royal*.

At the time that the torpedo was launched, it was about 800 yards away from the projected course of the *Bismarck*. It would take approximately 45 seconds, traveling at 32 knots, to reach the position where the *Bismarck* was expected to be. Alerted by a lookout on the starboard side, Captain Lindemann could see the Swordfish drop its torpedo well ahead of the *Bismarck's* course. Fearing a hit in the bow, which could seriously affect the speed and mobility of his ship, Lindemann ordered a hard turn to port, hoping to cut in front of the expected track of the torpedo. The huge twin rudders of the *Bismarck* reacted promptly, and the ship gradually turned to port. It was now a matter of sweating it out as the torpedo closed in on the *Bismarck*.

Actually, it was a well-aimed torpedo, which probably would have hit the *Bismarck* regardless of any evasive action that could have been taken by her crew. Had the *Bismarck* kept on course, the torpedo might have hit amidships against her armored belt and would have done relatively little damage. By turning to port, however, the *Bismarck* exposed her "Achilles' heel," the critical area near her screws and rudders. The torpedo plowed directly into the stern end of the *Bismarck* and exploded on the underside of the hull between her two rudders.

After the torpedo hit, the speed of the *Bismarck* did not appear to be affected, but the helmsman could not get the ship to respond to the wheel. The *Bismarck* merely kept turning in a counterclockwise direction as governed by the last set position of her rudders. Damage control parties were immediately sent into the stern to assess the damage, and the engineering staff pulled out its blueprints of the *Bismarck* to work out a procedure for correcting the problem.

At first, the reports coming back from the Swordfish pilots on their return to the *Ark Royal* cast a spell of doom over Admiral Somerville, Admiral Tovey, and the Admiralty. They knew that they had scored at least

Swordfish aircraft attacks *Bismarck* with torpedo. *Drawing by the author*

Swordfish turns back as torpedo hits stern of Bismarck. *Drawing by the author*

one hit on the *Bismarck*, but it appeared to have no effect on her operational performance. Then the commanders were confused by reports from the *Sheffield* as well as Swordfish observers concerning the erratic movements of the *Bismarck*. It seemed that the *Bismarck* was now steering in a northwesterly direction, away from the French coast, which did not appear to make much sense. The British continued to be in the dark about the *Bismarck's* strange movements until all of the pilots had returned to the *Ark Royal* and had been debriefed.

Despite the intense antiaircraft fire thrown at them by the *Bismarck*, all of the Swordfish were able to return to the *Ark Royal*, but one crashed on the deck of the carrier as it came in for a landing. As before, the landing had been difficult in the high swells and the planes were stretched out in making their landing attempts. It was not until 2230 that most of the pilots had been debriefed and it became known that one of the torpedoes might have hit the *Bismarck* in the starboard quarter of the ship. When Tovey received word of a probable torpedo hit in the stern, there appeared to be a glimmer of hope that they might yet bring the *Bismarck* to bay. Additional reports from the scene then seemed to confirm that the *Bismarck* had indeed been disabled.

Aboard the *Bismarck*, the news was not good. The explosion from the torpedo flooded the *Bismarck's* steering compartment and damaged her steering mechanism, causing her rudders to be jammed in their last set position, about 12° to port. After analyzing the situation, the engineers aboard the *Bismarck* considered the situation to be hopeless. It would be impossible to work on the rudders either from the inside of the ship or by divers sent over the stern. The possibility of using explosives to free the

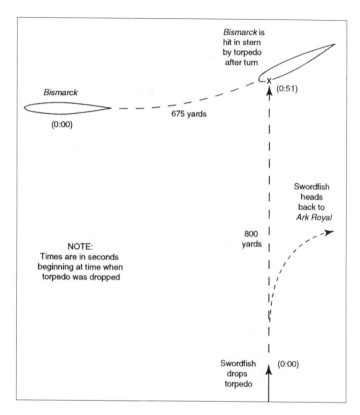

Track of fatal
torpedo.

rudders was rejected on the basis that the screws, which had not been affected by the torpedo blast, might now be damaged and render the ship totally helpless.

Captain Lindemann made every effort to control the movement of the *Bismarck* by different speed settings for her three engines, but this achieved only limited success. He could set his port engine for a higher speed than his starboard engine, thereby forcing the ship to turn to starboard, but as soon as some speed was attained, the twin rudders would bite into the sea and turn the ship back to port again. There was no way to achieve an equilibrium between the engines and the rudders so that the ship would move forward in a straight direction.

With the *Bismarck* steering an erratic course in a northwesterly direction instead of heading southeast toward the French coast, Admiral Tovey now became confident that his task force could do the job of destroying the ship. Besides his flagship, the *King George V*, he now had the older but more powerful battleship *Rodney*, which had just joined his force that afternoon with her destroyers *Tartar* and *Mashona*. He also had several cruisers and a bevy of destroyers at his disposal, including the *Norfolk*, which was ordered to join Tovey's task force after a quick refueling stop in Iceland. The heavy cruiser *Dorsetshire*, also a County-class cruiser and sister ship of the *Norfolk*, left a convoy to help locate the *Bismarck*, and she was now steaming north to participate in the final action against the enemy.

The *King George V* and *Rodney* were about 100 miles away from the *Bismarck* when she was stricken. Admiral Tovey could have reached the *Bismarck* in about four hours before total darkness set in, however, he preferred to wait until morning before beginning the action. He wanted to maneuver his squadron into a more favorable position so as to reduce the probability of being hit by his still very dangerous foe. While the *Bismarck* had been immobilized, she still had her full fighting capability intact, and the potency of her firepower had been amply demonstrated just two days before. Also, both the *King George V* and *Rodney* were running low on fuel, and Admiral Tovey's strategy would enable those ships to proceed to the scene at a more economical speed.

CHAPTER **22**

DESTROYER ATTACKS AND NIGHT VIGIL

RIGHT AFTER THE LAST AIR STRIKE BY PLANES FROM THE *Ark Royal*, the *Sheffield* moved up to obtain a visual sighting of the *Bismarck*, but she immediately came under fire from the German battleship. The *Bismarck* scored no hits on the British cruiser, but she did manage to achieve several straddles that sprayed the ship with shell splinters and knocked out her radar, leaving her unable to maintain contact with the *Bismarck* in the dark. Three men were killed by the shell splinters, and they were buried at sea on the following morning before the *Sheffield* resumed her duties.

Fortunately, however, Vian's five destroyers of the Fourth Destroyer Flotilla came onto the scene at 2200, and they were directed toward the stricken *Bismarck* by the *Sheffield*. The Polish destroyer *Piorun* was the first to sight the *Bismarck* at 2238, and she immediately came under fire from the German battleship. The *Zulu* then spotted the *Bismarck* at 2250 and sent out a sighting report. Vian recognized that his first duty was to keep the *Bismarck* under surveillance and to guide Tovey's task force to the stricken warship in the morning, so he first set up a perimeter around the *Bismarck* with one destroyer in each quadrant and the fifth bringing up the rear.

As complete darkness set in, Vian began to contemplate a coordinated torpedo attack on the *Bismarck* with all of his destroyers attacking the battleship from different angles at the same time, two from one side and three from the other. However, the rough seas and poor visibility weighed against such an organized attack due to the inability of the destroyers to even maintain contact with one another, so Vian had to settle for individual attacks when the opportunity to do so arose. By that time, the destroyers were receiving accurate fire from *Bismarck's* main and secondary batteries whenever they came into view, even at longer ranges. At 2342, Vian's flagship, the *Cossack* came under fire at 8,000 yards, and at 2350, the *Bismarck* straddled the *Zulu* with three salvos.

The first opportunity for an individual destroyer attack on the *Bismarck* occurred at 0100 when the *Zulu* was coming up unobserved on the port quarter of the German battleship. At 0121, the *Zulu* was able to fire off two torpedoes at 5,000 yards, but during her final approach, she was discovered and taken under fire, so her two torpedoes, fired while the ship was turning, had little chance of hitting their mark. At 0137, the *Maori* tried the same tactic, coming up on the port side of the *Bismarck*, and she was able to fire two torpedoes, one of which was believed to be a hit. While this was going on, Vian took advantage of the attention being given to the port side of the *Bismarck*, and had the *Cossack* fire three torpedoes at the German battleship at 6,000 yards from the starboard side, scoring what was believed to be another hit.

At 0148, *Zulu* reported that the *Bismarck* had stopped, or had at least slowed down considerably, reinforcing the belief that she may have been hit once or twice by torpedoes from the shadowing destroyers. *Bismarck* survivor Baron von Müllenheim-Rechberg, reported that the starboard turbine had been shut down for some unexplained reason at about that time, and that it took a while to start it up again after it had frozen in place. At 0218, the *Sikh* took advantage of the situation and fired all four of her torpedoes at the almost stationary target 7,000 yards away. The *Sikh* was credited with what was believed to be a probable hit.

At 0230, Admiral Tovey ordered Vian to begin firing star shells every half hour so that the flagship could confirm the reported positions of the *Bismarck* and to make sure that he was always steering toward the enemy ship. Vian obeyed at first, but the star shells were often obscured by the low clouds in the area, and they tended to illuminate his own ships, allowing them to be taken under accurate gunfire from the *Bismarck*. Not wanting to expose his ships unnecessarily to enemy fire for any slight benefit that the star shells might be to the task force commander, Vian ceased the practice by 0300. At that time, the *Cossack* made one last torpedo attack on the *Bismarck*, firing her last torpedo at 4,000 yards, but not scoring any hits.

At 0400, the destroyers lost contact with the *Bismarck* in the rain

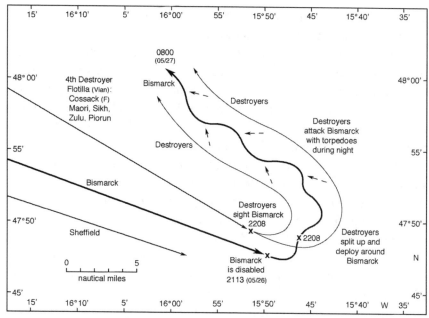

Destroyers attack during the night.

squalls and mist, but in view of the enemy's inability to maneuver or take off at high speed, it would just be a matter of time before they could relocate their quarry. At 0500, the *Piorun* was detached to refuel, but her commander was reluctant to leave the scene at that critical time. When nothing materialized in the next half hour or so, he finally gave up and headed for Plymouth to refuel. At 0550, the *Maori* sighted the *Bismarck* again, and when the German battleship emerged from a rain squall at 0625, the *Maori* illuminated her with a star shell. At about 0700, the *Maori* fired her last two torpedoes at the *Bismarck* at a range of 9,000 yards, but failed to score a hit.

With all of their torpedoes expended, the destroyers again took up their positions around the *Bismarck* and kept her under surveillance at a safe distance until the arrival of Tovey's task force. There was a question regarding the number of hits actually scored by Vian's destroyers during the night. *Bismarck* survivors claim that the ship had not been hit by any of the torpedoes, and that appears to have been accepted by the British authorities as probably being true. With the destroyers darting in from under cover, firing their torpedoes at beyond 2,000 yards, and then heading back for cover again to avoid *Bismarck's* accurate gunfire, the probability of scoring a hit was very remote.

As night fell, all aboard the *Bismarck* finally realized that their situation was hopeless. The fickle gods of war appeared to have turned toward the British after blessing the Germans for the last couple of days. The *Bismarck* was still some 500 miles away from Brest, the closest point on the French coast, and still beyond the range of Luftwaffe support. Her crewmembers were told by the German Naval High Command that U-boats were on their way to help them, but they knew that there was little that any U-boats could do to save the *Bismarck*. All they could do was wait for the end, which they fully expected would come in the morning, and they were under no illusions that they would be as lucky as they were when they met the *Hood* and *Prince of Wales*.

The officers and professional seamen accepted their ultimate fate in the tradition of the Kriegsmarine, as did the idealistic young cadets. Those who had families or had been conscripted into the service may have had other hopes than dying for the Fatherland and Third Reich. Some may have remembered that their comrades aboard the *Admiral Graf Spee* were spared that fate when the decision was made to scuttle their ship rather than face overwhelming odds, but that of course was a completely different situation. The *Bismarck* was still capable of putting up a fight and inflicting some damage on the enemy, so it would come down to everyone doing their duty regardless of the consequences.

The correspondents aboard the *Bismarck* were noncombatants, but they knew that incoming fire would not be able to distinguish between themselves and legitimate targets of war. They had plenty to write about, but had no way to file their reports. They undoubtedly interviewed many crewmembers of the *Bismarck* and had woven heroic tales of their exploits in the battle against the *Hood* and *Prince of Wales*, but they probably now realized that it could all be for naught. They were prepared to cover the forthcoming battle that was expected in the morning, but their own self-preservation now became uppermost in their minds.

During the night, there was an exchange of messages between the *Bismarck* and the German Naval High Command. At about 2100, Admiral Lütjens advised his superiors of the air strike, the fatal torpedo hit, and the inability of his ship to maneuver. In reporting the hopelessness of the situation, he added that he would fight to the last shell and ended with a greeting to the Führer. At midnight, Lütjens reported to Group West that the *Bismarck* was able to defend itself and that the propulsion plant was intact, but that the ship did not respond to steering with its engines. At 0113 on 27 May, Group West advised Lütjens of the dispatch of tugs to the scene and plans for Luftwaffe coverage in the morning, including the arrival of three Focke-Wulf 200 Condor reconnaissance aircraft by dawn, followed by three bomber groups between 0500 and 0600. At 0147, Group West also advised Lütjens that the supply ship *Ermland* would sail from the port of La Pallice at La Rochelle on the west coast of France at 0500 to assist the *Bismarck*. Lütjens, however, did not really expect that such support would arrive in time to save his ship.

The messages continued through the early morning hours. The German Naval High Command and Group West sent their best wishes to Admiral Lütjens. Even Hitler thanked the Fleet Commander in the name of the entire German nation for his devotion to duty. Hitler also addressed a message to the crew of the *Bismarck*, promising that everything possible would be done to save them and commending them for their performance of duty. Based on the recommendation of Lütjens, Lt. Comdr. Adalbert Schneider, the first gunnery officer of the *Bismarck*, was awarded the Knight's Cross by Hitler for his role in sinking the *Hood*.

Admiral Lütjens was convinced that the *Bismarck* would not survive the combined attack by units of the Royal Navy that was expected in the morning, and he was anxious to save the *Bismarck's* war diary (Kriegstagebuch), which would explain in detail everything that occurred during the sortie and therefore might be of help in planning future operations with surface ships. Lütjens ordered that the war diary be flown out by one of the aircraft carried aboard the *Bismarck*, and by 0600, an Arado 196 float plane had been hoisted out of its hanger, fueled and placed on its cradle on the port end of the catapult that stretched across the main deck between the funnel and after superstructure of the ship.

By controlling the speed of her engines, Lindemann was able to turn the *Bismarck* around until her starboard beam was into the wind. The pilot took the war diary on board with him and revved up the plane's engine until it was warm enough for takeoff. When the pilot signaled that he was ready, the catapult operator turned the control that should have sent compressed air into the system and hurled his aircraft outward into the sky, but nothing happened. Upon inspection, it was found that the

Captain Vian aboard HMS *Cossack*. *Photo courtesy of MaritimeQuest*

British Tribal-class destroyer HMS *Cossack* (1938). *Photo courtesy of MaritimeQuest*

catapult had been damaged and was unusable. The pilot exited the aircraft with the war diary, and the plane, loaded with fuel, was jettisoned off the end of the catapult to avoid it becoming a fire hazard during the upcoming battle, but not before its floats had been punctured to ensure that it would sink.

Admiral Lütjens then radioed Group West to send a U-boat to retrieve the war diary, and Group West responded that U-556 had been dispatched to perform that task. U-556 was the closest U-boat to the *Bismarck*, having just been passed by the *Ark Royal* and *Repulse* on their way to attack the *Bismarck*, but being without any torpedoes, she could do nothing to stop the British ships. The captain of the U-556 could see the occasional star shell bursts in the direction of the *Bismarck*, but being low on fuel, he could not undertake his assigned mission. When U-74 arrived on the scene, U-556 requested that the mission be reassigned to that ship, and it then headed back to its base. U-74 did not receive the reassignment before the final battle had begun, and the war diary went down with the *Bismarck*.

On the other side, morale was high on the British ships, and their crews knew that they would soon have the opportunity to avenge their ship-mates who went down with the *Hood* and those who were killed and injured on the *Prince of Wales*. The *Bismarck* was still a dangerous adversary, but there was no longer any question about the outcome of the forth-coming battle. Since the *Bismarck* was apparently going nowhere, the British could dictate the time and circumstances of their attack. With the *King George V* and *Rodney* being able to approach the *Bismarck* from differ-ent directions and divide her fire, it would be almost like a "turkey shoot." It would certainly be a far cry from the situation that the *Hood* and *Prince of Wales* had had to face a couple of days earlier.

CHAPTER **23**

BISMARCK IS SUNK

DURING THE EARLY MORNING HOURS OF 27 MAY, CAP-
tain Vian's destroyers kept the *Bismarck* under close surveillance, with the *Maori* sending out periodic reports on the position,
course, and speed of the *Bismarck* to the Admiralty and to the forces that
were closing in on the German battleship. With the *Maori's* position
reports, Admiral Tovey was able to plot his interception of the *Bismarck*
under the most favorable conditions for his battle force. Confident that
the *King George V* and the *Rodney* could do the job, and not wanting any
distraction from the task at hand, Tovey ordered Admiral Somerville to
keep Force H in the vicinity, but not closer than 20 nautical miles (40,000
yards) from the forthcoming battle arena.

Tovey had instructed Captain Dalrymple-Hamilton of the *Rodney* to
operate independently but in conformance with the movements of the
flagship, *King George V.* As they approached their quarry at 0708, Tovey
ordered his ships to increase their separation to six cables (1,200 yards) to
ensure that the *Bismarck* would have to divide its fire. After sailing almost
due south for most of the night, at 0737, Tovey turned his battle force
east to course 080° so as to arrive on the scene with the *Bismarck* silhouetted by the morning sunrise to the east.

Of the converging forces, the heavy cruiser *Norfolk*, coming down
from the north, arrived on the scene first. The *Norfolk* spotted the *Bismarck* at 0815 and then turned to the west, where a few minutes later, she
sighted the British battle force bearing down. The *Norfolk* then turned
north and circled around to the east where she could observe the fall of
shot of the British battleships and thereby aid in their gunnery.

At 0843, lookouts on the *King George V* sighted the *Bismarck* at about

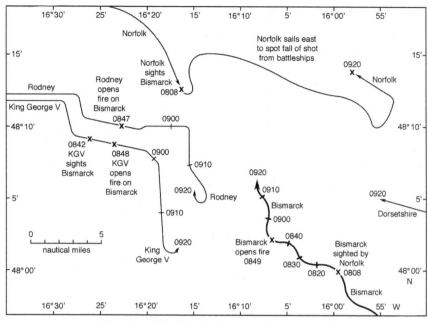

King George V and *Rodney* begin attack on *Bismarck*.

24,000 yards (12 nautical miles) ahead, and a minute later, the *Rodney* also had a bearing on the German battleship. The *King George V* headed directly toward the *Bismarck* in accordance with Tovey's plan to close to 15,000 yards and then engage the German ship with broadsides. The *Rodney* remained on the port quarter of the *King George V*, and then at 0847, she opened fire on the *Bismarck* with her two foremost turrets. A minute later, the *King George V* also opened fire with her forward turrets. The sharp angle of approach prevented the third turret on the *Rodney* and the after turret on the *King George V* from bearing on the enemy.

Lookouts on the *Bismarck* had seen the approach of the British battle group to the northwest, and the ship was ready to take on the challenge. Recognizing that the 16-inch guns of the *Rodney* posed the greater threat to their ship, the German gunners opened fire on her at 0849. Initially, the *Bismarck* was also limited to the use of only her forward turrets, but by engine power, she was able to turn to starboard sufficiently for her rear turrets to bear as well. With her third salvo, the *Bismarck* was able to straddle the *Rodney*, spraying the ship with shell splinters and causing some superficial damage to the ship.

Captain Dalrymple-Hamilton was anxious to deliver full broadsides against the *Bismarck* as soon as possible, so at 0852, he turned the *Rodney* to port sufficiently to allow her third turret to bear on the enemy ship. While increasing her firepower, the turn, however, also caused the *Rodney* to gradually increase the separation between her and the flagship. At 0854, the *Norfolk*, then about 13,000 yards northeast of the British battleships, opened fire on the *Bismarck* at a range of 22,000 yards, adding her firepower of eight 8-inch guns to the fray. A couple of minutes later, the *Rodney's* secondary battery of six 6-inch guns also began firing at the *Bismarck*.

Captain Dalrymple-Hamilton was in no hurry to dispatch the *Bismarck*, and he did not want to take any unnecessary risks with his own ship in dealing with his dangerous opponent. He therefore adopted the practice of steering toward the splashes of the last fall of shot from the *Bismarck* in the hope that the Germans would make the necessary corrections and the *Rodney* could thereby avoid the next salvo from the German battleship. This practice, however, interrupted the firing routine of the *Rodney*, and made it more difficult for her to achieve any hits on the *Bismarck*.

At 0900, with the range then down to 16,000 yards, the *King George V* turned south, allowing her rear turret to bear on the enemy. Seeing the

British battleship HMS *Rodney* (1927). *Photo courtesy of MaritimeQuest*

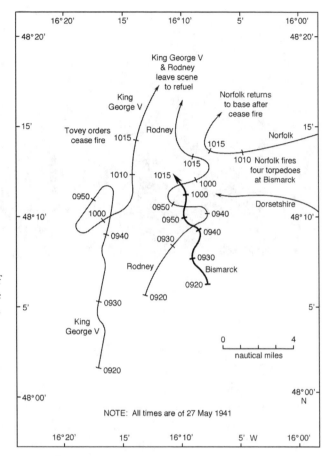

16° 20' 15' 16° 10' 5' 16° 00'

48° 20' 48° 20'

King George V
& Rodney
leave scene
to refuel

King
George V

Norfolk returns
to base after
cease fire

15' 15'

Tovey orders
cease fire 1015 Rodney Norfolk

1015

1015

1010 1015 1015 1010 Norfolk fires
four torpedoes
at Bismarck

0950 1000

1000

0950 Dorsetshire

48° 10' 0950 0940 48° 10'

1000 0940

0940

0930

0930

0940

0930 Bismarck

Rodney

0920 Bismarck

0920

5' 0930 5'

King
George V

0 4

nautical miles

0920

48° 00' 48° 00'
N

NOTE: All times are of 27 May 1941

16° 20' 15' 16° 10' 5' W 16° 00'

Final gunfire phase of
last battle to sink the
Bismarck.

King George V turn south, the *Rodney* followed suit a couple of minutes
later in compliance with Tovey's order to conform to the movements of
the flagship. Both British battleships were then firing full broadsides at
the *Bismarck* at decreasing ranges, but they were still not scoring any hits.
The *Bismarck* kept up a good fight for the first twenty minutes of the battle, but then she began taking hits that affected her ability to continue the
struggle.

With very little forward progress to help stabilize the ship, the *Bismarck* was wallowing in the swells of the sea, making it difficult for her
gunners to maintain an accurate rate of fire against any target. To make
matters worse, the main fire control director on the foretop of the ship
was hit and destroyed early in the engagement, forcing the transfer of cen-

Rodney fires at *Bismarck* during final battle. *Photo courtesy of MaritimeQuest*

tral fire control to either the forward or after fire control directors. The foretop was the post of Lt. Comdr. Adalbert Schneider, the first gunnery officer of the *Bismarck*, who was responsible for the sinking of the *Hood*.

At 0902, the *Bismarck* suffered a heavy hit on her forecastle that knocked her two forward turrets out of action. With the *Bismarck's* main fire control director and both forward turrets out of the fight, the after fire control director, commanded by Sr. Lieut. Burkard Baron von Müllenheim-Rechberg, the fourth gunnery officer of the *Bismarck*, was ordered to take over fire control of the after turrets Caesar and Dora. Technically, the third gunnery officer of the *Bismarck* was the antiaircraft officer, Sr. Lieut. Karl Gellert; however, for all practical purposes, the baron, being in charge of the after fire control director, was considered to be the third gunnery officer, and he was often referred to as such.

At 0905, the heavy cruiser *Dorsetshire*, coming onto the scene from the southeast, also opened fire on the *Bismarck* at a range of 20,000 yards, putting the German battleship under fire then from four different directions. At about the same time, the secondary battery of eight 5.25-inch guns on the *King George V* also opened fire on the *Bismarck*, adding to the weight of fire being directed at the German battleship.

At 0905, the *Bismarck* shifted targets with her remaining guns to the

Smoking
wreck of
Bismarck
gradually
sinking.
*Drawing
by the
author*

King George V. The baron was able to get off several salvos at the *King George V* with turrets Caesar and Dora at 12,000 yards, the last of which came uncomfortably close to the British flagship, but no hits were scored. Just as the baron determined the range for another salvo, the after fire control director suddenly received a violent shock. A shell had clipped off the top of the cupola, tearing away the heads of the optical sights and rendering the director useless. With no further contact with any of the fire control directors, fire control of turrets Caesar and Dora had to be put under local control.

From 0900-0910, the *Rodney* fired eight 24.5-inch super torpedoes at the *Bismarck* at 11,000 yards from her two underwater torpedo tubes, but without scoring any hits. The *Norfolk* also fired four standard 21-inch torpedoes at the *Bismarck* during the same period of time, but with the same results. At that time, the *Rodney* was continuing to sail in the opposite direction of the *Bismarck*, firing broadside after broadside to port at the German battleship.

At 0916, the *Rodney* was almost abreast of the *Bismarck*, and she began a 180° turn to starboard, bringing her stern around toward the enemy. As soon as the *Rodney* had competed its turn, she resumed firing broadsides at the *Bismarck*, which was now on her starboard side. The *King George V,* then at the end of her southward travel, also turned around almost 180°, but in her case to port toward the *Bismarck*, which deceased the range to the enemy ship. After completing her turn, she also resumed firing broadsides at the *Bismarck*. Hits scored by both British battleships had started numerous fires throughout the *Bismarck* in addition to the physical damage done by their exploding shells.

At 0920, the after turrets of the *Bismarck*, still on local control, turned on the *Rodney* again, but no hits were scored. At 0924, turret Dora was knocked out of action, but a couple of minutes later, one of the forward turrets of the *Bismarck* was able to get off a salvo before losing all power and remaining out of action thereafter. At 0931, turret Caesar fired its final salvo before it also was disabled, leaving only the *Bismarck's* secondary batteries to carry on the fight. Brief contact was then made with the forward fire control director, commanded by Lt. Comdr. Helmuth Albrecht, the second gunnery officer of the *Bismarck*, but all that Albrecht said was that his station had to be evacuated due to gas and smoke. Since the forward fire control director had been controlling the fire of the secondary batteries, those guns then had to go on local control as well.

Both the *King George V* and the *Rodney* kept pouring shells into the *Bismarck* over the next half hour, reducing the ship to a smoldering hulk. During that period, the *Rodney* fired her last two torpedoes at the *Bismarck*, but without scoring any hits. The 14-inch gun turrets on the flagship, however, were beginning to experience problems similar to those which plagued the *Prince of Wales* during the initial battle with the *Bismarck*. One turret was out of action for over 20 minutes and another turret for over five minutes due to mechanical breakdowns. The *Bismarck* was beginning to slow down even more as the engagement progressed, and the British battleships had to zigzag to keep from overrunning the target.

With no longer any means for the *Bismarck* to defend herself against the overwhelming firepower being directed at her, at about 1000, the order was given to set scuttling charges and abandon the ship. By that time, the ship had already taken a slight list to port as a result of flooding from the underwater hits that she received, but that did not guarantee that she would sink as a result. Teams set the charges with ten-minute delay fuses against the large cooling water intake pipes in the engine room, the destruction of which would allow sea water to gush in and rapidly fill the cavernous engine room and adjacent open spaces. Bulkhead doors were

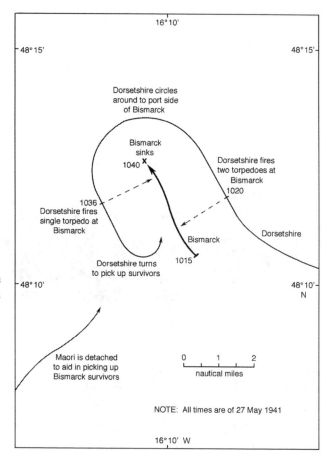

16° 10'

48° 15'

48° 15'

Dorsetshire circles
around to port side
of Bismarck

Bismarck
sinks

1040 ✗

Dorsetshire fires
two torpedoes at
Bismarck
1020

1036
Dorsetshire fires
single torpedo at
Bismarck

Dorsetshire

Bismarck

Dorsetshire fires
torpedoes after which
Bismarck sinks.

Dorsetshire turns
to pick up survivors

1015

48° 10'   48° 10'
                                          N

Maori is detached
to aid in picking up
Bismarck survivors

0   1   2

nautical miles

NOTE: All times are of 27 May 1941

16° 10' W

opened to facilitate flooding of the ship, and the crewmembers were then
ir own to leave the *Bismarck* as best they could.

At 1010, the *Norfolk* fired her last four torpedoes against the *Bismarck*,
but scored no hits. By that time, all of the *Bismarck's* guns had been
silenced and the ship was listing further to port. Scuttling charges were
beginning to detonate, and it was now just a matter of time before the
end would come. With the *Bismarck's* ensign still flying defiantly, however,
the British force had no other choice but to continue firing at the German
battleship, adding to the destruction and carnage already meted out to
the enemy. With firing ranges down to as low as 3,000 yards, at least one
hit was almost assured with every salvo fired at point-blank range.

Shortly after the battle commenced, Admiral Somerville decided to

Splashes of shells landing around smoking *Bismarck*. *Photo courtesy of MaritimeQuest*

send an attack force of Swordfish torpedo bombers to assist in the destruction of the *Bismarck*. At 0926, 12 Swordfish aircraft, carrying the last torpedoes on board the ship, took off from the *Ark Royal* and headed north toward the engagement. When they arrived on the scene, the battle was still going on, and Admiral Tovey was not yet ready to stop his gun bombardment of the *Bismarck*. Deeming it unsafe to attempt an aerial torpedo attack in the midst of heavy gunfire, the raid was called off and the aircraft returned to the *Ark Royal* after jettisoning their torpedoes.

Finally at 1015, Admiral Tovey ordered the British ships to cease fire, and with both the *King George V* and *Rodney* running dangerously low on fuel, he ordered the battle group to withdraw on course 027° to refuel at the nearest British naval base. Captain Vian provided the destroyer escort for the retiring British battleships with the destroyers *Cossack*, *Sikh*, and *Zulu*, leaving the *Maori* behind to assist the *Dorsetshire*. Admiral Tovey then ordered the *Dorsetshire*, the only ship with any torpedoes left, to finish off the *Bismarck*. The *Dorsetshire* closed in, and at 1020, she fired two torpedoes at the starboard side of the *Bismarck*, scoring one hit below the bridge. The cruiser then circled around to the port side of the *Bismarck* and at 1036, she fired her one remaining torpedo at 2,600 yards, scoring another hit on the German ship.

By then the *Bismarck*, filling rapidly with water, began to roll over on her port side until she was upside down and sinking by the stern. With little buoyancy left, the mighty ship disappeared from view at 1040. Hundreds of crewmen were able to escape from the ship and were now swimming in the water awaiting rescue. The cruiser *Dorsetshire* and the destroyer *Maori* were ordered to pick up survivors of the *Bismarck*. Both ships closed in amid the swarm of swimmers and threw down knotted ropes by which to climb onto the deck of the ships. In many cases crewmen on the ships helped to retrieve survivors when they were unable to pull themselves up.

Ever mindful of the U-boat threat to the British ships, Captain B.C.S. Martin of the *Dorsetshire* requested one of the *Ark Royal's* Swordfish aircraft in the area to maintain anti-submarine surveillance over area during the rescue operation. The British ships remained on the scene for over an hour rescuing *Bismarck* survivors when one of the lookouts on the *Dorset-*

Dorsetshire picks up *Bismarck* survivors. *Drawing by the author*

shire spotted a suspicious smoky discharge a couple of miles away. Fearing a U-boat in the area, Captain Martin ordered the *Dorsetshire* to get underway, and the *Maori* soon followed suit, leaving hundreds of survivors stranded in the water.

Although accounts differ to some degree, the *Dorsetshire* rescued some 80-85 survivors from the *Bismarck*, including four officers, and the *Maori* an additional 20-25 ratings for a total of 110-120. The U-74, which had been sent to the area to rescue the *Bismarck's* war diary, picked up three more survivors that evening, and the German weather ship *Sachsenwald* rescued two more survivors later that night. The exact number of persons aboard the *Bismarck* when she sank is unknown due mostly to non-crew additions, but it was greater than her basic complement of about 2,200 officers and men, including the Admiral's staff. This probably put her death toll at about 2,100 or more.

Ammunition expended by British forces to sink the *Bismarck* in the final battle included 380 16-inch shells fired by the *Rodney*, 339 14-inch shells fired by the *King George V*, 527 8-inch shells fired by the *Norfolk*, and 254 8-inch shells fired by the *Dorsetshire*. In addition, the *Rodney* fired 716 6-inch shells and the *King George V* fired 660 5.25-inch shells from their secondary armaments during the battle. It has been estimated that the *Bismarck* suffered direct hits by at least 100 large and medium caliber shells during her final battle. She was also the target of over 70 torpedoes fired at her with at least four hits.

CHAPTER 24

ADMIRALTY ENQUIRIES INTO
THE LOSS OF HMS *HOOD*

THE SINKING OF THE *HOOD*, THE PRIDE OF THE ROYAL Navy, and the turning away of the *Prince of Wales*, Britain's newest battleship, initially came as a tremendous shock to the Admiralty, the British government, and to the British people as a whole. The British task force, together with the *Norfolk* and *Suffolk*, constituted something like a two to one superiority over the German squadron, so how could such a disaster possibly happen? When it was later learned that the *Prince of Wales* still had most of her fighting capability intact, there was outrage in some circles, and this was followed by a demand that both Captain Leach and Admiral Wake-Walker be court-martialed for dereliction of duty. Didn't they realize that stopping the *Bismarck* was of the highest priority, and that it was even worth sacrificing the *Prince of Wales* to achieve that goal?

The First Sea Lord, Admiral of the Fleet Sir Dudley Pound, was a strong advocate for the court-martial of Captain Leach for breaking off the engagement with the *Bismarck*, and of Admiral Wake-Walker for not reengaging the *Bismarck* when the *Prince of Wales* was restored to near full serviceability. Admiral Tovey, however, supported the decisions of Captain Leach and Admiral Wake-Walker, and he threatened to resign if those commanders were court-martialed for their actions. Fortunately, the favorable outcome of the sinking the *Bismarck* without any further loss of life, or serious damage to the ships involved, weighed against such a court-martial, and the commanders received awards for their deeds instead. Had there not been a favorable outcome to the episode, it is most likely that a court-martial would have been convened.

Although there was no court-martial, immediate action was taken by the Admiralty to investigate the loss of the *Hood*. On 28 May, the day after the *Bismarck* was sunk, the First Sea Lord sent a memo the Third Sea Lord and Controller of the Navy, Vice-Admiral Bruce A. Fraser, requesting that a committee be established to review the possible causes of the explosion that sank the *Hood*. Sir Dudley Pound recalled that during the battle of Jutland in World War I, three other British battle cruisers were lost under similar circumstances, and he was concerned that there might be some connection between those incidents and the *Hood*'s loss.

A Board of Enquiry was promptly established with Vice-Admiral Sir Geoffrey Blake as its President and Captain C.F. Hammill and Captain C.H.J. Harcourt as its members. Testimony was taken primarily from eyewitnesses at the scene when the *Hood* exploded. The witnesses included Rear-Admiral Wake-Walker, Captain A.J.L. Phillips, and six other officers and ratings who were on the bridge of the *Norfolk* at the time; Captain Leach and seven other officers and ratings who were then on the bridge

First Sea Lord
Sir Dudley Pound.
*Photo courtesy of
MaritimeQuest*

of the *Prince of Wales*; and Midshipman W.J. Dundas, one of the three survivors of the *Hood*.

After weighing all of the evidence, the Board of Enquiry concluded that the explosion that sank the *Hood* was caused by one or more hits from the fifth salvo fired by the *Bismarck*. They also concluded that, in view of the magnitude of the explosion and short time it took for the ship to sink, one or more of the after magazines exploded, causing a large area to be blown out from the bottom of the ship. Although the explosion was seen by witnesses to be in the area of the mainmast, there are no magazines in that area, but the blast from a 4-inch HA ammunition magazine could have been vented to that location through the after engine room. An explosion of the 4-inch magazine could also cause the adjacent magazine containing ammunition for the *Hood's* main armament of 15-inch guns to blow up.

The Board of Enquiry further concluded that the warheads in the *Hood's* above water torpedo tubes did not explode, as some believed may have happened. They also deduced that the cordite fire on the shelter deck of the *Hood* was superficial, and it was not the cause for the ship to blow up. The Board finally concluded that the probable cause of the loss of the *Hood* was the direct penetration of its armor protection by one or more 15-inch shells fired by the *Bismarck* at a range of 16,500 yards, which resulted in the explosion of one or more of her after magazines. The fear that the *Hood* may have been sunk by plunging fire that penetrated her horizontal deck armor was apparently not an issue insofar as the Board of Enquiry was concerned.

The report by the Board of Enquiry on the loss of the Hood was completed just a few days later on 2 June, and on 7 June it was submitted to the Sea Lords, Sir Dudley Pound, and Bruce A. Fraser. On 12 June, a copy of the report was furnished to the Director of Naval Construction (DNC), Sir Stanley V. Goodall, for his comments before further distribution to the other departments of the Admiralty. The Director of Naval Construction was a senior civilian post in the Admiralty who was also the senior member of the Royal Corps of Naval Construction, which was responsible for the design and construction of all warships for the Royal Navy. As the chief marine architect for the Admiralty, his views on such issues carried much weight.

On 2 July, Goodall prepared a memorandum expressing his views on the report by the Board of Enquiry regarding the loss of HMS *Hood*. His first observation was that the report did contain the findings of the Board, but not the evidence on which those findings were based. He considered the findings of the Board to be premature in assuming that the possibility of the *Hood* blowing up in the manner that it stated was the way in which it actually happened. He went on to explain that is was also possible that the *Hood* may have been sunk by the detonation of the eight torpedo warheads, which contained 4,000 lbs. of TNT, that were stored on the upper deck of the ship if struck by a 15-inch shell from the *Bismarck*.

Goodall concluded that since his alternate explanation was entirely plausible, the findings of the Board should not be accepted as being final until the matter had been more thoroughly investigated. He then concluded with the statement that the doubts concerning the manner in which the *Hood* was lost should be cleared up as soon as possible so that appropriate measures could be taken to improve the armor protection of the older capital ships of the Royal Navy. He acknowledged, however, that it might not be possible to provide sufficient protection to ensure that the magazines of such ships could never be reached by modern shells and bombs.

The Controller disagreed with the views of the Director of Naval Construction and pointed out the reasons why he accepted the report of the Board of Enquiry as written. Fraser proposed that the findings of the Board be accepted and that the Commander-in-Chief of the Home Fleet, Admiral Tovey, be advised accordingly. On 18 July, the Vice Chief of the Naval Staff, Vice-Admiral Tom S.V. Phillips, weighed in with his comments, noting that the Board of Enquiry report did not include the evidence on which their conclusions were based and that the issues raised by the Director of Naval Construction should be resolved by a more searching enquiry than the one that was carried out. He proposed that a further Board of Enquiry be assembled as soon as possible and that every person who saw the *Hood* blow up be fully interrogated.

On 19 July, the First Sea Lord sent a memorandum to the First Lord of the Admiralty, A.V. Alexander, regarding the report of the Board of Enquiry on the loss of the *Hood*. In that memorandum, Sir Dudley Pound pointed out that the failure to take a verbatim record of the evidence of the witnesses to the incident was a handicap to the further investigation of the matter and that the technical departments might reach different conclusions than those reached by the Board. He proposed that a new Board of Enquiry be established to investigate the loss of the *Hood* with the assistance of a "Constructor" and an expert in explosives. Alexander immediately agreed to the calling of a new Board of Enquiry.

On 31 July, the Lords of the Admiralty established the Second Board of Enquiry into the loss of HMS *Hood* with Rear-Admiral Harold T.C. Walker, who had been the captain of the *Hood* from May 1938 until January 1939, as its President, and with Captain R.D. Duke (replacing Captain H.E. Morse) and Captain L.D. Mackintosh as its members. The Second Board of Enquiry took testimony from a total of 176 witnesses, including 71 from the *Prince of Wales*, 89 from the *Norfolk*, 14 from the *Suffolk*, and two survivors of the *Hood*. The testimony from those witnesses were taken on 12 August on board the HMS *Dorsetshire*, on 13 August on board the HMS *Suffolk*, and subsequently at the Admiralty office in Dorland House on Lower Regent Street near Piccadilly Circus in downtown London.

As part of his testimony, Captain Leach submitted a memorandum dated 4 June 1941 with an appendix that contained a detailed narrative of the operations against the *Bismarck* from the time that the *Prince of Wales* passed Hoxa Gate when exiting Scapa Flow on 22 May until the ship anchored at Hvalfjord on 27 May. On 12 June, Captain Leach submitted to Admiral Tovey the gunnery appendix to his narrative of operations against the *Bismarck*. The *Prince of Wales* salvo plot and an overall track chart of the *Prince of Wales* during the battle were provided as enclosures, and these documents were also made a matter of record by the Board of Enquiry.

The Board of Enquiry also received testimony from technical witnesses, including Captain J.F.B. Carslake of the Department of Torpedoes and Mining, Dr. Godfrey Rotter representing the Chief Superintendent of the Research Department, and Mr. D.E.J. Offord, the Chief Constructor of the Naval Construction Department. Information derived from the interrogation of *Bismarck* survivors was of particular interest to the Director of Naval Intelligence, Vice-Admiral John Godfrey, and the Director of Naval Construction, Sir Stanley V. Goodall, and extracts from the survivor statements were incorporated into the proceedings of the Board.

The work of the Second Board of Enquiry into the loss of HMS *Hood* was completed on 12 September 1941, and its report was submitted to the Admiralty office in Rex House, also on Regent Street in downtown London. The report included a summary of the evidence gathered and a discussion of the various possible causes of the explosion that led to the destruction of the *Hood*. One key issue was the fact that several witnesses testified that the explosion occurred near the base of the main (rear) mast, which was far removed from any magazines.

The Second Board of Enquiry concluded that the sinking of the *Hood* was caused by a 15-inch shell from the *Bismarck* hitting in or adjacent to the magazines with ammunition for the *Hood's* 4-inch and 15-inch guns, causing the magazines to explode and wreck the after part of the ship. They believed that the 4-inch magazines probably exploded first. The Board stated that, although the possibility still existed, there was no conclusive evidence that one or more torpedo warheads exploded concurrently with the magazines. The Board also concluded that the fire observed on the *Hood's* boat deck, involving the detonation of ready use ammunition stored in that area, was not the cause of the *Hood's* destruction. While the Second Board of Enquiry came up with substantially the same conclusions as the First Board, its results were deemed to be more credible in view of the more comprehensive nature of the enquiry.

The report was reviewed with much interest by the new Assistant Chief of Naval Staff (Weapons), Rear-Admiral Rhoderick R. McGrigor, who had just been promoted and reassigned to that position from being the Captain of the battle cruiser *Renown*, which was the flagship of Force H in its recent encounter with the *Bismarck*. McGrigor observed that British capital ships were susceptible to having their igniters (primers) set off by the flash from enemy shell hits while the Germans used brass cases to protect their charges. The problem was overcome on ammunition for 8-inch and smaller guns by avoiding powder igniters and using foil-wrapped one-inch tube igniters.

The Permanent Secretary to the Admiralty, Henry V. Markham, responded to McGrigor's comments with the thought that the magazines of British ships should be provided with as much protection as necessary to prevent enemy shells from penetrating them, and that ammunition that was not likely to be detonated by enemy fire should be provided to all ships. The Controller, Vice-Admiral Bruce A. Fraser, noted the remarks of the Permanent Secretary and commented that the magazines in Britain's newer ships were good, but that they were poor in older ships. He added that some additional armor had been installed in "R"-class ships, but that it was not very satisfactory. Fraser was referring to battleships of the *Royal Sovereign*-class, whose names began with the letter "R", i.e., *Ramillies, Resolution*, and *Revenge*, and possibly also the battle cruisers *Renown* and *Repulse.*

The First Sea Lord, Sir Dudley Pound, concurred with the recommendation of the Permanent Secretary that the report by the Board of Enquiry be brought before the Board of the Admiralty, but he believed that the Board of the Admiralty should also have two additional reports available to it. One report would be on the lessons learned from the destruction of the *Hood* and the action taken in response to those lessons. The other report would be on why present igniters used on 8-inch and smaller caliber guns could not be used on guns over 8-inch and how the tinfoil covered igniters were likely to prevent a magazine from blowing up. Also, what action was being taken to get a charge that could not be ignited by an enemy shell for guns over 8-inch, and was such action being taken with a sufficient degree of urgency?

The First Sea Lord also commented that, in view of the remarks by the Director of Naval Construction regarding the ability of the *Bismarck* to withstand all of the damage that she did, it would be all the more necessary to determine why the *Prince of Wales* suffered so severely from at most two torpedoes when the *Bismarck* was able to stand up to five torpedoes. The First Lord of the Admiralty, A.V. Alexander, concurred in the recommendations of the First Sea Lord and directed that necessary action be taken accordingly.

In addition to the Lords of the Admiralty, the report was also well received by the various technical departments with a view toward making improvements in the design of new warships and the refit of older warships to make them less susceptible to catastrophic explosions resulting from hits by enemy warships. The technical reviewers included the Director of Naval Equipment, Vice-Admiral Charles E.B. Simeon; the Director of Naval Construction, Stanley V. Goodall; the Director of Naval Ordnance, Captain Oliver Bevin; and the Director of Torpedoes and Mining, Henry C. Phillips.

CHAPTER **25**

AFTERMATH OF THE BATTLE

WHEN THE BRITISH ANNOUNCED THAT THE *BISMARCK* had been sunk and the Germans could no longer make contact with the ship, Admiral Raeder advised the Führer of the battleship's probable loss. While this setback was obviously a disappointment to Hitler, it was partially offset by recent German triumphs in Greece and Yugoslavia, including the successful airborne invasion of Crete on 20 May 1941. Hitler's thoughts at the time, however, were concentrated primarily on plans and preparations for the forthcoming invasion of the Soviet Union, which was less than four weeks away.

After leaving the scene of battle with the *Bismarck*, Admiral Tovey's force of the battleships *King George V* and *Rodney*, escorted by Captain Vian's destroyers *Cossack*, *Sikh*, and *Zulu*, headed for the nearest British naval base to replenish their fuel. The nearest base was at Loch Ewe on the west coast of Scotland, and at 1600 on the following afternoon of 28 May, 11 additional destroyers, dispatched by the Admiralty to bolster the anti-submarine protection for the task force, met up with Tovey's battle group. Admiral Tovey's force safely reached Loch Ewe at 1230 on 29 May with their fuel tanks almost empty.

The heavy cruiser *Dorsetshire* headed for Newcastle to deliver the 80-85 *Bismarck* survivors aboard, including the fourth gunnery officer, Senior Lieutenant Burkard Baron von Müllenheim-Rechberg, and engineering officer, Sr. Lieut. Gerhard Junack, to the authorities. The *Dorsetshire* arrived in Newcastle on 30 May, and the prisoners were immediately transported by rail to London where they were taken to the London District Cage at the Kensington Palace Gardens for interrogation by intelligence officers.

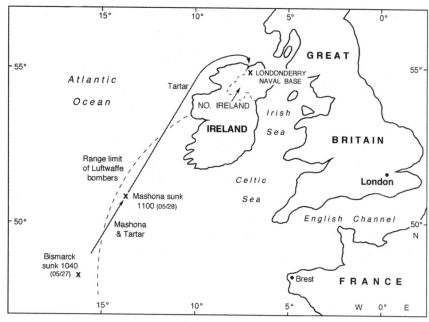

Loss of the destroyer *Mashona*.

The London District Cage was one of nine prisoner of war "cages" established throughout the British Isles by the Prisoner of War Interrogation Section (PWIS) of the War Office for the initial interrogation of prisoners of war. At these cages, incoming prisoners of war were identified, processed, and evaluated as to the amount of intelligence they might provide. The London District Cage had accommodations for 60 prisoners and five interrogation rooms, and it was staffed by some 20 intelligence officers and interpreters. Prisoners deemed to be of little value for intelligence purposes were then sent directly to prisoner of war camps established throughout the country.

The destroyer *Maori* delivered her 25-30 *Bismarck* survivors to the Firth of Clyde, where they were taken to the local district "cage" for their initial interrogation and then sent to a POW camp. In the meantime, the *Maori* resumed her convoy escort duties.

Senior officers, such as Baron von Müllenheim-Rechberg, were singled out for further questioning at the Combined Services Detailed Interrogation Centre (CSDIC) in Trent Park. The CSDIC, also known as Cockfosters Camp No. 10 or Trent Park Camp No. 11a, was located in the

Cockfosters District of London between the London Boroughs of Enfield and Barnet at the northern end of the Piccadilly Underground line. The CSDIC was housed in a large three-story mansion, which had accommodations for the prisoners at the Centre as well as staff functions.

The Centre also had 12 large rooms in the common areas of the house that were wired for sound to pick up unguarded conversations between the prisoners. The CSDIC was staffed by highly qualified interrogators who were capable of conducting comprehensive interrogations to extract the most information from the prisoners, as well as numerous recording technicians, interpreters, and support personnel.

After weeks of interrogation at Cockfosters, Baron von Müllenheim-Rechberg was taken north to Prisoner of War Camp No. 15, the Shap Wells Hotel near Penrith in Cumberland. The camp was one of the earliest prisoner of war camps among the over 600 eventually established in Great Britain during the war. The Shap Wells Hotel had been a resort that was requisitioned by the War Office early in February 1941 to serve as a POW camp for officer personnel. The Shap Wells was returned to private use after the war, and it is now a three-star Best Western Hotel serving the tourist trade in the region.

British Tribal-class destroyer HMS *Tartar* (1939). *Photo courtesy of MaritimeQuest*

Officer prisoners were usually treated far better than their enlisted counterparts, receiving superior accommodations and food, and often given more freedom of movement. Enlisted prisoners of war were housed mostly in semi-cylindrical-shaped Nissen huts constructed of corrugated sheet metal and set up in parks and open fields. The Nissen hut was invented by Major Peter N. Nissen of the British Royal Engineers during World War I, and it later became the model for the American Quonset hut.

In March 1942, Baron von Müllenheim-Rechberg was among a group of prisoners designated to be sent to a POW camp in Canada. They were taken to Greenock on the River Clyde where they boarded the 17,000-ton transport *Rangitiki* that was destined for Halifax, Nova Scotia. Built in 1929 by John Brown as a liner for the New Zealand Shipping Company, the *Rangitiki* had been in use since the beginning of the war as a troop transport. From Halifax, the baron and his group were transported by rail to the Prisoner of War Camp No. 30 at Bowmanville, about 40 miles east of Toronto, where they remained in captivity until after the war.

Prisoner of War Camp No. 30, officially the Lake Ontario Officers' Camp–Bowmanville, was one of 40 POW camps established in Canada during World War II. It had been a home for delinquent boys on the northeast side of the town, but soon after the outbreak of war it was taken over by the Canadian government and converted into a prisoner of war camp for officers. It had a number of brick and stucco buildings to accommodate the prisoners, and it also had a swimming pool for their recreation. The site was enclosed with barbed wire, however, to discourage escape attempts.

In October 1942, the prisoners at Camp 30 revolted against their guards when the latter attempted to shackle them in retaliation for Germany's new Commando Order, which directed the killing of all Allied commandos henceforth taken into custody and ordered the shackling of nearly 1,400 Allied prisoners, mostly Canadians captured in the Dieppe raid. Several on both sides were injured in the ensuing brawl, which was finally brought under control by the deployment of high-pressure fire hoses directed against the prisoners.

The baron was well versed in the English language, and he subscribed to the Toronto-based *The Globe and Mail*, one of the leading daily newspapers in Canada, to keep up with world events during his imprisonment at Bowmanville. One morning in the summer of 1943, he picked up his copy of the paper and was astonished to see on the front page a photograph of the *Bismarck* taken from the air while it was at anchor in Grimstadfjord near Bergen, Norway. It was a rude awakening for him to learn that the British were fully aware of the *Bismarck's* movements that early in the operation, and he now knew for sure that the *Suffolk* and *Norfolk* were not in the Denmark Strait by chance at the time, and why the *Hood* and *Prince of Wales* were able to intercept the German squadron so soon after that.

After the *Prinz Eugen* was detached from the *Bismarck* during the evening of 24 May, she continued steaming south toward a rendezvous with a German tanker. At 1700, she had 1,350 tons of fuel oil left, 42% of her capacity, but not enough to engage in extended raiding operations and still return to base. At 2111, Captain Brinkmann sent a short signal to Group West indicating the urgent need for the *Prinz Eugen* to refuel from either the tanker *Spichern* or the *Esso Hamburg*. By 0800 on the following morning of 25 May, her fuel tanks were down to 1,145 tons, 35% of capacity. At 0921, the *Prinz Eugen* turned to course 188° in the direction of the quadrant that the tanker *Spichern* was reported to be in by Group West.

The *Prinz Eugen* finally met up with the *Spichern* on the morning of 26 May and took on fuel oil all day until 2230 that evening. At midnight, the *Prinz Eugen* set a course to the west in search of the scout ship *Kota Pinang*, which with the *Gonzenheim* had been ordered to reconnoiter in advance the proposed operational area of the *Bismarck* and *Prinz Eugen*. The *Kota Pinang* and *Gonzenheim* were then given instructions to determine shipping routes and report on ship movements every six hours to Group West. Later on 27 May, the *Prinz Eugen* was able to obtain some needed supplies from the *Gonzenheim*.

At 1850, a message was received from Group West that an Italian submarine reported large British naval activity in the area, suggesting that they may be on the hunt for the *Prinz Eugen*. Apparently what the submarine saw were the ships that had participated in the sinking of the *Bismarck* and were now returning to their bases to refuel. With a British heavy cruiser having been sighted off the Portuguese coast and American patrol activity in the west, the only evasive action that could then be taken by the *Prinz Eugen* was to the south where the tanker *Friedrich Breme* would be able to refuel and re-supply the ship. Shortly after midnight, the *Prinz Eugen* made contact with the tanker *Esso Hamburg* and took on 680 tons of fuel oil.

It was Captain Brinkmann's intent that the *Prinz Eugen's* fuel tanks be topped off daily so that the ship would always have the maximum cruising range possible in the event that a long high-speed run became necessary. At 1400 on 29 May, the *Prinz Eugen* rendezvoused with the *Kota Pinang*, and new written orders were delivered by pouch to the scout ship. The *Kota Pinang* was to reconnoiter a new quadrant for enemy shipping, but first sail to the *Gonzenheim* and pass on similar orders for her to scout the adjacent area. The scout ships were directed to report to Group West and the *Prinz Eugen* on steamer routes and ship sightings by type, number, speed, direction, and time of sighting. Further specific redeployments were to be made if no further word was received from the *Prinz Eugen* by 4 June.

Captain Brinkmann recorded his growing concern about the condition of *Prinz Eugen's* engines in the ship's war diary on 29 May. His most serious concerns include steam leaking from a flange in the main steam line preventing the port engine from achieving flank speed, the starboard engine drive being placed under strain by a damaged propeller blade, a defective main water cooling pump amidships, and the sudden and complete failure of the port engine, which could only partially be restored. Since the *Prinz Eugen* could now make only 29 knots and extensive repairs were required on her power plant, Brinkmann expressed the need to return to a port for repairs.

After exploring the various alternatives, Brinkmann determined that steaming for a French port would provide the best opportunity for the *Prinz Eugen* to avoid contact with British naval forces, so he ordered the *Prinz Eugen* to turn east in the direction of the French coast. At 0600 on the morning of 30 May, her fuel oil status was 2,657 tons, 82% of capacity. The *Prinz Eugen* continued to sail due east on course 90° at a speed of 29 knots during the day to rendezvous with the Fifth Destroyer Flotilla in the designated quadrant. At 0800 on the following morning, 31 May, her fuel oil stores were down to 1,976 tons, 61% of capacity, and at 0810, Brinkmann advised Group West that the *Prinz Eugen* could not steam at a speed of more than 28 knots and that he intended to go to a French port on the Bay of Biscay.

On the morning of 1 June, the *Prinz Eugen* continued to sail eastward, and she began to zigzag at dawn (0600). Shortly thereafter, three Heinkel aircraft appeared to provide air cover for the cruiser. The *Prinz Eugen* had rendezvoused with the Fifth Destroyer Flotilla in the designated quadrant, and at 0605, the destroyers escorted the cruiser to Point Rosa 21, where they were released at 1525. From there, *Sperrbrecher 13* took over the task of leading the *Prinz Eugen* to Brest. By 0800, the ship's fuel tanks were down to 1,269 tons, 39% of capacity, but she was almost home. At 1930, the *Prinz Eugen* entered the harbor at Brest and docked after having traveled a total of 7,000 nautical miles at an average speed of 24 knots and having consumed a total of 6,410 tons of fuel oil.

Shortly after his arrival at Brest, Captain Brinkmann of the *Prinz Eugen* reported to his superior, Vice-Admiral Hubert Schmundt, Commander of Cruisers (Befehlshaber der Kreuzer). Brinkmann provided him with the *Prinz Eugen's* war diary, the ship's battle diagram, and a set of photographs taken from the cruiser during the battle. After reviewing the documents, Admiral Schmundt submitted a report to the German Naval High Command, Office of Naval Operaiions (Oberkommando der Marine, Seekriegsleitung) on 16 June 1941 stating his position on the issues raised in those documents.

First of all, Admiral Schmundt stated that he could not acccpt the explanation that the departure of the *Bismarck* and *Prinz Eugen* from home waters may not have been known by the enemy in view of ample opportunities for such information to reach them. The bombing of anchorages near Bergen was another indication that the British knew of the German ships being on the move. Second, he was critical of Admiral Lütjens for not waiting for further intelligence on the disposition of British warships at the Scapa Flow naval base before undertaking the operation from Norway.

Admiral Schmundt was critical of Captain Brinkmann for not placing the *Prinz Eugen* on the lee-side of the *Bismarck* during the battle. Admiral Schmundt apparently came to that conclusion based on the photographs showing the *Bismarck* on the starboard side of the *Prinz Eugen*, which of course would have placed the cruiser toward the enemy from the *Bismarck*. If, however, the photographs had been printed in their correct orientation, they would have shown that the *Prinz Eugen* was actually on the lee-side of the *Bismarck*, as prescribed by German naval operating procedures.

Admiral Schmundt's criticism of Captain Brinkmann did not make much sense anyway. The records show that the *Prinz Eugen* made two hard turns to starboard beginning at 0603, which actually placed the cruiser further away from the enemy. Therefore, if anyone was responsible

Prinz Eugen arrives at Brest (bow view). *Photo courtesy of MaritimeQuest*

Prinz Eugen arrives at Brest (stern view). *Photo courtesy of MaritimeQuest*

for the *Prinz Eugen* being on the wrong side of the *Bismarck* during the battle, it would have been Admiral Lütjens, and not Captain Brinkmann of the *Prinz Eugen*. There was no sound reason for the *Bismarck* to turn away from the *Prince of Wales* when she was getting the better of the one-sided exchange of gunfire and then sail behind the *Prinz Eugen* on the cruiser's starboard side.

Certainly, the *Bismarck* would not have come racing up on the port side of the *Prinz Eugen* only to turn and sail behind the cruiser, leaving the cruiser exposed to direct fire from the *Prince of Wales* for several minutes before returning to the port side of the *Prinz Eugen* again, just before the German ships ceased fire. It makes no sense whatsoever, and yet there are some who are willing to believe that this happened.

Captain Brinkmann was also criticized for not having launched any torpedoes against the *Prince of Wales* during the window of opportunity when it appeared that she was within range of 14,000 meters (15,300 yards) and before the British battleship turned away. Brinkmann made no mention of any contemplated torpedo attack on the *Prince of Wales* in the *Prinz Eugen's* war diary. While the photographs initially placed the *Prinz Eugen* in the open and toward the enemy, the *Bismarck* coming up on her port side would have precluded a torpedo attack by the *Prinz Eugen* against the *Prince of Wales*.

The *Prinz Eugen's* first torpedo officer, Sr. Lieut. Reimann, later tried to explain away the failure of the cruiser not launching a torpedo attack against the *Prince of Wales* by claiming that he had difficulty acquiring the proper range and bearing to the target. Captain Brinkmann attributed the failure to insufficient training of the crew in firing torpedoes under all possible conditions. Admiral Schmundt countered these excuses by observing that torpedoes should have been fired at the *Prince of Wales* under any circumstances as soon as the British battleship came within range.

Admiral Schmundt was critical of the *Prinz Eugen's* battle diagram, which he declared to be worthless since the position of the *Prince of Wales* in relation to that of the *Prinz Eugen* could not be determined. He was also critical of first gunnery officer Paulus Jasper for failing to recognize the enemy ships as capital ships and therefore using base-fuse shells instead of point-fused ammunition, which could have inflicted more severe damage on the *Hood* and *Prince of Wales*.

On 12 June 1941, Vice-Admiral Otto Schniewind, who had been the

Director of Sea Warfare (Seekriegsleitung) since 1938, was reassigned as the Chief of the Fleet, replacing Admiral Günther Lütjens, who along with his staff went down on the *Bismarck*. Schniewind reviewed Admiral Schmundt's report, and on 22 July he submitted his own position statement to the new Director of Sea Warfare, Vice-Admiral Kurt Fricke, who had been his Chief of Naval Operations at Seekriegsleitung. In his position statement, Schniewind agreed with nearly all of the statements made by Admiral Schmundt, but he did not want to get involved in the details of the report, preferring to address in general the various risks involved in any future breakouts by surface vessels for raiding operations in the North Atlantic.

Admiral Rolf Carls, Commander of Naval Group North, also weighed in by disagreeing with some of the conclusions reached by Admiral Schmundt. Carls stated that the deployment of the *Prinz Eugen* under the circumstances was entirely proper and productive. He also stated that the criticism of the *Prinz Eugen's* first gunnery officer, Jasper, for initially believing that the *Hood* and *Prince of Wales* were merely cruisers, was unjustified since the far distance and steep angle of approach made identification very difficult.

CHAPTER 26

SUBSEQUENT LOSS OF SHIPS
INVOLVED IN THE OPERATION

T HE TOLL OF HUMAN LIFE AND SHIPS FOR THE EPISODE
did not end with the sinking of the *Bismarck*. On the following morning of 28 May, the Germans sent a flight of bombers to attack
any British ships leaving the scene where the *Bismarck* went down, but
they found only the destroyers *Mashona* and *Tartar* of the Sixth Destroyer
Flotilla heading for Londonderry at slow speed to conserve fuel. The German bombers attacked the hapless destroyers and succeeded in hitting the
Mashona, which sank with the loss of nearly 50 officers and men. The *Tartar* was able to rescue the *Mashona's* 170 survivors, including her skipper,
and bring them to Londonderry in Northern Ireland, with her fuel supply
nearly exhausted.

With the sinking of the *Bismarck*, and the battleships *Scharnhorst* and
Gneisenau and heavy cruiser *Prinz Eugen* being holed up in Brest and under
surveillance by British air and submarine patrols, the immediate German
surface threat to convoys bringing supplies to Great Britain had been virtually eliminated. It was now safe to leave only destroyers to escort convoys
for anti-submarine protection, thereby allowing larger units the freedom
to pursue other tasks. One of these tasks was to eliminate the network of
German tankers and supply ships stationed in the Atlantic Ocean to support surface raiders and U-boats. At the beginning of June 1941, a concerted effort was undertaken by the Royal Navy to hunt down those
German tankers and supply ships, and it met with considerable success.

On 3 June, the German tanker *Belchen* was sunk by the British light
cruisers *Aurora* and *Kenya* in the North Atlantic south of Greenland. On
the following day, 4 June, the tankers *Esso Hamburg* and *Egerland* were

scuttled in the South Atlantic to avoid being captured by the heavy cruiser *London* and the auxiliary cruiser *Brilliant*. On the same day, the scout ship *Gonzenheim* escaped from the British auxiliary cruiser *Esperance Bay*, but was later scuttled when she was intercepted by the battleship *Nelson* and light cruiser *Neptune*. Also on that day, the supply ship *Gedania* was captured by the British auxiliary cruiser *Marsdale* in the mid-Atlantic.

On 12 June 1941, the tanker *Friedrich Breme* was scuttled in the mid-Atlantic to avoid capture by the light cruiser *Sheffield*, and on 15 June, the light cruiser *Dunedin* captured the tanker *Lothringen*. On 3 October 1941, the scout ship *Kota Pinang* was scuttled to avoid capture by the cruisers *Sheffield* and the *Kenya*, and on 13 March 1942, the tanker *Spichern* was scuttled after being intercepted by the sloop *Scarborough*. The supply ship *Ermland*, later renamed the *Weserland*, remained on the loose until 3 January 1944, when she was scuttled after being intercepted by the American destroyer USS *Somers* in the South Atlantic.

After discharging her dead and wounded crewmen and refueling at the British naval base of Hvalfjord in Iceland in early June 1941, the *Prince of Wales* sailed to the Royal Dockyard at Rosyth on the River Forth near Edinburgh, Scotland for necessary repairs. When the ship was moved into a dry dock, Admiralty officers had the first opportunity to fully assess the damage done to the ship by German gunfire. To their surprise, they found an unexploded 15-inch shell still inside the hull of the ship. The shell was the first of four hits scored by the *Bismarck* on the *Prince of Wales*, and it struck the ship amidships, about a foot above the bilge keel on the starboard side.

An analysis of the hit indicated that the shell traveled about 80 feet underwater and struck the side of the *Prince of Wales* 28 feet below the water level. It then traveled another 12 feet within the hull before being stopped by the protective bulkhead. A hole had to be cut in the bottom of the hull so that the shell could be lowered onto a rubber-tired ammunition trolley for removed by bomb disposal personnel. The failure of the shell to detonate was attributed to a defective fuse.

The damage caused by a 15-inch shell going through the compass platform of the *Prince of Wales* was assessed, and it was concluded that the 15-inch shell that hit the support for the forward high-angle antiaircraft directors came from the same salvo as the shell that hit the compass platform. The fourth 15-inch shell hit on the *Prince of Wales* did considerable

Prince of Wales arrives at Singapore. *Photo courtesy of MaritimeQuest*

splinter damage in addition to damaging the starboard crane and destroying or damaging some of the boats. The three 8-inch shell hits scored by the *Prinz Eugen* were also analyzed with a view toward minimizing the damage caused by such hits in the future.

After the damage inflicted by the *Bismarck* and *Prinz Eugen* had been repaired, the *Prince of Wales* returned to service. In August 1941, she carried Prime Minister Winston Churchill and his staff to Newfoundland for his famous meeting with President Roosevelt, which culminated in the Atlantic Charter. The *Prince of Wales* was then sent to the Mediterranean for convoy duty. In October of that year, still under the command of Captain John C. Leach, she was ordered to sail for Singapore with the destroyers *Electra* and *Express* as Force Z under the overall command of Admiral Sir Tom S.V. Phillips, the former Vice Chief of Naval Staff. The objective of Force Z was to deter any Japanese aggression against British interests in the area in view of the growing Japanese threat to southeast Asia.

The battle cruiser *Repulse*, which had been on convoy duty in the Indian Ocean, was ordered to join Force Z at Ceylon, and from there, the ships sailed together for Singapore, arriving there on 2 December 1941. There the force was joined by two additional destroyers, the *Encounter* and *Jupiter*. Force Z was also assigned an aircraft carrier, but with the accidental grounding of the new carrier *Indomitable* off Jamaica and the sinking of the *Ark Royal* by a U-boat near Gibraltar, no other carrier could be spared. The situation had become ominous with the sighting by an RAF reconnaissance plane of a large Japanese convoy with a heavy naval escort heading south along the Indo-China coast on 4 December. Two days later, it was approaching British Malaya.

On 8 December, the British naval commanders met at Singapore to assess the Japanese threat and to plan appropriate countermeasures. They had just received news of the Japanese attack on Pearl Harbor a few hours earlier (7 December in Hawaii), and they now anticipated an attack against Malaya. Shortly before nightfall, Force Z set sail in a northerly direction to intercept the reported Japanese convoy. The destroyers *Encounter* and *Jupiter*, both of which needed repairs, had been replaced by two older ships, the *Tenedos* and the Australian *Vampire*. The next day, the Japanese launched an air attack against targets in Malaya, which caused the evacuation of the only airfield that could provide air cover for Admiral Phillips' Force Z.

On 9 December, Force Z was spotted by a Japanese submarine and later by naval aircraft launched from Japanese cruisers. The Japanese attempted to mount an air attack on Force Z that night, but in the dark-

Ark Royal sinking after being torpedoed. *Photo courtesy of MaritimeQuest*

ness they could not find the British ships. In the meantime, the destroyer *Tenedos* was running low on fuel and had to return to Singapore, leaving Phillips with only three destroyers to cover his force. On the morning of 10 December, Admiral Phillips received a report that the Japanese were making a landing at Kuantan, much further down the Malay coast and closer to Singapore. Sensing this to be an even greater threat, he turned his squadron around and headed southwest toward the reported landing site.

At about 1000, the Japanese discovered the *Tenedos* on her way back to Singapore and subjected her to high-level bombing attacks, but without success. The *Repulse* launched her Walrus seaplane to make a reconnaissance flight in the area of the reported landing at Kuantan, but the pilot could see nothing unusual—the earlier report had evidently been false. Admiral Phillips soon learned of the air attack on the *Tenedos,* and shortly before 1100, a Japanese aircraft was sighted in the distance. He ordered Force Z to be brought up to full alert and to increase speed in anticipation of an air attack against the force. He did not have to wait long before a large flight of enemy aircraft was spotted on radar approaching Force Z.

At about 1115, the first squadron of Japanese bombers appeared on the scene and attacked the *Repulse.* They scored one hit and several near misses and caused some moderate damage to the ship. Some fifteen minutes later, the *Prince of Wales* became the target of a combined bombing and torpedo attack, and was hit by two torpedoes on her port side. One of the torpedoes struck in the stern area, damaging her rudder and drive shafts, and the other one hit amidships, causing some flooding. The two torpedo hits left the *Prince of Wales* in a crippled condition and listing to port.

At about noon, the *Repulse* was again attacked and hit by several torpedoes. These hits inflicted fatal wounds on the old battle cruiser, and a half an hour later, she sank. The destroyers *Express* and *Vampire* were ordered to pick up survivors. They managed to rescue nearly 800 persons, including the skipper, Captain William G. Tennant, from the *Repulse's* complement of about 1,310 officers and men. Over 510 officers and men, however, went down with the ship.

The Japanese then turned their full attention to the *Prince of Wales,* which received two more torpedo hits and several near misses by bombs that caused further underwater damage to the ship. This additional damage left the *Prince of Wales* in a sinking condition, and the order was given to abandon ship. The destroyer *Electra* came alongside to take off her crew, but the *Prince of Wales* capsized and sank before that operation could be completed. In all, nearly 1,300 officers and men were rescued out of a total complement of over 1,600. Among the some 325 officers and men that perished with the *Prince of Wales* were Admiral Phillips and Captain Leach.

In late 1941 and early 1942, Great Britain lost a number of ships involved in the *Bismarck* operation due to enemy action. The destroyer *Cossack* was torpedoed in the North Atlantic by U-563 on 23 October 1941, and she sank four days later while under tow with a total loss of 159 members of her crew.

After the operation against the *Bismarck*, the aircraft carrier *Ark Royal* returned with Force H to Gibraltar. While on convoy duty in the Mediterranean, she was attacked many times by German bombers hoping to avenge the *Bismarck*, but she survived all of those attacks without being hit. On 13 November 1941, the *Ark Royal* was hit by a single torpedo from an Axis submarine near Gibraltar, but that hit proved to be fatal. Nearly all of her crew were rescued by her destroyer escort as she slowly listed on her starboard side. On the following morning, the *Ark Royal*, one of the most renowned ships of the Royal Navy, turned over and sank.

The destroyer *Electra*, which had rescued the three survivors from the *Hood* and later had taken hundreds of officers and men from the sinking *Prince of Wales*, returned to Singapore with the *Prince of Wales* survivors. When the Japanese ground forces came down the Malay Peninsula and approached Singapore, the *Electra* was dispatched to reinforce the Allied Western Striking Force defending the Dutch East Indies from Japanese invasion. On 27 February 1942, the *Electra* was one of the Allied warships sunk by a superior Japanese naval force during the Battle of the Java Sea. Of her crew of nearly 150 officers and men, over 90 were lost.

The heavy cruiser *Dorsetshire*, which struck the last blow against the *Bismarck* with her three torpedoes and helped to send her to the bottom, was also sent to the Far East to bolster the British fleet operating in the Indian Ocean. On 5 April 1942, Easter Sunday, the *Dorsetshire* and her sister ship, the *Cornwall*, came under attack by Japanese dive bombers off Ceylon. Both ships received multiple bomb hits and sank with a heavy loss of life.

CHAPTER **27**

END OF THE GERMAN SURFACE
THREAT TO ALLIED SHIPPING

AFTER THE LOSS OF THE *BISMARCK*, THE GERMAN NAVAL High Command realized that the chances for surface raiders to have any success in the North Atlantic had become very remote due primarily to the increasing effectiveness of British radar. The loss of nearly all of the German tankers and supply ships in the area further weighed against additional operations of surface ships in the North Atlantic. The final blow came with America's entry into the war, which allowed all of the resources of the U.S. Atlantic Fleet to be added to those of the Royal Navy in their campaign against the raiders.

Early in 1942, Hitler ordered the remaining surface vessels of the Kriegsmarine currently in French ports to be returned to Germany via the shortest route through the English Channel so that they could operate from Norwegian bases to attack convoys bringing essential war material to Russia. Although the German Naval High Command thought that the Channel route was too risky, they proceeded with the planning and preparation for what became known as Operation Cerberus (Unternehmung Zerberus), named for the mythical three-headed dog that guarded the gates of Hades, or by the term "Channel Dash." The operation, which came under the jurisdiction of Naval Group Command West headed by Fleet Admiral Alfred Saalwächter in Paris, was placed under the direct command of Vice-Admiral Otto Ciliax, the Commander of Battleships, a new post created on 18 June 1941 after the loss of the Fleet Commander on the *Bismarck*.

At around midnight on 11 February 1942, the battleship *Scharnhorst*, commanded by Captain Kurt C. Hoffmann and flying the flag of Admiral

Ciliax, and the battleship *Gneisenau*, commanded by Captain Otto Fein, accompanied by the heavy cruiser *Prinz Eugen*, still commanded by Captain Helmuth Brinkmann, set sail from Brest. The ships were escorted by six destroyers of the Fifth Destroyer Flotilla, including the Z-29, which flew the flags of both Rear-Admiral Erich Bey, the Commander of Destroyers, and Captain Fritz Berger, the flotilla commander. The other five destroyers in the flotilla were the *Richard Beitzen* (Z-4), *Paul Jacobi* (Z-5), *Hermann Schoemann* (Z-7), *Friedrich Ihn* (Z-14), and Z-25.

The squadron circled around the Pointe de St. Mathieu, and headed north and then east toward the English Channel while avoiding detection by a British submarine patrol in the area. They arrived off the island of Alderney at 0515, and between 0530 and 0630, they sailed off Cherbourg and the Cotentin Peninsula, still undetected by British air patrols established to cover the movements of the German ships at Brest. At 0845, Luftwaffe fighters began to fly air cover over the German squadron, and at 0930, five torpedo boats from the Second Torpedo Boat Flotilla arrived from Le Havre to provide additional protection for the ships.

At 1042, the German ships were finally sighted off Le Touquet by RAF Spitfires, but they were not reported until the planes, under strict orders to maintain radio silence, returned to their home base at 1109. Once word of the breakout had been received, British air and naval activities, under the overall command of Vice-Admiral Sir Bertram Ramsey, began to plan and order attacks on the German squadron. The first British force to be deployed was a small group of motor torpedo boats from Dover, which began their attack at 1150 when the squadron was off Cape Gris Nez, but they were quickly driven off by the firepower of the German force.

At about the same time, eight torpedo boats from the German Third Torpedo Boat Flotilla at Dunkirk arrived to provide further protection to the squadron as it traversed the narrowest part of the English Channel. At 1219, the South Foreland Battery of coastal defense guns in the Dover area began firing at the German ships, but due to poor visibility, the fall of shot could not be observed. The guns fired a total of 33 rounds, but no hits were scored. At 1300, the German squadron was attacked by another group of British motor torpedo boats from Ramsgate, but they were also kept at too great a distance by heavy defensive fire to be effective.

At 1220, six Swordfish torpedo planes of No. 825 Squadron of the Fleet Air Arm under the command of Lt. Comdr. Eugene Esmonde, which had earlier attacked the *Bismarck* from the aircraft carrier *Victorious*, took off from Hatston Naval Air Station in the Orkney Islands, to which it had recently been deployed, to attack the German squadron. The squadron began its attack at 1400, but failed to score any hits. In the process, it lost all of its aircraft and most of its crewmen, including Esmonde and his crew, due to heavy and accurate antiaircraft fire from the ships.

At 1431, the *Scharnhorst* struck a mine, which temporarily stopped the ship and caused Admiral Ciliax to transfer his flag to the destroyer Z-29, where he joined Admiral Bey. Some time later, her engineers were able to restore sufficient power to allow the ship to get underway again.

At 1700, the German squadron came under a combined air and surface attack from British forces. The destroyers *MacKay*, *Whitshed*, *Walpole*, and *Worcester* of the 16th Destroyer Flotilla and the *Campbell* and *Vivacious* of the 21st Destroyer Flotilla, all based at Harwich, were able to launch a salvo of torpedoes against the German ships, but again the combined firepower of the German squadron kept the ships at too great a distance to fire their torpedoes effectively, and no hits were scored. In the exchange, the *Worcester* was seriously damaged and suffered 24 dead and 45 wounded. The destroyers made no further attempt to close with the German squadron and fire additional torpedoes.

At the same time, only 39 out of a total of 242 RAF Bomber Command aircraft that participated in the operation were able to find and attack the ships through the overcast skies below. The attacking force of Hudson and Beaufort aircraft dropped their bombs almost blindly, and they were not able to score any hits. This was the last opportunity for British forces to stop the German squadron, which was rapidly getting out of range of British bombers, and darkness would soon set in.

The German squadron was not yet home free, and at 1955, the *Gneisenau* hit a mine, temporarily bringing the ship to a stop. Fortunately, the *Gneisenau* had set off a magnetic mine that exploded some distance from the ship, and it therefore caused little damage. Her engineers were able to get the *Gneisenau* going again in about a half hour. The last blow to the German squadron came at 2134 when the *Scharnhorst* hit a second mine. There again, the setback was only temporary, and the ship was soon on her way, arriving at the naval base at Wilhelmshaven at 1000 on the following morning.

In the meantime, the *Gneisenau* and the undamaged *Prinz Eugen* headed for Brunsbüttel at the mouth of the Elbe River and southern terminus of the Kiel Canal (Nordsee-Ostsee Kanal), arriving there at 0930 on the morning of 13 February. The *Gneisenau* continued up the canal to Kiel where it went into dry dock at the Deutsche Werke shipyard to be repaired. Two days later, the *Scharnhorst* arrived to have her damaged hull repaired in an adjacent dry dock at the same shipyard.

The *Prinz Eugen* remained at Brunsbüttel until 19 February to be replenished with fuel and ammunition and to take on additional supplies before heading to her new assignment in Norway. The *Prinz Eugen*, accompanied by the armored cruiser (pocket battleship) *Admiral Scheer*, sailed up the western coast of Denmark and across the Skagerrak to Norway and then traversed the inner waterways along the Norwegian coast to avoid detection by RAF air patrols over the area. Upon reaching the open sea again, after a stop in the familiar Grimstadfjord near Bergen, the two ships, escorted by only two destroyers, steered a course for the major German naval base at Trondheim, unaware that the British submarine *Trident* was on patrol in the area.

When the *Prinz Eugen* and *Admiral Scheer* got to within torpedo range of the *Trident* on the morning of 23 February, the submarine fired a spread of torpedoes at the two ships, and then it quickly departed the area before the destroyers could react to the attack. One of the torpedoes hit the *Prinz Eugen* in the stern, damaging the cruiser's rudder and leaving the after end of the ship sloping downward. The *Prinz Eugen* was ultimately able to limp into Trondheim under the protection of hastily organized air cover and additional escort vessels.

The *Prinz Eugen* was later fitted with a temporary rudder fabricated by the Kiel Naval Shipyard, and she headed back to Germany for repairs. During the passage along the Norwegian coast, the *Prinz Eugen* was subjected to numerous bombing and aircraft torpedo attacks, but managed to escape without being hit. She eventually arrived at the Deutsche Werke shipyard in Kiel where she underwent extensive repairs to her stern section. Repairs were completed in October 1942, and the *Prinz Eugen* set sail for Gotenhafen for training exercises. After two unsuccessful attempts to return to Norway undetected, the *Prinz Eugen* remained in Baltic waters for the remainder of the war.

In the meantime, on the evening of 26 February 1942, less than two weeks after arriving at Deutsche Werke in Kiel, the *Gneisenau* was hit by a bomb during an RAF raid. The bomb set off an explosion of powder stored in turret Anton, the foremost turret of the ship, blowing the turret off its base and starting a fire that engulfed the entire forward part of the ship. The *Gneisenau* was eventually able to make it to Gotenhafen, where it was planned to repair the ship and rearm it with six 15-inch guns, but repairs proved to be too extensive and the ship was never restored to service.

Repairs on the *Scharnhorst* were completed in October 1942, but it was not until March of the following year that she was finally able to reach Norway undetected. After numerous stops along the way, the *Scharnhorst* reached Altafjord, where she joined *Bismarck's* sister ship, the *Tirpitz,* to engage in raiding operations against convoys heading for Murmansk to deliver war supplies to the Soviet Union. On 6-9 September 1943, the *Scharnhorst* and the *Tirpitz*, with their accompanying destroyers, heavily bombarded Spitsbergen (Svalbard) off the northeastern coast of Greenland after a force of exiled Norwegians from Great Britain had occupied the island.

In late December 1943, German aerial reconnaissance planes spotted Convoy JW-55A, which consisted of 19 ships bringing vital war supplies to the Soviet Union, on its way from Loch Ewe to Murmansk. Attempts were made to bomb the convoy by Junkers Ju-88 bombers, but these were unsuccessful and no hits were scored. In view of the importance of keeping those supplies from reaching the Soviet forces, the German Naval High Command ordered that a task force consisting of the *Scharnhorst* and a number of destroyers be dispatched to attack the convoy. The task force was to be commanded by Rear-Admiral Erich Bey, the Commander of Destroyers, but who would be flying his flag on the *Scharnhorst*.

At about 1900 on the evening of 25 December 1943, a task force comprised of the battleship *Scharnhorst,* now commanded by Captain Heinz Hintze, and five destroyers (Z-29, Z-30, Z-33, Z-34, and Z-38) of the Fourth Destroyer Flotilla sailed north from Altafjord to intercept the convoy. As the task force reached the open sea, it was met by stormy conditions which hindered the progress of the *Scharnhorst's* destroyer escort, so on the following morning, the destroyers were released to return to calmer waters off the northern coast of Norway.

Shortly after noon on 26 December, the *Scharnhorst* ran into the convoy's cruiser screen, including the heavy cruiser *London* and the light cruisers *Belfast* and *Sheffield*. In the subsequent exchange of gunfire, both the

London and the *Scharnhorst* were hit and suffered some damage, but the *Scharnhorst* lost its forward radar from shell splinters during the action. Not wanting to risk any further damage to his flagship, Admiral Bey decided to break off the engagement and return to base. Unbeknown to Admiral Bey, however, a task force comprised of the new British battleship *Duke of York*, the light cruiser *Jamaica*, and four destroyers, under the command of Admiral Bruce Fraser, the former Third Sea Lord and Controller of the Admiralty, was nearby to provide back-up support to convoys in the area.

Upon learning of the cruisers' encounter with the *Scharnhorst*, the *Duke of York* raced to intercept the German battleship, and she arrived on the scene at about 1700. Illuminated by star shells from the British destroyers, the *Scharnhorst* was taken under fire by the *Duke of York,* and she soon received several hits. With her three-knot speed advantage, however, the *Scharnhorst* was able to outdistance the British battleship. The accompanying destroyers then raced ahead and were able to score four torpedo hits on the fleeing *Scharnhorst*, bringing her to a virtual stop.

When the *Duke of York* caught up with the *Scharnhorst*, she began to pound the German battleship with her 14-inch shells. The cruisers *Jamaica* and *Belfast* soon joined in with their guns, and the destroyers continued to fire torpedoes at the *Scharnhost* until the stricken battleship finally turned over and sank off the North Cape of Norway at 1945. Out of her crew of 1,968 officers and men, only 36 were saved. Admiral Bey, Captain Hintze, and all of the other officers aboard the German vessel went down with their ship.

With Germany's now almost complete reliance on U-boat operations to slow down the flow of war supplies to Great Britain, on 30 January 1943, Hitler replaced Grand Admiral Erich Raeder with Grand Admiral Karl Dönitz, the former Commander of U-boats, as the Commander-in-Chief of the German Navy. Raeder resigned from the Kriegsmarine in May 1943.

The German battleship *Tirpitz*, sister ship of the *Bismarck*, was the only capital ship left in the German Navy after the loss of the *Scharnhorst*. The *Tirpitz* became fully operational in late 1941, and for a while she was the flagship of the German Baltic Fleet with Kiel as her home base. While at Kiel, the *Tirpitz* had already become the target of numerous RAF bombing raids, and plans were made to send her to Norway. After having her antiaircraft defenses improved, the *Tirpitz* set sail for Norway on 14 February, arriving at Faettenfjord just north of Trondheim on the 17th.

The *Tirpitz* made two unsuccessful sorties on convoys off the Norwegian coast in March and July 1942, but on both occasions, she was driven off by superior British naval and air forces. In September 1942, the *Tirpitz* participated with the *Scharnhorst* in the attack on Spitsbergen to destroy the facilities on the island after its occupation by Norwegian exiles. During the following year, the Royal Navy made a number of attempts to neutralize the German battleship with bombs from carrier aircraft, but they were for the most part unsuccessful. On 22 September 1943, British frogmen operating from midget submarines (X-craft) were successful in attaching explosive charges to the hull of the *Tirpitz* while at Altafjord, causing extensive damage to the ship.

On 3 April 1944, just when the damage had been repaired, the British launched a massive air attack on the *Tirpitz* with some 40 Fairey Barracuda bombers and an equal number of fighter escorts from two fleet carriers and four escort carriers. They scored 15 direct hits and two near misses on the *Tirpitz*, which put the ship out of action again for several months. During that period, the Royal Navy continued to conduct a series of attacks on the *Tirpitz* with carrier aircraft, but little additional damage was done, even when the aircraft were able to penetrate the defenses around the ship's anchorage at Altafjord.

On 15 September 1944, RAF Bomber Command was partially diverted from its primary mission of bombing industrial targets in Germany to help eliminate the threat posed by the *Tirpitz* to convoys bringing critical war materiel to the Soviet Union. A flight of 17 Avro Lancaster bombers, each carrying a single new type of six-ton bomb, known as the "Tallboy", took off from a base in Russia, accompanied by six other Lancasters carrying mines, to attack the *Tirpitz*. They scored one hit on the bow of the ship, again causing severe damage that would require another nine months of work to repair.

The Germans patched up the bow of the *Tirpitz*, and on 15 October the ship was able to sail down to Tromso under her own power. On 29 October, the RAF conducted another bombing raid on the ship at Tromso with Lancaster bombers and "Tallboy" bombs, but this time, they only scored a near miss, which caused some underwater damage and flooding. By that time, there was little hope that the *Tirpitz* could ever be made fully operational again, and she was being prepared as a floating fortress guarding the approaches to Tromso harbor.

Two weeks later, on 12 November 1944, the RAF made a third attempt to destroy the *Tirpitz* with "Tallboy" bombs. The Lancasters dropped a total of 29 of the huge bombs on the ship, and scored two direct his and one near miss. One hit amidships on the port side blew a large hole in the side and bottom of the ship, causing considerable flooding. The *Tirpitz* gradually began to list to port at an increasing rate, and finally just before 1000 she capsized, taking some 1,000 officers and men with her to a watery grave. Of her survivors, 82 were saved by cutting holes into the overturned bottom of the ship.

With the Norwegian coast so vulnerable to air attack, the Germans kept the remainder of their major surface vessels, including the armored cruisers (pocket battleships) *Lützow* and *Admiral Scheer,* the heavy cruisers *Admiral Hipper* and *Prinz Eugen*, and the light cruisers *Nürnberg* and *Emden*, in the Baltic region out of range of British bombers during the last two years of the war. As Soviet forces appeared on the offensive along the coast of East Prussia, the ships were used for shore bombardment of Russian positions to assist in the defense of the Fatherland.

On 9 April 1945, the RAF conducted a major raid on German naval facilities at Kiel, dropping numerous bombs on the Deutsche Werke ship-yard. The *Admiral Scheer*, received a direct hit and capsized at her dock. The *Admiral Hipper* was severely damaged in the raid and was later scuttled by depth charges on 1 May. The light cruiser *Emden* was likewise severely damaged and was towed to nearby Heikendorfer Bay (Bucht) where she was scuttled on 3 May. On 16 April, the armored cruiser *Lützow* (ex-*Deutschland*) was heavily damaged in a Lancaster raid on Schweine-münde on the Baltic coast. She continued to be used for shore bombardment of advancing Soviet forces, but when ammunition ran out, she also was scuttled on 4 May.

The light cruiser *Leipzig* had been seriously damaged when she was accidentally rammed amidships by the heavy cruiser *Prinz Eugen* on 15 October 1944. She was never restored to full service, and after that was used mostly as a training ship. She also was used to bombard Soviet forces along the Baltic Sea, but at the end of March 1945, she was moved to Abenra Harbor in Denmark near the German Border 38 miles north of the German town of Schleswig. At the end of the war, she surrendered to the British and was later moved to the German naval base at Wilhelm-shaven. She was scuttled in the North Sea on 16 December 1946.

Thus ended the surface threat to Allied shipping in the Atlantic. By that time, the battle against the U-boats was also being won with increasing U-boat losses as a result of improved anti-submarine weapons and tactics, coupled with unabated merchant ship production. Six months later, the war would be over with the surrender of German land forces on 8 May 1945.

CHAPTER **28**

POSTSCRIPT

A LBERT VICTOR (A.V.) ALEXANDER WAS FIRST LORD OF
the Admiralty from 11 May 1940 to 25 May 1945, a post
that he had held earlier from 7 June 1929 to 24 August 1931 and later
from 3 August 1945 to 4 October 1946. He was elected to Parliament in
November 1922, and he later became a spokesman for the Labour Party.
Overshadowed by his predecessor and then Prime Minister, Winston
Churchill, Alexander was nevertheless effective in managing the Admiralty
during World War II. He was later elevated to the rank of Viscount, and
in 1963, he became Earl Alexander of Hillsborough.

Admiral of the Fleet Sir Dudley Pound was appointed First Sea Lord
on 31 July 1939. He was credited with conducting the successful campaign against U-boats in the North Atlantic, but his subordinate commanders had mixed feelings about him, especially after he had advocated
the court martial of Captain Leach and Rear-Admiral Wake-Walker over
their actions in the battle with the *Bismarck*. In ill-health, Pound retired
from the Royal Navy in October 1943 and was replaced by Admiral of
the Fleet Sir Andrew Cunningham, who had been the Commander-in-
Chief of the Mediterranean Fleet.

Admiral John Cronyn "Jack" Tovey was appointed Commander-in-
Chief of the Home Fleet in November 1940, and in May 1941 he headed
the task force consisting of the battleship *King George V*, the battle cruiser
Repulse, the aircraft carrier *Victorious*, and a number of destroyers that
pursued the German battleship *Bismarck* after it had sunk the *Hood*. In
June 1943, he became Commander-in-Chief of The Nore, a Royal Navy
area command responsible for naval activities along the east coast of Great
Britain, and in August of that year he was promoted to Admiral of the

Fleet. In 1946, he retired from the Navy and later that year he became a baron.

Rear-Admiral A.T.B. Curteis, the commander of the Second Cruiser Squadron during the hunt for the *Bismarck*, was promoted to Vice-Admiral and assigned as commander of the Second Battle Squadron of the Home Fleet and second-in-command of the Home Fleet on 1 July 1941. With his flag on the battleship *Duke of York*, he commanded one of the two heavy cover forces for convoy PQ-12 en route to Murmansk, and he helped to thwart an attack on the convoy by the German battleship *Tirpitz* under Operation Sportpalast in March 1942. Curteis was succeeded as Commander, Second Battle Group, by Admiral Bruce Fraser in May 1942, and he retired from the service in 1944.

Vice-Admiral Sir James Somerville, the commander of Force H during the *Bismarck* operation, went on to become the Commander-in-Chief, Eastern Fleet, as a full Admiral in March 1942. He was replaced by Admiral Bruce Fraser in August 1944, and he was then placed in charge of the British Admiralty Delegation in Washington, DC. Somerville was promoted to Admiral of the Fleet on 8 May 1945, and he retired from the service after the war. In August 1946, he was made Lord Lieutenant of Somerset.

Vice-Admiral Bruce Austin Fraser was appointed as Third Sea Lord and Controller of the Navy in 1939, and he held that post until May 1942 when he became the commander of the Second Battle Squadron of the Home Fleet. A year later, in May 1943, he was promoted to the rank of full Admiral and appointed Commander-in-Chief of the Home Fleet. In December 1943, he commanded the task force consisting of the battleship *Duke of York*, the light cruiser *Jamaica*, and four destroyers that intercepted and sank the German battleship *Scharnhorst* off the North Cape of Norway. In 1946, he was elevated to the peerage as Baron Fraser of North Cape, and as Admiral of the Fleet, Sir Bruce Fraser served as First Sea Lord from 1948–1951.

Rear-Admiral William Frederick Wake-Walker was the commander of the First Cruiser Squadron from January 1941 until February 1942. In May 1941, he commanded the heavy cruisers *Norfolk* and *Suffolk*, and later also the damaged battleship *Prince of Wales*, in tracking the *Bismarck* through the Denmark Strait and into the North Atlantic. In April 1942, he was promoted to Vice-Admiral, and in May, he was appointed as Third

Sea Lord and Controller of the Navy, replacing Vice-Admiral Bruce Fraser. On 8 May 1945, the day on which Germany surrendered, he was promoted to full Admiral, and in September of that year, he was appointed as Commander-in-Chief in the Mediterranean. He died suddenly at his home in London a short time later on 24 September 1945.

Rear-Admiral Rhoderick Robert McGrigor was appointed as the Assistant Chief of Naval Staff (Weapons) on 9 September 1941, and he was involved in the Second Enquiry into the Loss of HMS *Hood*. Beginning in late 1943, he held several commands at sea throughout the remainder of the war. On 1 October 1945, as a Vice-Admiral, he became the Vice Chief of Naval Staff, and from 1948 until 1950, as a full Admiral, he was Commander-in-Chief of the Home Fleet. From 1950-1951, McGrigor was Commander-in-Chief, Plymouth, a Royal Navy area command responsible for naval activities in the English Channel, and in 1953, he was promoted to Admiral of the Fleet and appointed as First Sea Lord, replacing Admiral of the Fleet Sir Bruce Fraser.

Captain Philip Vian had been the commander of Fourth Destroyer Flotilla of Tribal-class destroyers since early 1940. After participating in the final battle against the *Bismarck*, Vian was promoted to the rank of Rear-Admiral in July 1941. In September 1941, Vian commanded Force K in its successful attack on the Norwegian islands of Spitsbergen (Svalbard) in the belief that it was occupied by the Germans. In October of that year, Vian was given the command of the 15th Cruiser Squadron in the Mediterranean, where he was responsible for defending the island of Malta and intercepting Axis convoys bringing supplies to German and Italian forces in North Africa. He was later the commander of one of the naval task forces supporting the Allied landings in Normandy, and in November 1944 he was promoted to Vice-Admiral and placed in charge of air operations of the British Pacific Fleet. Vian became the Fifth Sea Lord in charge of naval aviation in 1946, and in 1948, he was appointed to be the Commander-in-Chief of the Home Fleet, replacing Admiral of the Fleet Sir Rhoderick McGrigor. Vian was promoted to Admiral of the Fleet on 1 June 1952.

Captain Frederick Dalrymple-Hamilton had been the commander of the battleship *Rodney* since 21 November 1939. After his participation in the sinking of the *Bismarck*, he was promoted to Rear-Admiral, and on 5 September 1941, he was appointed to be the Admiral Commanding Iceland. From 31 October 1942 to December 1943 he served as Naval Secretary to the First Lord of the Admiralty. Dalrymple-Hamilton was then appointed commander of the 10th Cruiser Squadron from 3 March 1944 to 1 April 1945, when he became Vice-Admiral Malta and Flag Officer Central Mediterranean. After the war, he was appointed Flag Officer Commanding Scotland and Northern Ireland from 1946-1948.

Sub-Lieutenant Ludovic H.C. Kennedy was the son of Captain Edward C. Kennedy, the commander of the auxiliary cruiser *Rawalpindi*, which was sunk by the German battleships *Gneisenau* and *Scharnhorst* on 23 November 1939. In May 1941, Ludovic Kennedy was serving on HMS *Tartar*, one of the destroyers that accompanied the battleship *Rodney* during the hunt for the *Bismarck* after it had sunk the *Hood*. The *Tartar* rescued the survivors of her companion destroyer *Mashona* when it was hit by German bombers on the morning after the *Bismarck* was sunk. After the war, Kennedy became a journalist and wrote the highly acclaimed book, *Pursuit—The Chase and Sinking of the Bismarck*. He was knighted for his contribution to journalism in 1994, and died in 2009.

After her battle with the *Bismarck*, the British battleship *Rodney* sailed to the Boston Naval Shipyard where she underwent a complete refit of her machinery. That work had been scheduled before the battle, and the ship was tied up for several months before she could rejoin the fleet. The *Rodney* survived the war, as did the battle cruiser *Renown*, until both were scrapped in 1948.

The battleship *King George V* was kept in service until 1957 before she was scrapped. The carrier *Victorious* was rebuilt in 1950 and again in 1958, but she was also scrapped in 1969 after 28 years of service with the Royal Navy. The *Norfolk* and *Suffolk* both survived the war and were eventually scrapped in the 1948-49 time frame. The *Sheffield* also survived the war and was scrapped in 1967.

After the war, Grand Admiral Erich Raeder, former Commander-in-Chief of the German Navy, was charged with war crimes for his involvement in the planning for the invasion of Norway, and he was tried by the International Military Tribunal at Nuremberg. Raeder was sentenced to life imprisonment, but his sentence was later reduced, and he was released from prison on 26 September 1955 due to ill health. He died in 1960.

Vice-Admiral Karl Dönitz was the Commander of U-boats at the time of the *Bismarck* operation, but on 30 January 1943 he replaced Grand

Admiral Raeder as the Commander-in-Chief of the Navy and was himself promoted to Grand Admiral. Not trusting his Army and Luftwaffe generals to run the nation, Hitler named Dönitz to be the President of Germany, and Supreme Commander of the Armed Forces (Wehrmacht) upon his death. When Hitler committed suicide on 30 April 1945, Dönitz automatically became the head of the nation. All that he could do, however, was to preside over the surrender of German forces to the Allied powers during the next two weeks. The Dönitz government ceased to exist on 23 May 1945, and its leaders were arrested by the Allied Control Commission in Flensburg.

Like his predecessor, Dönitz was also charged with war crimes and was tried by the International Military Tribunal at Nuremberg. He was found guilty of planning, initiating, and waging wars of aggression and of crimes against the laws of war, but he was found not guilty of conspiracy to commit crimes against peace, war crimes, and crimes against humanity. He was also found not guilty of waging unrestricted submarine warfare when evidence was presented that the Allies were also involved in such activity, especially against Japan. Dönitz served ten years in Spandau Prison near Berlin before being released on 1 October 1956.

Admiral Otto Schniewind was the Director of Sea Warfare (Seekriegsleitung) at the time of the *Bismarck* operation, but he was appointed as Fleet Commander to replace Fleet Admiral Günther Lütjens when he went down with his entire staff in the *Bismarck*. Schniewind was then assigned as Commander, Naval Group North on 2 March 1943, replacing Admiral Rolf Carls. He served in that post until 30 July 1944, when it was disbanded, and he received no further assignments. At the end of the war, Schniewind was charged with war crimes related to the German invasion of Norway, but he was acquitted and released.

Admiral Rolf Carls was the Commander of Naval Group North at the time of the *Bismarck* operation, and he held that post until his retirement on 2 March 1943, when he was replaced by Admiral Schniewind. Nominated by Grand Admiral Erich Raeder to be his replacement as the Commander-in-Chief of the German Navy, Carls lost out to Admiral Dönitz as Hitler's choice for the position. Carls was killed in an Allied air raid near Hamburg on 15 April 1945.

In September 1942, German Fleet Admiral Alfred Saalwächter, Commander of Naval Group West, was replaced by Fleet Admiral Wilhelm

Marschall, and he resigned from active service in November of that year. At the end of the war, he was taken prisoner by the Russians, tried and convicted for war crimes, and executed by a firing squad in December 1945. He was later exonerated by a Russian court in 1994.

Captain Helmuth Brinkmann remained as the commander of the heavy cruiser *Prinz Eugen* until 31 July 1942, when the ship was about to undergo extensive repairs at the Deutsche Werke shipyard in Kiel after being torpedoed by the British submarine *Trident*. Brinkmann was then reassigned as the Chief of Staff of Naval Group Command South on 5 August, and he was promoted to Rear-Admiral on 1 September 1942. From 22 November 1943 to 9 November 1944, he served as Commanding Admiral of the Baltic Sea with the rank of Vice-Admiral. Brinkmann was taken into custody by Allied authorities on 31 May 1945, and after spending 30 months in captivity he was released on 29 November 1947.

The heavy cruiser *Prinz Eugen* was one of only two major warships of the Kriegsmarine to survive the war intact, the other being the light cruiser *Nürnberg*, which was captured by Russian forces and incorporated into the Soviet Navy as the *Admiral Makarov*. The *Prinz Eugen* surrendered to British forces at Copenhagen in May 1945, and she was subsequently taken to Wilhelmshaven where she was turned over to the U.S. Navy. In January 1946, the *Prinz Eugen* sailed with a joint German-American crew to Boston, and then she steamed with a totally American crew through the Panama Canal into the Pacific. There she became one of the target ships during the atomic bomb tests at Bikini Atoll in the summer of that year. The *Prinz Eugen* survived that test and was towed to Kwajalein Atoll where she sank unexpectedly in December 1946 as the result of latent underwater damage sustained in the test.

At the beginning of March 1946, the *Bismarck's* fourth gunnery officer, Sr. Lieut. Burkard Baron von Müllenheim-Rechberg, and a group of other German prisoners of war held at Camp No. 30 at Bowmanville, Ontario were designated to be returned to Europe. On 5 March 1946, the group arrived in Halifax, Nova Scotia and boarded the 13,500-ton steamship *Letitia* for their voyage to Liverpool. The *Letitia* was built at the Fairfield Shipyard in Govan, Scotland in 1924 as a liner for the Anchor-Donaldson Line, but it was requisitioned by the Admiralty on 9 September 1939, just after the outbreak of war, and converted to an auxiliary cruiser. On 7 June 1941, the *Letitia* was withdrawn from service as a cruiser and was then used as a troop transport for the remainder of the war.

The *Letitia*, now being used mostly for repatriating Canadian service personnel, arrived at Liverpool with the German prisoners of war on 18 March 1946. After stopping briefly at a camp in Nottingham, the group was sent to POW Camp No. 18, Featherstone Park Camp, at Haltwhistle, about 40 miles west of Newcastle-upon-Tyne in Northumberland, at the end of March. On 5 November 1946, the baron was transferred to Prisoner of War Camp No. 23 at Sudbury near Derby in Derbyshire to be processed for repatriation to Germany. On 20 November, he was transported from Sudbury to Hull (Kingston-upon-Hull) on the east coast of England, where he boarded the steamer *Empire Spearhead*.

Despite its dynamic name, the *Empire Spearhead* was only a small, 7,200-ton Type C-1 cargo ship built in 1944 by Consolidated Shipyard in California, with few amenities, but for a one-day trip, it really didn't matter that much to the baron. The *Empire Spearhead* arrived at Cuxhaven at 1730 on 21 November, returning the baron to his native land after five and a half years in captivity. After two days of processing at the port, the baron took the train to Hanover and then a local to Nienburg, about 50km (30 miles) northwest of Hanover, where he took up residence for the time being.

The baron vowed to overcome the initial hardships that he now faced in a country that was devastated by Allied bombing during the war. In 1949, he took his state examination and in 1952, he entered the Foreign Service of the new Federal Republic of Germany. Over the years, he held a number of diplomatic posts, and ironically in 1968, he became the German Consul General in Toronto, just 40 miles away from Bowmanville where he had spent four years in captivity as a prisoner of war. The baron retired from the Foreign Service in 1975, and he and his wife settled down in Herrshing am Ammersee, about 40km (25 miles) southwest of Munich.

The baron spent much of the remaining years of this life in researching material on the *Bismarck* and finally publishing a book on the subject. The book, *Battleship Bismarck* (*Schlachtschiff Bismarck*), in which he writes about his experiences while serving on the *Bismarck* and being a prisoner of war after its sinking, received international acclaim. He was invited to participate in the National Geographic expedition to find the wreck of the *Bismarck* in June 1989, but he had to decline due to the illness of his wife. The baron died on 1 June 2003.

Paul Schmalenbach, the second gunnery officer on the *Prinz Eugen*, became the primary historian for the *Prinz Eugen*, writing several books and articles on the subject after the war. Recalling his own observations and actions during the battle with the *Hood* and *Prince of Wales*, he made a major contribution to the solution of the disagreement regarding the deployment of the German ships during the battle. By indicating that the *Bismarck* was on the port side of the *Prinz Eugen* from 0600 until after 0609, when the *Prinz Eugen* ceased fire, he added credence to the so-called "reversed photo theory."

In 1960, the British war movie "Sink the *Bismarck*," starring Kenneth More and Dana Wynter was released. The film covers mostly efforts by the Admiralty in deploying Royal Navy units to stop the *Bismarck*. Shortly thereafter, the American country music singer Johnny Horton, inspired by the film, came out with his hit song "Sink the *Bismarck*." The German folk song "Muss i' denn," played by the Fleet Band as the *Bismarck* left Gotenhafen to begin her sortie, was made popular in America by Elvis Presley and Joe Dowell as "Wooden Heart" in 1961. Both the German and English versions of the song can now be heard on You Tube.

In July 1988, a little over 47 years after the *Bismarck* was sunk, the same underwater research team that had found the wreck of the *Titanic* in 1985 undertook an expedition to find the remains of the *Bismarck*. This team was headed by Dr. Robert D. Ballard of the Woods Hole Oceanographic Institute on Cape Cod and was sponsored by the National Geographic Society. The first try was unsuccessful, but on the team's second attempt one year later, one of the cameras on the underwater robot vehicle *Argo* began to pick up debris on the ocean floor in the vicinity of the *Bismarck's* last reported position.

After searching the area for the next few days, the team finally came across the hulk of the *Bismarck* at a depth of a little over 15,000 feet on the morning of 9 June 1989. Dr. Ballard's team spent another couple of days making detailed observations of the main part of the wreckage and combing the surrounding area for other parts of the *Bismarck*. Photographs were taken and compared against earlier pictures of the ship to identify the secondary objects discovered and to assess the damage sustained by the ship. Much of her superstructure was blown away, and scores of hits could be seen on her hull, armored command center, and two upper decks. Her four large 15-inch gun turrets, which fell out of her hull when she capsized, landed some distance away from the main part of the ship.

The tip of her stern section, undoubtedly weakened by the torpedo hit that crippled her, had broken off when the *Bismarck* hit the ocean floor and landed nearby. The *Bismarck's* tower battle mast and funnel were missing, probably having broken off as the ship capsized. With their allotted time running out, the team left the scene and sailed back to their home port of Cadiz, Spain. The visual observations made by Dr. Ballard and his team, together with the photographic evidence brought back by them, revealed the true extent of the damage inflicted on the *Bismarck* in her last battle with the Royal Navy.

In June 2001, the wreck of the *Bismarck* was visited again by Deep Ocean Expeditions headed by Australian Michael McDowell. Transported to the scene on the Russian scientific research ship *Akademik Keldysh*, McDowell's team used two manned submersibles to view the wreck. Each submersible could carry two observers in addition to the pilot, and representatives of the media, as well as private individuals, could be accommodated on some of the dives. Two *Bismarck* survivors were also on board to help identify portions of the ship that came into view.

In July 2001, an expedition sponsored by British television stations and led by David Mearns discovered the wreck of the *Hood* broken apart into several sections at a depth of 10,000 feet on the ocean floor. The bow section was broken off forward of turret "A" and landed on its port side, while the heavily damaged middle section of the ship landed upside down with the keel up. The smaller stern end of the ship, blown off by the magazine explosion, was sticking up from the bottom. The *Hood's* rudder was set at an angle, which confirmed that she was still in the midst of a turn to port when fatally stricken. The *Hood's* armored conning tower was located some distance from the main part of the wreck, and other bits of wreckage were scattered in basically two separate debris fields.

In May 2002, James Cameron, noted director of the award-winning film "Titanic," headed an expedition to survey the wreck of the *Bismarck*, using remote-controlled underwater vehicles to resolve questions as to how exactly the ship was sunk. He was able to photograph at close range much of the damage done to the *Bismarck*, and he came up with certain conclusions that cleared up some of the issues regarding its sinking. One of his conclusions was that the fatal torpedo that had earlier crippled the

Bismarck came in from the starboard side of the ship, contradicting the opinion of several experts who maintained that the fatal torpedo came in from the port side of the ship.

There continues to be considerable interest in the battle of the Denmark Strait and in the ships that participated in that engagement. Members of several Internet forums are currently active in exchanging detailed information on almost every aspect of the ships involved, and models of those ships are still quite popular among naval history enthusiasts. Although this book goes far deeper into the battle than any previous account of the action, it will probably not be the final word in the matter, but just another step in the never-ending process of reinterpreting naval history.

APPENDICES

APPENDIX A
ANALYSIS OF INTERCEPTION REPORTS

Reports from both sides on the interception of the German squadron by the British battle force in the Denmark Strait on 24 May 1941 lack sufficient detail to understand the exact circumstances of that event. It is, however, possible to reconstruct the confrontation between the two battle groups based on a detailed technical analysis of the data and information currently available. The objective of this analysis was to determine who saw what, when did they see it, and what was the significance of that information.

To start with, we need to establish the distance separating the two opposing forces on a minute-by-minute basis from 0400 to 0600. We know that the British force approached the scene of battle at a speed of 28 knots and on a course of 240°. At 0537, the British force turned 40° to starboard on course 280°, and at 0549, it made an additional 20° turn to starboard on course 300°. At 0555, the British force made a 20° turn to port, back to course 280°, and at 0559, Admiral Holland ordered another 20° turn to port to course 260°, but that turn was never completed by 0600 when the *Hood* was stricken. The German squadron steamed at 27 knots on course 220° from 0400 until 0521, when it turned 50° to port on course 170°. It then returned to course 220° eleven minutes later at 0532 and stayed on that course until 0600.

The rate of convergence for each segment of the total time from 0400 to 0600 can be readily calculated from the angle of convergence, using the average of the two rates of speed (27.5 knots) for each of the two vectors in the vector analysis. Since the actual range of 25,000 yards at 0553, when the *Prince of Wales* opened fire, is perhaps the most accurate of reported distances between the opposing forces, that was be established as the base point from which to work backwards and forwards to cover the entire time period from 0400 to 0600. Once we have this chart laid out, we will know the separation between the two opposing forces at any point in time between 0400 and 0600 on 24 May 1941.

The next step is to determine the distance to the horizon from any point on each ship based on the vertical distance of that point from the waterline of the ship. There is a simple formula for making that determination. When you multiply the square root of the height of the point in feet by a factor of 1.17, you get the nautical miles from that point to the horizon. Multiplying the nautical miles by 2025 gives you the distance in yards. For example, the main director at the foretop of the *Bismarck* was 108 feet above the waterline of the ship, and therefore its distance to the horizon was 12.2 nautical miles or 24,600 yards.

When we want to find out how much of a ship could be seen from an observation point on another ship at a certain point in time, we first have to determine the separation of the two ships at that point in time. For example, when the *Prince of Wales* sighted the *Bismarck* at 0535, the separation between the two forces was 41,600 yards. The distance from the forward main director on the *Prince of Wales* to the horizon was 22,200 yards. Therefore, the difference of 19,400 yards represents the distance from the *Bismarck* to that same point on the horizon. We then have to determine the height corresponding to a distance of 19,400 yards to the horizon.

A distance of 19,400 yards is equivalent to 9.58 nautical miles, and if we divide this figure by the factor of 1.17, we get 8.19. By squaring 8.19, we get 67 feet, the height above the waterline on the *Bismarck*. Therefore, everything on the *Bismarck* above the height of 67 feet could be seen from the forward main director of the *Prince of Wales* at 0535.

At 0535, the observers on the *Prince of Wales* spotted a "suspicious object" which they concluded to be part of the *Bismarck* or *Prinz Eugen*, but they could not identify the nature of that suspicious object. At the time, the *Bismarck* and *Prinz Eugen* were still way over the horizon, so the suspicious object could be nothing other than the massive forward tower battle mast of the *Bismarck* or *Prinz Eugen* that measured over 20 feet across and extended down below the level of the bridge of the ship. This highlights the fact that the western sky was still so dark as to make it impossible to identify such a large structure from a distance of a little over 40,000 yards (8 nautical miles).

This in sharp contrast with the German lookouts who could make out the thin main (after) masts of the British warships as far away as 50,000 yards (25 nautical miles) when they were silhouetted by the light of the eastern horizon. This analysis goes far in explaining why the *Hood* gunners initially fired on the *Prinz Eugen* instead of the *Bismarck*. Not only was there the darkness factor, but the analysis also shows that the *Bismarck* and *Prinz Eugen* did not come into full view on the horizon until after the *Hood* had opened fire on the German squadron. The main armament director of the *Hood* was located over the armored conning tower before the bridge structure, 65 feet above the waterline of the ship, and it therefore was at a distance of 19,000 yards from the horizon. The *Hood* opened fire when the range to the target was 25,000 yards, 6,000 yards beyond the horizon.

Lt. Comdr. Colin McMullen, the first gunnery officer on the *Prince of Wales*, correctly identified the *Bismarck* at the onset of the battle. With the sky in the west still being quite dark, it was obviously very difficult to compare the two enemy ships under those conditions, but he focused on the areas that showed the greatest variation between the two ships. First of all, the *Bismarck* was 140 feet (20%) longer than the *Prinz Eugen* and her main armament gun turrets were very much bulkier than those of the cruiser.

Another distinguishing feature was the different aircraft catapult configurations of both ships. In the case of the *Bismarck*, there was a conspicuous 33-foot gap between the after edge of the funnel and the after superstructure of the ship to accommodate the fixed basic catapult frame across the main deck of the ship. The Arado Ar-196 floatplane had a wingspan of 40 feet, so it had to be launched from an extension to the basic catapult frame. The *Prinz Eugen*, however, had a more conventional rotating catapult mounted atop the superstructure of the ship aft of the funnel.

McMullen had a slight advantage of height over the *Hood's* gunners. The main director on the *Prince of Wales* was 88 feet above the waterline of the ship, allowing him to see the horizon at 22,200 yards away, 3,200 yards further than the distance that the *Hood* gunners could see. By the time that the British ships opened fire, the German ships were almost fully on the horizon and they were therefore more easy for McMullen to distinguish than the *Hood* gunners could.

Many historians speculated that Admiral Holland ordered the 20° turn from a course of 280° to 300° at 0549:00, three and a half minutes before the *Hood* opened fire at 0552:30, to traverse the zone of the *Hood's* vulnerability to plunging fire more quickly even though it would "wooden" the after turrets of the British ships so that they could not bear on the enemy. It now appears that this conclusion was untrue, and upon reflection, it actually does not make much sense.

Holland's mission was to stop the *Bismarck* at all costs, and that is exactly what he tried to do. He would need his full firepower to bear on the *Bismarck*, and he would not have limited it merely to improve the safety of his own ship from the possibility of plunging fire. The simple fact is that the *Hood's* gunners could still not positively identify which ship was actually the *Bismarck*, and he needed to be sure that he would be firing at the correct target. As it turned out, they were still unable to make that determination by the time the range dropped to 25,000 yards and it was ready to open fire, and they wound up firing at the wrong target.

Some attributed the *Hood's* firing on the *Prinz Eugen* to the similarity of silhouettes between the two German ships, but that is only part of the story. True, their silhouettes were similar, but the gunners on the *Hood* were well drilled to identify the peculiarities between the silhouettes of all German warships. The fact that the gunners could still not see the hulls of the two ships, and the other distinguishing features of the ships were obscured by the darkness of the western sky, certainly contributed to the error. McMullen's 23-foot height advantage over the main fire control director of the *Hood* enabled him to compare the hull sizes of the two ships earlier and thereby positively identify the *Bismarck* as being the right-hand ship before the *Prince of Wales* opened fire.

APPENDIX B
ANALYSIS OF *PRINCE OF WALES* SALVO PLOT

The *Prince of Wales* salvo plot (ADM 199-1187) was Enclosure No. 4 to the Gunnery Appendix to Captain Leach's Narrative of Operations Against *Bismarck* contained in Admiralty Report ADM 234-509: Official Dispatch of Admiral J. Tovey, Commander-in-Chief, Home Fleet – Pursuit of the *Bismarck*. The salvo plot shows the track of the *Prince of Wales* during the battle, and it shows lines representing each of the 18 salvoes fired by the *Prince of Wales* under central control against the *Bismarck*. Each of those lines is annotated with the bearing and range of each salvo fired, and the fall of shot for each salvo, as they appeared from the *Prince of Wales*, is marked on the plot.

The salvo plot also contains various notes, the first of which indicates that the *Prince of Wales* approached the battle on a course of 300° and at a speed of 28 knots. The plot then shows a 20° turn to port at 0555, with the *Prince of Wales* maintaining a course of 280° until 0602. The plot shows a salvo being fired every minute from 0553 to 0602 with a second salvo being fired less than half a minute after the first salvo in each group, for a total of 18 salvoes in a period of nine minutes.

In view of the greater range at the beginning of the battle, i.e., 25,000 yards or more, and therefore longer flight times of the projectiles fired, compared to the range at the end of the battle, i.e., 14,500 yards according to Admiralty reports, and correspondingly shorter flight times, the time between groups of salvoes would have been much greater at the beginning of the battle than toward the end. Since the second salvo in each group was based on the recycle time for reloading the guns, its timing after the first salvo in each group would have remained relatively constant.

Since the combination flight time of the projectiles and reaction time was about a minute at the beginning of the battle compared with a constant recycle time of 30-35 seconds, the 18 salvoes fired by the *Prince of Wales* had to go well beyond the time of 0602, as shown on the plot. This further substantiates the conclusion that the first 16 salvoes were fired between 0553 and 0605 with the remaining two salvoes fired between 0605 and 0606, while the *Prince of Wales* was turning away from the scene of battle.

Another indication that the *Prince of Wales* salvo plot may not have been completely accurate in the timing of salvoes is that the plot shows salvo 12 being fired at about 0558 or shortly thereafter. Admiralty Report ADM 234-509 states that after the *Prince of Wales* fired salvo 12, a heavy hit was felt on its starboard side. The earliest time that a shell from the *Bismarck* could have struck the *Prince of Wales* would have been around 0601, after the *Hood* had received her fatal hit at 0600. This again indicates an extension of at least three minutes in the *Prince of Wales* completing her 18 salvoes.

The salvo plot also shows the *Prince of Wales* making about a 90° turn to port at 0602, and then sailing on a meandering course, roughly parallel to that of the *Bismarck*, until 0605. While not indicated, the turn shown at that time was obviously to circle around the wreck of the sinking *Hood*. Next to this section of the ship's track is the notation: "'Y' TURRET LOCAL CONTROL 3 SALVOES." This notation is obviously incorrect since the forward main director was not yet "wooded" at the time and the *Prince of Wales'* "Y" turret was not placed under local control until after the ship had completed its second 90° turn to port to retire from the scene of battle at 0606.

The salvo plot then shows the *Prince of Wales* beginning her second 90° turn to port at 0605 and completing it a minute later on course 160° at 0606. It is during this turn that the *Prince of Wales* actually fired her 17th and 18th salvoes instead of between 0601 and 0602, as shown on the plot. With this turn, the forward main director became wooded and the aft main director could not acquire the target due to smoke, necessitating the after "Y" turret to go on local control.

The *Prince of Wales* salvo plot also provides significant information on the *Bismarck*. The *Bismarck's* track, based on the fall of shot of the *Prince of Wales's* salvoes, indicates that the *Bismarck* traveled about 10 percent further than the *Prince of Wales* during the course of the battle, which would confirm that the *Bismarck* was traveling at her maximum speed of 30 knots at the time.

Another note on the *Prince of Wales* salvo plot estimates that the *Bismarck* had been traveling on course 212° during the battle, however, when calculated and plotted, the eight-degree difference between the course of the *Prinz Eugen* (220°) and the 212° figure would have put the *Bismarck* much too far over to port of the *Prinz Eugen* as they progressed during the battle. At that angle, the *Bismarck* would have been traveling 140 yards to port while gaining only 100 yards on the *Prinz Eugen* each minute during that period. A five-degree difference in courses would be more consistent with the photographic evidence, and it is most likely that the *Bismarck* actually traveled on a course of 215° during the battle.

The plot also shows that the *Bismarck* was firing in the direction of about 60° off the port bow, or 30° forward of the port beam of the ship, indicating that he *Prince of Wales* was still slightly ahead of the *Bismarck* at 0602 and therefore able to prevent the *Bismarck* from sailing past her even with the *Bismarck's* two knot superior speed. This confirms the soundness of Admiral Holland's decision to take advantage of his slight lead and immediately close with the enemy to prevent the *Bismarck* and *Prinz Eugen* from slipping away with their superior speed over the *Prince of Wales*.

APPENDIX C
ANALYSIS OF *PRINZ EUGEN'S* WAR DOCUMENTATION

The *Prinz Eugen's* war documentation consists primarily of three documents, i.e., her war diary (Kriegstagebuch), her battle diagram (Gefechtsskizze), and her speed chart, each of which complements the other documents and contributes to a better understanding of how the battle of the Denmark Strait was fought. It were these documents, in addition to the photographs taken from the *Prinz Eugen* during the battle, that were presented by Captain Brinkmann to his superior, Admiral Schmundt, the Commander of Cruisers, upon *Prinz Eugen's* return from her sortie.

The war diary of German warships was the official record of the significant events that took place on each day during wartime operations. It was typed on letter-size forms that contained three columns, the first of which was for the date and time. The second column was used for the entry of such information as the location of the ship, wind conditions, weather conditions, sea conditions, light conditions and visibility, sky conditions, moonlight, etc. The last column was for recording the events that occurred during the day, including any changes in course or speed of the ship. The captain of the ship would then sign off on the report after the last entry for the day, and the first entry for the next day would follow immediately thereafter if space permitted.

The war diary was subject to review by higher authorities, so every effort was made to make it as accurate and complete as possible. Since it was prepared at the end of the day rather than being a running log of events, the war diary had to be based on any logs maintained on the ship, notes written during or immediately after each event, and the memories of key personnel involved in those events. Due to the delay in preparing the final report for the day, there was also the opportunity to enhance the image of the ship by emphasizing information favorable to the performance of the crew and minimizing or even omitting any unfavorable circumstances.

The war diary usually contained only the report by the captain of the ship, but for 24 May 1941, *Prinz Eugen's* war diary included separate reports by Paulus Jasper, the first gunnery officer, and Paul Schmalenbach, the second gunnery officer, in addition to the report by Captain Brinkmann. The diary also contained a number of hand-written notes next to some entries, apparently afterthoughts concerning the events subsequent to the preparation of the report. The *Prinz Eugen's* war diary was generally a straight-forward document that provided a reasonably accurate account of what happened during the battle of the Denmark Strait from the viewpoints of the captain and for 24 May, also of both gunnery officers of the ship.

The *Prinz Eugen's* battle diagram was prepared on large-size drafting paper on a scale of 1:50,000 (1cm = 500 meters or 1-inch = 1390 yards) at some time after the battle, and probably in conjunction with the preparation of the ship's war diary. It shows the *Prinz Eugen* traveling on a course of 220° from about 0540 until 0603, after which the ship made three hard turns, first to starboard, then to port, and then back again to starboard before straightening out on a course roughly parallel to that of the *Bismarck*. The diagram shows the turns as having been completed at about 0609.

The battle diagram does not show the track of the *Bismarck*, but it does show the tracks of the *Hood* and *Prince of Wales* in relation to that of the *Prinz Eugen*. The diagram indicates a distance of 17 nautical miles (34,400 yards) and bearing of 337° to the *Hood* at 0541, a distance of 30,000 meters (32,800 yards) to the *Prince of Wales* at 0550:30, a distance of 20,700 meters (22,600 yards) to the *Hood* at 0557:30, and a distance of 19,700 meters (21,600 yards) to the *Prince of Wales* at 0559:30. In addition, the diagram shows torpedo noises at 0603 and 0607, and air alarms at 0610 and 0612.

The *Prinz Eugen's* speed chart was a record maintained of the speed of the ship, probably as a measure of its fuel consumption and the wear and tear on the components of its power plant, drive shafts, and related items. Changes in speed were first recorded separately, and the speeds were then drawn on graph paper with each square representing a half-knot increment vertically and a 10-minute time interval horizontally. For 24 May 1941, the speed chart indicates that the *Prinz Eugen* traveled at a constant speed of 27.0 knots from 0000 to 0610, which includes the entire period of the battle that began at 0553 and ended at about 0610.

The next significant bit of information on the speed chart was the increase in the speed of the *Prinz Eugen* from 27.0 knots to its maximum speed of 32.5 knots at 0610. This is consistent with this version of the battle which shows the *Bismarck* to be several hundred yards ahead of the *Prinz Eugen* at 0610, requiring the *Prinz Eugen* to go to maximum speed for ten minutes to catch up with the *Bismarck* and again take the lead of the German squadron as directed by Admiral Lütjens. The chart shows that the *Prinz Eugen* maintained the speed of 32.5 knots for 10 minutes until 0620, when her speed was cut back to 30.5 knots.

This suggests that the *Prinz Eugen* probably passed the *Bismarck* at about 0620, at which time Lagemann took several pictures of the *Bismarck*, and then the cruiser gradually moved ahead to take the lead of the German squadron. Twenty minutes later, at 0640, the *Prinz Eugen* reduced her speed to a more economic 26 knots, presumably at the order of the Fleet Commander, Admiral Lütjens, with the *Bismarck* following suit. Speed changes between 0800 and 1020 reflect the efforts by the *Prinz Eugen* to drop back and disperse the trail of oil leaking from the *Bismarck's* damaged fuel tank. From 1020 to 1810, both German ships continued to sail in unison at a speed of 26.0 knots.

The increase in *Prinz Eugen's* speed from 26.0 to 31.0 knots at 1810 coincides with her successful second breakout attempt at 1814. The *Prinz Eugen* maintained the speed of 31.0 knots until 2000, when it was reduced to 29.0 knots for the next four hours. By midnight, it was safe to return to the more economical speed of 26.0 knots as the *Prinz Eugen* continued on her mission alone.

There is one major issue with the war diary regarding the latter phase of the battle. In his entry into the war diary for the time of 0603-0614 on 24 May, Captain Brinkmann reported that the *Prinz Eugen* successfully avoided the tracks of three torpedoes, the noises of which had been reported by the hydrophone listening room. The report further states that the tracks of the second and third torpedoes were actually seen by the ship's commander after they had passed by the ship. In his report, Paulus Jasper states that during the battle, the *Prinz Eugen* made three hard turns, but he does not state the direction of those turns. The battle diagram, however, shows that these turns were made to starboard beginning after 0603, and they apparently were in response to the reported torpedo noises.

Jasper stated that the *Prinz Eugen* had turned so far that the target was obscured from the foretop by the funnel smoke of his own ship, and that the forward turrets of the ship were at their maximum degree of rotation. With a moderate (level 3) wind coming from the east at the time, funnel smoke could have interfered with visibility to the southeast from a ship turning to starboard, whereas turning to port would have caused the smoke to be swept away from the target. Turning to starboard would also have reduced the arcs of the forward turrets aiming at the enemy, whereas turning to port would have placed the ship steaming toward the enemy and provided unrestricted rotation for the turrets. These comments by Jasper tend to confirm that the *Prinz Eugen's* turns were indeed made to starboard, away from the enemy.

The war diary indicates that the torpedoes were believed to have come from the *Hood*, but that ship had no opportunity to launch any torpedoes against the German squadron before she was sunk, and there is no indication from British sources that the *Hood* had fired any torpedoes during the battle. The *Prince of Wales* was not even equipped with torpedo tubes, so the torpedoes could not have come from that source. It has generally been concluded by historians that no torpedoes had ever been launched against the German ships during the battle, and that the entries in the war diary regarding those torpedo tracks were not factual.

The turns made by the *Prinz Eugen*, as shown on the battle diagram, did not constitute standard torpedo avoidance maneuvers. The turns were relatively shallow, not exceeding much more than 45°, and thereby leaving a relatively wide target for the torpedoes to hit. The normal practice to avoid torpedoes is for a ship to turn directly toward the oncoming torpedoes in an attempt to "comb their tracks," i.e., steer between the torpedoes, which are generally fired in a spread pattern to increase the odds of scoring a hit. Another alternative is to steer away from the oncoming torpedoes and present the smallest target by presenting only its stern end toward the source of the torpedoes.

Turning to starboard, away from the enemy, also placed the *Prinz Eugen* at a farther distance from the *Prince of Wales*, and it made it impossible for her to launch her own torpedoes at the British battleship. So the questions remain as to why non-existent enemy torpedoes were used as the excuse for the *Prinz Eugen* to make her turns, and why Captain Brinkmann stated that he actually saw the tracks of two of those torpedoes when that was obviously not the case.

If the *Bismarck* was indeed steaming up on the port side of the *Prinz Eugen* to come between the cruiser and the *Prince of Wales* to protect the *Prinz Eugen* in accordance with established German naval operating procedures, by 0603 the *Bismarck* would have been getting close to passing the *Prinz Eugen*. With shells from the *Prince of Wales* often falling over the *Bismarck*, there was a distinct possibility that the *Prinz Eugen* might be hit by one of those "overs." Under those circumstances, it would have been prudent for the *Prinz Eugen* to increase the lateral separation between her and the *Bismarck* by moving a greater distance to starboard.

After the first series of turns seemed not to offer adequate protection, a second turn to starboard was ordered to bring the *Prinz Eugen* at an even safer distance away from the *Bismarck*. As for Brinkmann witnessing the two torpedoes go by the *Prinz Eugen*, it probably seemed to him more heroic to say that the turns were made to avoid torpedoes than to say that it was merely to get out of the way of stray enemy shells? His report of actually having seen the torpedoes would certainly have added credibility to the story. If the *Prinz Eugen* had actually been on the port side of the *Bismarck*, as some claim, the cruiser could have easily launched torpedoes at the *Prince of Wales* when the British battleship came within torpedo range, but instead, the *Prinz Eugen* turned to starboard, away from the enemy.

The timing of the turns by the *Prinz Eugen*, as shown in her battle diagram, is not consistent with that statement made by Paulus Jasper in the war diary. Jasper stated that after the ship completed her turns, the *Bismarck* appeared in his line of sight to the *Prince of Wales*. Then the order came down not to shoot over the *Bismarck*, and right after that, the order was given to cease fire. Fire was terminated at 0609. For that series of events to take place by 0609, it would appear that the *Prinz Eugen* would have completed her turns a minute or two earlier than the time of 0609 as shown on the battle diagram, making her turns even shallower than as shown on the diagram.

The *Prinz Eugen's* battle diagram's depiction of the tracks of the *Hood* and *Prince of Wales* during the battle is not consistent with the actual tracks of those ships as reported in official British accounts of the action. The tracks do not appear to be based on actual time and range determinations, but rather just a loose artistic interpretation of the tracks of those ships. This led Admiral Schmundt to condemn the battle diagram as being "worthless" when he later reviewed the document.

The battle diagram also shows the *Prinz Eugen* making a wide turn to starboard at 0613 and then another wide turn back to port at 0617, which is not consistent with the other evidence in the case. The *Bismarck* was ahead of the *Prinz Eugen* at the time, and the *Prinz Eugen's* speed chart shows that the cruiser increased her speed from 27.0 knots to 32.5 knots from 0610 until 0620, presumably to catch up with the *Bismarck* and again take the lead of the German squadron. There are several photographs taken after the battle that show the *Prinz Eugen* passing the *Bismarck* off the starboard side of the flagship at about 0620 and then gradually taking the lead of the German squadron.

Presumably the *Prinz Eugen* was ordered to take the lead of the German squadron right after the battle at 0610, in which case, she would have headed directly for the *Bismarck*, coming up on the starboard side of the flagship, where she had been all along. After reaching the *Bismarck* at 0620, the *Prinz Eugen* slowed down to 30.5 knots, and with the flagship now able to steam at only 29.0 knots, gradually advanced to the van of the formation.

With the maximum speed of the *Bismarck* being 30.0 knots, the most that the *Bismarck* could gain on the *Prinz Eugen* while both ships were traveling in the same general direction was 3.0 knots, or about 100 yards per minute. This is important since other versions of the battle show the *Bismarck* traveling at up to 33 knots, doubling the rate of closure between the two ships to 200 yards per minute and portraying maneuvers that the *Bismarck* was not actually capable of performing within that time constraint.

APPENDIX D
ANALYSIS OF CEASE FIRE TIMES BY BRITISH AND GERMAN FORCES

There is no specific time cited in any of the Admiralty reports as to when the *Prince of Wales* actually ceased fire. In his report to the Second Board of Enquiry into the loss of HMS Hood, Captain J. C. Leach of the *Prince of Wales* mentioned that the ship's compass platform was hit at 0602, and he described the subsequent hit on the boat deck that seriously upset the starboard after H.A. Director. Leach then stated that "it was considered expedient to break off the action and consolidate the position, and the ship, after being maneuvered round the remains of "Hood", turned away behind a smoke screen." He concluded by stating that "Y" turret fired in local during the turn as smoke blanked the after director.

The *Prince of Wales* salvo plot indicates that the ship's turn to course 160° began at 0605, which would have given Captain Leach sufficient time to recover from experiencing the hit on the compass platform, return to the bridge, assess the situation, and then make the decision to call off the action. In the meanwhile, first gunnery officer McMullen was continuing to fire at the *Bismarck*, even as the *Prince of Wales* was beginning to turn south. The Gunnery Appendix to Captain Leach's Narrative states that salvos 17 and 18 were ragged as the ship was under full wheel at the time, which would have been between 0605 and 0606.

After the *Prince of Wales* straightened out on course 160°, the second gunnery officer in the after main armament director took over central control of the main armament system, but he had difficulty in acquiring the target due to the smoke screen deployed to conceal the ship from *Bismarck's* fire. The crew commander of "Y" turret, however, was able to see the *Bismarck* under the smoke screen, and on his own initiative, he fired his turret on local control. The Gunnery Appendix also states that "Y" turret fired four rounds under local control after the 18th salvo, after which the shell ring jammed. Photographs taken from the *Prinz Eugen* show the splashes of two single shells exploding 23 seconds apart near the *Bismarck*, indicating that these were probably among the last shots fired by the *Prince of Wales* at about 0608.

The only specific cease-fire time mentioned for any of the ships involved in the battle of the Denmark Strait was for the *Prinz Eugen*. According to the *Prinz Eugen's* war diary, the *Bismarck* came into view in the sights of first gunnery officer Paulus Jasper of the *Prinz Eugen* at about 0607-0608 while he was engaged in firing on the *Prince of Wales*. Then the order was given not to shoot over the *Bismarck*, and right after that, the order was given to cease fire. According to her war diary, the *Prinz Eugen* ceased fire at 0609. Some historians assumed that this time also applied to the *Bismarck*, but that is not necessarily true. The photographs themselves indicate that the *Bismarck* was still firing even after having passed the *Prinz Eugen*.

Baron von Müllenheim-Rechberg states in his book "Battleship *Bismarck*" that when the range increased to 22,000 meters (24,100 yards) after the *Prince of Wales* turned away from the scene of battle, Admiral Lütjens gave the command to cease fire on the enemy battleship. Evidence indicates that the *Prince of Wales* turned away at 0605 and that the minimum range at that time was 14,500 yards. Traveling at 27 knots (910 yards per minute) directly away from the course of the *Bismarck*, it would have taken the *Prince of Wales* 10.5 minutes, or not until 0615:30, for the ship to reach a point 22,000 meters away from the *Bismarck*. The time of 0615 for the *Bismarck* to have ceased fire is not consistent with the other evidence in the case.

In his message to Group West after the battle, Admiral Lütjens reported the *Bismarck's* expenditure of only 93 heavy 15-inch shells in defeating the *Hood* and *Prince of Wales*. The Gunnery Appendix to Leach's Narrative states that "*Bismarck* appeared to fire the whole of her fore group (i.e. "A" and "B" turrets) followed by the whole of her aft group (i.e. "C" and "D" turrets). Toward the end of the morning action, guns in a group were definitely observed to 'ripple' as if one or more turrets were in gunlayers' firing."

The *Bismarck* fired six full salvos at the *Hood*, which would account for 48 shells, and that would leave only 45 shells for the *Prince of Wales*. It would seem logical that initially the *Bismarck* would have continued to fire full salvos against the *Prince of Wales* until she turned away at 0605 and was no longer a threat to the German squadron. Assuming that the *Bismarck* fired two salvos per minute from 0601 to 0605, that would represent an expenditure of 72 shells. Even with a reduced level of firing after 0605, it is not very likely that the *Bismarck* ceased fire much after 0610.

The *Prinz Eugen's* speed chart shows that the cruiser increased her speed from 27.0 knots to 32.5 knots at about 0610. The battle film shows the *Bismarck* initially becoming gradually smaller, indicating that the *Bismarck* was traveling faster than the *Prinz Eugen* and pulling away from the cruiser. However, toward the end of the battle film segment, the image of the *Bismarck* gradually grew in size, which would be consistent with the *Prinz Eugen* increasing her speed and closing back in on the *Bismarck*. It would seem to logical for Lütjens to order the *Prinz Eugen* to again take the lead of the German squadron immediately after the cease fire and as things returned to normal.

It appears that the battle film included the final salvo fired by the *Bismarck* at the *Prince of Wales*, and since the same segment of battle film includes the splashes from the individual shells fired by the *Prince of Wales* at about 0608, it is concluded that the *Bismarck* actually ceased fire at about 0610. No further salvos were filmed by Lagemann or the motion picture cameraman after that, and it would appear that both would have done so if the battle had still been in progress.

APPENDIX E
ANALYSIS OF THE STILL PHOTOGRAPHS OF THE *BISMARCK*

Seldom in the annals of naval history have events that occurred during a naval battle between surface vessels been documented by such a wealth of photographic material as in the case of the battle of the Denmark Strait. The *Prinz Eugen* had a staff photographer named Lagemann who took about a dozen still photographs of the *Bismarck* during the battle with his 35mm camera. He was accompanied by a motion picture cameraman who shot film segments of the *Bismarck* during the battle with his 16mm film camera. Both photographers covered the last two minutes of the battle, and this provided vital clues as to how the overall battle was actually fought. In addition to recording events that took place on a second-by-second basis, the battle film also establishes the exact sequence and relative timing of the still photographs taken during the same period of time.

Photographs, however, are subject to interpretation, and it is therefore necessary to ensure that the photographs are carefully analyzed to determine their validity, freedom from alteration, and proper orientation to permit an accurate depiction of events during the battle. This appendix is intended to provide an explanation as to how this photographic material was used in the development of this scenario of the battle and how it is related to the other documentary evidence available.

The photographs in question consist primarily of two sets of pictures, one set showing the *Bismarck* coming up on the port side of the *Prinz Eugen* to the point of almost passing the cruiser, and the second set showing the *Bismarck* on the starboard side of the *Prinz Eugen*. None of the photographs, however, show the *Bismarck* making any turns, nor do they give any other indication as to how the *Bismarck* transitioned from the port side of the *Prinz Eugen* to the starboard side of the cruiser.

U.S. Naval History and Heritage Command (formerly the U.S. Naval Historical Center) Photo **NH-69722** is the first photograph in the overall series. It shows the *Bismarck* firing on the *Hood* at about 0555 while the *Bismarck* was directly astern of the *Prinz Eugen*. There is a huge cloud of smoke extending 200 feet high and 400 feet outward from the guns that have just fired. This photograph was obviously taken from the starboard side of the *Prinz Eugen* looking aft. Lagemann then went over to the port side of the ship, where he took his position near the after 105mm antiaircraft gun mount. From there he snapped most if not all of the additional photographs taken during the battle.

The next photograph, **NH-69729**, showing the *Bismarck* coming up on the port side of the *Prinz Eugen*, was probably taken at about 0558 while the *Bis-*

marck was still firing at the *Hood*. This photograph also shows a huge cloud of smoke created by the *Bismarck* firing a broadside with her main armament guns. There is an almost identical photograph available from the German National Archives (Bundesarchiv), BA 146-1990-061-27, taken a few seconds earlier and which is slightly blurred due to camera motion. Lagemann probably took the second photograph of the same salvo sensing that the earlier one might be blurred due to camera motion. The smoke cloud in NH-69729 is about one third larger than the one in BA 146-1990-061-27, confirming that it was taken somewhat later than BA 146-1990-061-27.

The third photograph, **NH-69730**, taken at about 0601, shows the *Bismarck* firing at the *Prince of Wales* after the *Hood* had blown up. This photograph is the famous starboard bow view of the *Bismarck* being silhouetted by the flash of the guns in her after turrets firing. In the upper right corner of this photograph, the muzzle ends of the nearby twin 105mm antiaircraft guns can just be seen.

The fourth and final photograph showing the *Bismarck* coming up on the port side of the *Prinz Eugen* is Bundesarchiv photo BA 146-1984-055-13. It was taken at about 0603, when the *Bismarck* was nearly off the port beam of the *Prinz Eugen*, and it shows the *Bismarck* immediately after firing a full salvo with both of her forward and after turrets. This clearly places the timing of that photograph near the beginning of the *Bismarck's* action against the *Prince of Wales* when the *Bismarck* was still firing full salvos at the British battleship.

The series of pictures described above is consistent with other factual evidence, such as the *Prince of Wales* salvo plot, which shows the *Bismarck* moving up on the port side of the *Prinz Eugen* on an estimated course of 212°, eight degrees to port of the *Prinz Eugen's* baseline course of 220°. According to the *Prince of Wales* salvo plot, the *Bismarck* maintained the course of 212° until 0602, confirming that the *Bismarck* was some distance on the port side of the *Prinz Eugen* up until at least that time.

The *Prince of Wales* salvo plot also shows that the *Bismarck* traveled a distance at least 10% greater than that of the *Prince of Wales* during the battle, confirming that the *Bismarck* must have been traveling at her top speed of 30.0 knots. With the *Prinz Eugen* traveling at 27.0 knots throughout the battle, according to her official speed chart, the *Bismarck* could gain a maximum of 100 yards per minute on the *Prinz Eugen* at a speed differential of 3.0 knots. The timing of the photographs is consistent with the degree to which the *Bismarck* is seen to advance between successive photographs at the rate of 100 yards per minute.

At about 0603, the *Prinz Eugen* began to make a series of three hard turns, first to starboard, then to port, and then back to starboard again before straightening out on a course roughly parallel to that of the *Bismarck*. For all practical purposes, that ruled out the taking of any photographs for the next three to four minutes. Not only was the ship in the process of turning rapidly, but also her deck was tilted sharply during the turns, making it virtually impossible to take clear photographs or steady motion pictures during that period. It also explains why there are no further still photographs showing the *Bismarck* on the port side of the *Prinz Eugen* after BA 146-1984-055-13.

The second set of photographs show the *Bismarck* on the starboard side of the *Prinz Eugen*. These six photographs were probably taken between 0608:00, just after the *Prinz Eugen* straightened out from her sharp turns, and 0610:30, after both German ships ceased fire. The still photographs are fairly sharp, indicating that they were taken from a reasonably stable platform. All of the five photographs showing the *Bismarck* on the starboard side of the *Prinz Eugen* are essentially silhouette views of the *Bismarck* since the image of the *Bismarck* is dark and lacking sufficient detail to positively establish its orientation.

The brightest part of the sky on these views of the *Bismarck* is directly over the horizon. Considering the fact that these photographs were taken shortly after dawn, it would appear that the camera taking these photographs would have been aimed to the east in the direction of the rising sun that would illuminate the horizon so brightly. Since the *Bismarck* and *Prinz Eugen* were traveling in a southerly direction, east would be off the port side of those ships. The starboard side of the *Prinz Eugen* would therefore have been facing west, where the sky was still dark at the dawn hour. In fact, the darkest part of the sky would be directly over horizon to the west, totally different from the situation in the east.

If these views of the *Bismarck* had actually been taken from the starboard side of the *Prinz Eugen*, the sky would have been darkest over the horizon rather than being the brightest in that direction, as shown in the photographs. This would seem to indicate that the photographs may have been printed in reverse, and that they should be showing the *Bismarck* on the port side of the *Prinz Eugen* rather than the starboard side of the cruiser. There is still further evidence that the *Bismarck* was indeed on the port side of the *Prinz Eugen* when these photographs were taken, as explained below.

Since the photographs are essentially silhouette views of the Bismarck, it is possible to view the photographs as being either port bow views of the *Bismarck* coming toward the *Prinz Eugen* or port quarter views of the *Bismarck* sailing away from the *Prinz Eugen*.

The first still photograph showing the *Bismarck* on the starboard side of the *Prinz Eugen* is **NH-69728**. This photograph shows the *Bismarck* silhouetted against a lighter sky just above the horizon and at a considerably further distance away from the *Prinz Eugen* than shown in BA 146-1984-055-13, the last previous photograph. There are three large separate puffs of smoke over the stern end of the ship, indicating the firing of three turrets a few seconds apart. The inclination of the *Bismarck* indicates that the *Bismarck* was by then somewhat ahead of the *Prinz Eugen*. A large shell splash is seen about a ship length aft of the *Bismarck*, apparently from a single shell fired by the *Prince of Wales* while retreating from the scene of battle.

The left edge of the photographic image is slightly fogged, indicating that the image may have been on the first frame of a new roll of film installed in the camera and not turned sufficiently to fully take up the film leader. This of course would support the possibility that Lagemann took the opportunity of reloading his camera while the *Prinz Eugen* was making her hard turns between 0603 and 0607, making it impossible for him to take any pictures during that period of time anyway. If the *Bismarck* had continued on her course while the *Prinz Eugen* was turning, that would have placed the *Bismarck* somewhat ahead of the *Prinz Eugen* but some distance further away from the cruiser laterally than she had been at 0603.

The next photograph in the series is BA 146-1968-015-26, which was taken just five seconds after NH-69728. It shows the same image of the *Bismarck* silhouetted against a lighter sky just above the horizon, but with the three puffs of smoke seen in NH-69728 further behind the ship and partially dissipated. The following photograph is BA 146-1968-015-12, which was taken 18 seconds after BA 146-1968-015-26. Again the *Bismarck* is silhouetted against a lighter sky just above the horizon, but there also is a large shell splash off the port bow of the ship, indicating another single round fired by the *Prince of Wales* during her retreat. The inclination of the *Bismarck* is slightly smaller in this photograph, indicating that the *Bismarck* might be slowly moving further ahead of the *Prinz Eugen*.

The next photograph, **NH-69726**, is the most significant of the six photographs showing the *Bismarck* on the starboard side of the *Prinz Eugen*. It provides the evidence that clearly establishes the direction in which the *Bismarck* was firing and the orientation of the *Bismarck* in all of those six views.

Photograph NH-69726 was taken 29 seconds after BA 146-1968-015-12, and like the immediately preceding photographs, it is also a silhouette view of the *Bismarck*. The photograph shows a huge fireball directly above the stern of the *Bismarck* that brightly illuminated certain portions of the ship. However, all of the portside surfaces of the hull and superstructure, even those near the fireball, were completely in the dark, indicating that the *Bismarck* must have been firing to starboard and not to port when the picture was taken.

Further indications that the *Bismarck* was firing to starboard when photo

NH-69726 was taken are the lack of a reflection from the fireball in the water on the near (port) side of the ship and the absence of any blast effect on the surface of the water on the near side of the ship. The fireball of expanding hot gases would normally have extended down to the level of the water, but in this case the fireball seems to be above the hull of the *Bismarck*. The rear end of turret "Dora" is clearly visible near the bottom of the fireball, but the entire turret area would have been obscured by a fireball on the port side of the ship.

The pattern of illumination of other areas of the *Bismarck* would have been possible only if the ship had been firing to starboard with the fireball on the far side of the ship. The two bright identical patches of light seen amidships at deck level are consistent with the location, size and shape of the center and rear dual 150mm gun turrets and their barbettes. Both of these turrets are outboard on the main deck close to the edge of the side of the hull and are therefore subject to the same level of illumination. The forward dual 150mm gun turret is not visible in NH-69726 since it is more inboard and shielded from the flash by the surrounding forward superstructure of the ship.

When both illuminated secondary gun turrets are greatly magnified together, the rearmost turret is found to be slightly but measurably larger than the foremost turret, indicating that the photograph must be a port quarter view of the *Bismarck* and not a port bow view as some believe. This also confirms that the two secondary gun turrets illuminated in the photograph were in fact the center and after secondary gun turrets of the *Bismarck* and not the forward and center secondary gun turrets. If the fireball had been on the port side of the *Bismarck*, surely all of the three secondary gun turrets on that side of the ship would have been illuminated, not just the two.

The right half of the tower battle mast is seen to be illuminated in NH-69726, which is consistent with the rear surface of the control tower reflecting the flash from the *Bismarck* firing her rear main armament guns as seen in a port quarter view of the *Bismarck*. The rear surface of the control tower is essentially unobstructed from under the foretop platform down to the walkway between the control tower and the funnel. The partially illuminated structure on the port side of the control tower is also consistent with the edge of the upper antiaircraft gun position reflecting the flash from the *Bismarck* firing her rear guns to starboard.

The large vertical strip of illumination seen just to the left of the tower battle mast in NH69726 is consistent with the size, shape and location of the armored globe-topped forward port antiaircraft director as illuminated by the flash of the *Bismarck* firing her after guns to starboard. As with the upper antiaircraft gun position, the light from the flash would have been able to pass through the gap between the rear edge of the control tower and front edge of the funnel to illuminate the forward port antiaircraft director.

The next photograph was part of the Paul Schmalenbach collection, but there are no known Naval History, Bundesarchiv, or Imperial War Museum catalog numbers associated with that photograph. It was taken 36 seconds after NH-69726, and it shows the *Bismarck* totally silhouetted against the light sky just above the horizon. A large cloud of black smoke is seen over the after part of the ship, apparently from the *Bismarck* firing her forward turrets at the retreating *Prince of Wales* and the smoke drifting to the rear as the *Bismarck* progressed ahead.

The next and final photograph showing the *Bismarck* on the starboard side of the *Prinz Eugen* is **NH-69727**. This photograph was taken just five seconds after the photograph described above was shot, and it also shows the *Bismarck* totally silhouetted against the light sky just above the horizon. The large cloud of smoke is now seen directly over the stern end of the ship as a result of the forward movement of the *Bismarck* in the elapsed period of time between the two photographs.

In all of the photographs showing the *Bismarck* on the starboard side of the *Prinz Eugen*, the sky is brightest just above the horizon, which would seem to indicate that the scenes were shot toward the east in the direction of the rising sun that would have occurred at dawn when the battle took place. At that time in the morning, the sky to the west would still be dark, with the darkest part directly over the western horizon. With the German squadron sailing in a predominantly southerly direction, east would be to the port side of the ships, while their starboard sides would be facing west.

For the *Bismarck* to have been on the starboard side of the *Prinz Eugen*, it would had to have been on the west side of the cruiser where the sky would have been the darkest, not the lightest. This is perhaps the most irrefutable proof that the photographs showing the *Bismarck* on the starboard side of the *Prinz Eugen* had to have been reversed.

If the orientation of the *Bismarck* can be positively established in any one of the photographs showing the *Bismarck* on the starboard side of the *Prinz Eugen*, the same orientation would apply to all six photographs since they were all taken less than two minutes apart. Since NH-69726 clearly proves that the photograph is a port quarter view of the *Bismarck* by virtue of a comparison of the size of the two illuminated secondary gun turrets, all six photographs must also be port quarter views of the *Bismarck* and not port bow views as others have claimed.

Furthermore, if it can be positively established that the *Bismarck* had been firing in a certain direction in any one of those photographs, that direction of firing would apply to all six photographs showing the *Bismarck* on the starboard side of the *Prinz Eugen*. Since the evidence presented above clearly establishes that the *Bismarck* was firing to starboard in NH-69726, it was also firing to starboard in each of the other photographs showing the *Bismarck* on the starboard side of the *Prinz Eugen*.

Since the British force was always to port of the German squadron, the *Bismarck* could not have been firing to starboard, as shown on the still photographs, and therefore those still pictures had to have been printed in reverse. All of the evidence now clearly points to the fact that the photographs showing the *Bismarck* on the starboard side of the *Prinz Eugen* had to have been reversed.

When the starboard views of the *Bismarck* are turned around so that the *Bismarck* is seen in its correct orientation on the port side of the *Prinz Eugen*, the photographs match perfectly with the earlier photographs showing the *Bismarck* coming up on the port side of the *Prinz Eugen*. The complete set of photographs can finally be placed in true chronological order showing the *Bismarck* coming up on the port side of the *Prinz Eugen*, passing the cruiser off its port beam, and

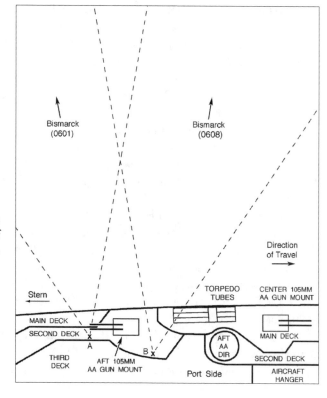

continuing to move ahead of the *Prinz Eugen* until the cease fire at 0609-0610.

The orientation of the *Bismarck* in the still photographs, showing the *Bismarck* on the starboard side of the *Prinz Eugen*, is not consistent with the other evidence that clearly places the *Bismarck* on the port side of the *Prinz Eugen* during the latter phase of the battle. The reports by the *Prinz Eugen's* first and second gunnery officers in the ship's War Diary positively place the *Bismarck* between the *Prinz Eugen* and the *Prince of Wales*, i.e., on the port side of the *Prinz Eugen* after 0607. Paul Schmalenbach's original battle diagram, published after the war, shows the *Bismarck* on the port side of the *Prinz Eugen* from 0600 until after 0609.

There are no other photographs showing the *Bismarck* on the starboard side of the *Prinz Eugen* during the battle, and there are no photographs showing the *Bismarck* making any turns or changing position with the *Prinz Eugen*. Since the *Prinz Eugen's* photographer Lagemann was taking photographs at an average rate of about one per minute during the battle, the absence of photographic evidence to support any turns by the *Bismarck* obviously makes that version of the battle highly questionable.

The still photographs are also not consistent with the documentary evidence presented in the official *Prinz Eugen's* war diary. In that document, *Prinz Eugen's* first gunnery officer, Paulus Jasper, reported that after the series of hard turns by the cruiser, the *Bismarck* came into his sights. That sighting indicated that the *Bismarck* would soon be directly between the *Prinz Eugen* and the *Prince of Wales*, leading to the order for the *Prinz Eugen* not to shoot over the *Bismarck*.

According to the *Prinz Eugen's* war diary, right after that the order was given to cease fire, and fire was terminated at 0609. This report clearly indicates that the *Bismarck* was already on the port side of the *Prinz Eugen* some time before the cruiser ceased fire at 0609. As pointed out above, it would have taken the *Bismarck* several minutes coming up on the port side of the *Prinz Eugen* to reach the point where she could come into Jasper's line of sight to the *Prince of Wales*.

Prinz Eugen's second gunnery officer, Paul Schmalenbach, reported in the *Prinz Eugen's* war diary that he took an occasional look at the *Bismarck* during the battle, This would not have been possible if the *Bismarck* had been on the opposite (starboard) side of the *Prinz Eugen* away from the target area. Schmalenbach later prepared a battle diagram based on his recollection of events which placed the *Bismarck* continually on the port side of the *Prinz Eugen* from 0600 to after 0609.

It is interesting to note that no other recognized author, not even Paul Schmalenbach, has been able to arrange all of the still photographs in chronological order, as would be normal for anyone describing a naval battle. Schmalenbach shows the many photographs in a completely random pattern, while other authors merely show two or three photographs scattered amid the text. In his book, *Pursuit*, Ludovic Kennedy does not even show any of the photographs taken of the *Bismarck* from the *Prinz Eugen* during the battle.

This all testifies to the inability of anyone to arrange all of the still photographs, as originally printed, in a logical time sequence. While some have attempted to do so, the results are not consistent with the time constraints imposed by the limitation of the *Bismarck* being able to gain only 100 yards every minute on the *Prinz Eugen* while both ships are traveling in the same general direction. Only by reversing the starboard views of the *Bismarck* can the entire set of still photographs be arranged in proper chronological sequence and be in conformance with the other documentary evidence in the case.

One may wonder whether it is feasible to have six photographs in a row all printed in reverse. One, yes, and two, maybe, but all six, not very likely. There is, however, a rational explanation as to how this could have happened. The photographs were taken with a 35mm film camera, and after 35mm film is developed, it is usually cut into strips of four to six frames for easier handling when using an enlarger. It is therefore possible that the strip containing the six photo-

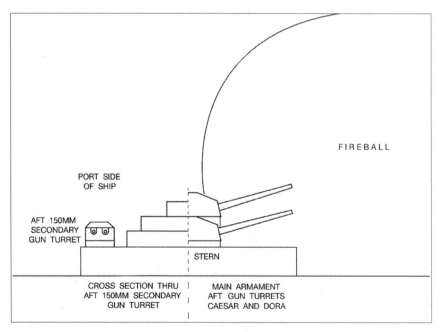

Showing illumination from fireball on starboard side..

graphs in question was inadvertently turned upside down in the enlarger, causing all of the six frames on that strip to be printed in reverse. This possibility is heightened by the fogging seen at the front edge of photo NH-69728, indicating that it was the first frame on a new roll of film as well as being the first of the six frames on the filmstrip.

In addition to the photographs mentioned above, there are two photographs of note taken by Lagemann in the direction of the British task force toward the southeast. One photograph, **NH-69724**, shows the Hood engulfed in a huge cloud of smoke just after her magazines exploded when hit by a shell from the *Bismarck*. The second photograph, **NH-69731**, which was taken about 30 seconds later, shows the splashes from the *Bismarck's* sixth salvo, fired just before the *Hood* exploded, directly in front of the smoke cloud that still hung over the sinking *Hood*. Both photographs show the smoke plumes from the funnel of the *Prince of Wales* still to the left of the *Hood* after the *Prince of Wales* turned toward the German squadron and before she sailed around the wreckage of the *Hood*.

The latter photograph was erroneously captioned in other publications as indicating that the splashes came from shells fired by the *Prince of Wales* that fell well short of the German ships. That caption is of course completely ridiculous for a number of reasons, and yet it is accepted by some as being the truth. The *Prince of Wales* salvo plot accounted for every salvo fired by the British battleship, and after the *Prince of Wales* once got the range on the *Bismarck*, her misses were never more than about one thousand yards off. The splashes shown in the photograph are near the horizon, over 15,000 yards (8 nautical miles) away from the vantage point of the photographer. Just looking at the photograph should be sufficient to discount those other captions.

APPENDIX F
ANALYSIS OF *BISMARCK* BATTLE FILM

In addition to the still photographs taken of the *Bismarck* from the *Prinz Eugen* during the battle of the Denmark Strait, there was also a motion picture film taken of part of the action at the same time. A digital version of that battle film was used for this analysis, and it covers a period of about two minutes and ten seconds. The authenticity of this version of the battle film was verified by comparison with the corresponding still pictures that have generally been accepted as being genuine.

The battle film was taken with a hand-held, 16mm motion picture camera with a normal focal length lens and a speed of 16 frames per second. In digital form, individual frames of the battle film could be printed in full-page size (8-1/2 x 11-inch) for detailed analysis. Since the frames are consistent in size, they allow for direct comparison with one another, which is not always possible with enlarged still pictures due to the possibility of cropping.

There are several gaps in the battle film, probably caused by the temporary cessation of filming or by splicing. To improve the accuracy of the time-line for the events depicted in the battle film, an attempt was made to account for the gaps in the film. When comparing the frames on both sides of the splices, it was noted that in each case the *Bismarck* had moved a further distance away from the near edge of a clearly defined smoke cloud created by the firing of her main guns. A series of measurements was made throughout the entire film segment, and they were sufficiently consistent to establish an empirical formula to determine the approximate size of the gaps in the film.

It was found that each 1/60-inch unit of measure represented an average of 2.1 frames with a range of values from 1.9 to 2.3 frames. That range of values constitutes a margin for error of 10 percent, which is far better than simply ignoring the gap. This formula would, of course, only be applicable to the specific set of circumstances depicted in the battle film itself. Factors such as smoke cloud expansion, wind direction and velocity, and ship inclination would certainly vary under different circumstances, and therefore a separate analysis would be required for each situation.

As a result of this effort, an additional 13 seconds were accounted for, and it was then determined that the segment of battle film on hand actually encompassed a total period of time of about 130 seconds. While the time difference between events seen on the film can be accurately determined to within a fraction of a second, tying these events to specific clock times is considerably more difficult.

An analysis of the battle film would be more meaningful if it could be correlated to a specific time period during the battle. Only in that way can the full potential value of the battle film be realized in arriving at the most probable scenario of the battle. The battle film is an essential element in the integration of all of the documentary evidence into a fully supported concept of how the battle of the Denmark Strait was fought.

The battle film could not possibly have been taken between 0553 and 0602 for the following reasons. Photo NH-69722 clearly shows the *Bismarck* still at least 1000 yards directly astern of the *Prinz Eugen* at about 0555 when the *Bismarck* opened fire on the *Hood*. Photo NH-69729 shows the *Bismarck* moving up on the *Prinz Eugen* on a course somewhat to port of the track of the *Prinz Eugen* at about 0558. Photo NH-69730 shows the *Bismarck* directly off the port quarter of the *Prinz Eugen* at about 0601 and Photo BA 146-1984-055-13 shows the *Bismarck* almost off the port beam of the *Prinz Eugen* at 0603.

The position of the *Bismarck* on the port side of the *Prinz Eugen* from 0553 to 0602 is also confirmed by the official *Prince of Wales* Salvo Plot, which shows the location of the *Bismarck* in relation to the *Prince of Wales* during that period. The *Prince of Wales* Salvo Plot shows the *Bismarck* as traveling on a straight-line course estimated to be 212 degrees from 0553 to 0602. This course was eight degrees to port of the course of 220 degrees sailed by the *Prinz Eugen*, and it is consistent with the other evidence.

The battle film could not possibly have been taken between 0603 and 0608. At 0603, the *Prinz Eugen* began a series of three hard turns, which would have made picture taking, especially motion pictures, impossible. Those turns are documented on the *Prinz Eugen's* Battle Sketch as well as in the *Prinz Eugen's* War Diary. The battle film, on the other hand, reflects a very steady progression of frames with no radical movements by either the *Bismarck* or the *Prinz Eugen* throughout the more than two-minute period covered by the battle film. This would seem to indicate that the battle film could only have been taken between 0608:00 and 0610:30.

The images on the 16mm battle film, while significantly smaller than 35mm still photo negatives, are surprisingly sharp, indicating that the battle film was taken while the *Prinz Eugen* was sailing on a steady course and providing a stable platform for picture-taking. In fact, after filming of the battle film segment began, the photographer held the *Bismarck* in the center of his viewfinder for a sustained period of 29 seconds. If the *Prinz Eugen* had been making any sharp turns, the images on the battle film would have been blurred due to unavoidable camera movements in trying to track the *Bismarck*.

The movie photographer began shooting the battle film shortly after the platform became stable enough to permit picture taking. The first few frames of the battle film are slightly blurred as the *Prinz Eugen* settled down after her last hard turn. *Prinz Eugen's* still photographer, Lagemann, began taking photographs 35 seconds later when he took NH-69728.

The firing of the *Bismarck's* main armament guns is characterized in the battle film by an initial frame that is mostly obscured by a brilliant flash that completely overexposed the film by the intensity of the light. The flash then quickly diminishes in succeeding frames until it disappears and a clearly defined fireball is seen for several additional frames. The fireball is then transformed into a cloud of smoke that is created when the hot gases from the ignited propellant are cooled down by the surrounding air. The location of the fireball distinguishes the specific group of turrets that fired, whether forward or aft.

The salvo pattern fired by the *Bismarck* is known to have changed during the battle. Baron von Mullenheim-Rechberg, in his book *Battleship Bismarck*, quoted the first gunnery officer as ordering "full salvos good rapid" against the *Hood*. Full salvos undoubtedly continued to be fired against the *Prince of Wales*, at least until 0603, as evidenced by the Photo BA 146-1984-055-13 taken of the *Bismarck* just after she fired both her fore and after turrets at the same time.

Admiralty Report ADM 234-509 states: "Bismarck appears to have fired all of her fore group (i.e. "A" and "B" turrets) followed by the whole of her aft group ("X" and "Y" turrets). Toward the end of the morning action, guns in a group were definitely observed to "ripple" as if one or more turrets were in gun layers' firing." The pattern of salvos shown in the battle film is consistent with the observations from the *Prince of Wales* and further establishes the battle film as covering basically the last two minutes of the battle.

The first frame of the battle film shows two puffs of smoke directly above the stern of the *Bismarck*, indicating that she had just fired separate salvos from her two after turrets in quick succession. At three seconds into the battle film (T+3), one of the *Bismarck's* forward turrets fired a salvo characterized by two separate flashes. This indicates that there was a slight delay between the firing of the individual guns of that turret.

At T+13 seconds, the *Bismarck* fired a salvo from her other forward turret, and at T+28 seconds, one of the *Bismarck's* forward turrets fired another salvo, and at T+40 seconds, the other forward turret fired a salvo.

The separation of 25 seconds between the first and third salvos and the separation of 27 seconds between the second and fourth salvos from the *Bismarck's* forward turrets is consistent with the established rate of fire for her guns. Under ideal conditions, the guns of the *Bismarck* could fire a round every 20 seconds, but under sustained combat conditions, some slight delays for various reasons could be expected.

The four salvos fired by the *Bismarck's* forward turrets were then followed by a salvo from one of her after turrets at T+43 seconds, and at T+82 seconds, the *Bismarck* fired one of her forward turrets again. This was followed by the firing of one of her after turrets at T+86 seconds and other firing by one of her after turrets one second later at T+87 seconds.

The very short duration of the flash during the firing of the last few salvos could indicate that the *Bismarck* may have been firing individual guns rather than two-gun salvos, further supporting the observations made from the *Prince of Wales* of the "ripple" effect of her firing. No more salvos were fired from the after turrets of the *Bismarck* in the 43 seconds remaining to the end of the film segment, indicating that the *Bismarck* was coming close to a cease fire.

One more salvo was fired from both forward turrets at T+119 seconds, possibly just to clear the guns if they had already been loaded. The slackening of fire from the *Bismarck* at this time suggests that it was becoming too difficult to acquire the *Prince of Wales* while she was retreating under a smoke screen and that this was probably the last salvo fired by the *Bismarck*. The segment of battle film ended 10 seconds later at T+129 seconds, and the *Bismarck* ceased fire at about 0610.

The *Bismarck* hit the *Hood* with its fifth salvo at 0600, causing the *Hood's* after magazines to explode and the ship to sink. The *Bismarck* had already fired its sixth salvo just before the *Hood* was seen to blow up, so the earliest that the *Bismarck* could have fired on the *Prince of Wales* was close to 0601. At a range of 16,000 yards, the time of flight of *Bismarck's* shells would have been 25 seconds. It is highly unlikely that the *Bismarck* could have hit the *Prince of Wales* four times in less than one minute before the latter purportedly turned away at 0602. All of the hits occurred at an angle, making it highly probable that they occurred over a somewhat longer period of time, probably between 0602 and 0604.

Admiralty Report ADM 234-509 states that the *Prince of Wales* fired 18 salvos in 8.58 minutes for a rate of fire of 1.895 salvos per minute. While the number of salvos is confirmed by other reports, including the *Prince of Wales* salvo plot, the time frame is questionable for the reasons cited above. The hit on the compass platform at about 0602 temporarily disrupted the "con" of the ship for a couple of minutes while Captain Leach recovered and reestablished control on the bridge of the *Prince of Wales*. Under the circumstances, it is unlikely that maintaining an accurate record of time was of high priority.

The battle film shows conspicuously the huge columns of water created when two shells from the *Prince of Wales* landed 23 seconds apart near the *Bismarck*, reaching their peak at T+35 seconds and T+58 seconds, respectively. The first shell is seen to land at T+26 seconds, but the fall of the second shell was out of camera range and was therefore estimated to land at T+49 seconds, nine seconds earlier than the time of the peak of the splash at T+58 seconds.

Since no further splashes are seen during the last 72 seconds of the battle film, those two shots apparently were the independent rounds fired by the *Prince of Wales* after her final turn away from the *Bismarck* at 0605. At a range of 14,500 yards, as reported in Admiralty Report ADM 234-509, the time of flight of the *Prince of Wales'* shells would have been about 22 seconds, placing the time of firing for the first shell at T+4 seconds and the second shell at T+27 seconds. Since the shots were apparently fired by the *Prince of Wales* at some time after 0607, the splashes seen in the battle film clearly places the battle film as having been taken during the very last phase of the battle.

While the distance to the *Bismarck* from the *Prinz Eugen* cannot be determined with any degree of accuracy merely by looking at the battle film, it is possible to determine changes in that distance, and thereby relative movement between the two ships, with some degree of accuracy. A vertical measurement is essential to avoid errors resulting from changes in ship inclination, and therefore the height of the *Bismarck* from the waterline to the top of her tower battle mast served as the reference for all measurements.

To measure the height of the *Bismarck* in the various frames analyzed, the images were first enlarged to twice their printed size to provide a larger image to work with. A fine line was then drawn along the bottom of her bow wave and stern wake parallel to the horizon to establish a common base line. From that line, the height of the tower mast above the water line to the top of the range finder was measured using a drafting scale with divisions of 1/60-inch. Several measurements in both directions were made and then averaged to achieve a margin of error of three percent.

The height measurements of the *Bismarck* declined slightly from 55 units (23mm) at the beginning of the film segment to 52 units (22mm) at T+11 seconds and 50 units (21mm) at T+27 seconds. The height remained 50 units at T+41 seconds and T+56 seconds, but then it increased to 52 units at T+66 and T+81 seconds. The height measurements continued to increase to 53 units (22.5mm) at T+94 seconds, 55 units (23mm) at T+97 seconds, 57 units (24mm) at T+103 seconds, 57 units at T+109 seconds, and 59 units (25mm) at T+114 seconds.

There is a gap in the battle film after T+115 seconds when the camera was suddenly pointed downward. When the filming resumed, the *Bismarck* was at the very top of the frame, and the first possible height measurement was 66 units (28mm). When earlier measurements are plotted, and the curve extended to the first reading after the gap, the curve reaches the value of 66 units at T+121 seconds, indicating the gap was about six seconds. This would be just enough time for the photographer to rewind the spring motor on the movie camera, if that was indeed the reason for the temporary halt in filming.

While the height measurements do not reflect precise distances between the *Bismarck* and the *Prinz Eugen*, actual measurements are provided to show the order of magnitude of the changes. When plotted against time, these height measurements indicate that the *Bismarck* was moving away from the *Prinz Eugen* at the beginning of the battle film segment, but after T+56 seconds, the *Prinz Eugen* began to pick up speed and draw closer to the *Bismarck*. By T+127 seconds, near the end of the battle film segment, the *Prinz Eugen* was slightly closer to the *Bismarck*.

According to the *Prinz Eugen's* official speed chart, the *Prinz Eugen* maintained a steady speed of 27.0 knots throughout the battle, but at 0610 after the action, she increased her speed to 32.5 knots and maintained that speed until 0620. While adequate for tracking fuel consumption and certain other purposes, the scale used for the *Prinz Eugen's* speed chart cannot be regarded as very precise with respect to establishing the exact times of speed changes.

From a practical point of view, the *Prinz Eugen* could not have increased her speed from 27.0 knots to 32.5 knots instantaneously. It would take at least a couple of minutes to do so, and therefore the process could have begun as early as 0609, making the battle film entirely consistent with the speed chart. This would indicate that the decision to cease fire was made at about the same time that the *Prinz Eugen* began to pick up speed to catch up to the *Bismarck* and again take the lead of the German squadron.

Inclination is the angle at which the *Bismarck* appears to be traveling as seen from the *Prinz Eugen*. An inclination angle of 0 degrees indicates that the *Bismarck* is traveling along the line of sight from the *Prinz Eugen*, either directly toward or directly away from the *Prinz Eugen*. An inclination angle of 90 degrees indicates that the *Bismarck* was traveling perpendicular to the line of sight from the *Prinz Eugen*.

It is possible to determine the inclination angle of the *Bismarck* to the line of sight from the *Prinz Eugen* within a degree or two by trigonometric means. The actual ratio between the overall length of the *Bismarck* to its height from the waterline to the top of the tower mast is 7.35. When the ratio of the measured length to height of the *Bismarck* in a particular battle film frame is divided by the figure of 7.35, the result is the sin of the inclination angle, which can then be readily determined with a scientific calculator.

The inclination angle of the *Bismarck* to the line of sight from the *Prinz Eugen* was calculated to be 53 degrees at T+27 seconds into the battle film, 54 degrees at T+41 seconds, 51 degrees at T+56 seconds, 52 degrees at T+67 seconds, 50 degrees at T+81 seconds, 45 degrees at T+94 seconds, 40 degrees at T+103 seconds, and 36 degrees at T+114 seconds. As can be seen, the inclination angle is relatively constant for the first 80 seconds or so of the battle film segment, but then it begins to decrease slightly after that.

As with the height measurements, the inclination calculations were then disrupted by the gap in the film at 115 seconds. The first possible determination of the angle of inclination of the *Bismarck* to the line of sight from the *Prinz Eugen* after filming resumed resulted in a value of 30 degrees. When the earlier values of the inclination angle were plotted, and the curve extended to the value of 30 degrees, the curve intersected that value at about the same time as the height measurement, further confirming that the gap in the film was about six seconds.

The slow and gradual changes in the *Bismarck's* inclination angle indicate that the *Bismarck* was sailing on substantially a straight-line course throughout the more than two-minute period covered by the battle film. Any turns by the *Bismarck* would surely have been reflected by rapid and drastic changes in her inclination angle.

The battle film offers a number of clues as to the direction in which the *Bismarck* fired her guns during the battle. The battle film shows no bright illumination of the portside surfaces of the *Bismarck* when her big guns are fired, although a couple of frames show faint illumination of the portside surfaces of the *Bismarck* from the hot gases of the fireball escaping to the rear. If the *Bismarck* had been firing to port, the portside surfaces of the ship would have been brilliantly illuminated by the flash.

The huge smoke cloud generated by the *Bismarck* firing her big guns extends for some 400 feet outward along the surface of the water, yet in no frame of the battle film does any smoke appear to be on the near (port) side of the ship. In many frames, the stern wake of the *Bismarck* is clearly visible with the smoke behind it on the far (starboard) side of the ship. If the *Bismarck* had been firing to port, a large portion of the ship, especially along the waterline, would have been obscured by the smoke cloud.

Another phenomenon associated with a battleship firing its big guns is the blast effect on the surface of the water. The blasts churn up the surface of the water into a white froth extending outward for several hundred feet from the source of the blast and lasting for at least a couple of seconds, long enough to be picked up on a number of frames of the battle film. Yet the battle film shows no signs of any blast effect that would have been seen if the *Bismarck* had been firing to port and toward the camera.

There is a complete lack of any reflection of the fireball created by the *Bismarck* firing her big guns in the water on the near (port) side of the ship. If the

Bismarck had fired to port, as some claim, surely a large oval reflection of the fireball would have been seen on the near (port) side of the ship in a number of frames of the battle film, but there is no sign of any reflection of the fireball on the water. If the *Bismarck* fired to starboard, however, the reflection of the fireball would have been obscured by the ship itself.

There is clear evidence on several frames of the battle film that when the *Bismarck* fired her forward main gun turrets, the fireball created by that firing was partially obscured by the superstructure of the ship. The front tower structure and funnel are both silhouetted by the fireball on the far (starboard) side of the ship in those frames. Some have tried to explain the bright areas surrounding the tower and funnel as fire from the *Bismarck's* secondary gun turrets, but most of those bright spots are not even located near the secondary gun turrets.

As a result of this analysis, it must be concluded that the images in the battle film show port quarter views of the *Bismarck* firing to starboard. Since the British force was always on the port side of the German squadron, the battle film must have been processed in reverse. When properly oriented, the battle film conforms to the other documentary evidence relative to the battle and it supports the concept of the battle that envisions the *Bismarck* sailing in a straight line course along the port side of the *Prinz Eugen* throughout the battle. The battle film establishes the events that occurred during the latter phase of the battle to within half a minute or less in actual time.

APPENDIX G
ANALYSIS OF THE FATAL TORPEDO HIT ON THE *BISMARCK*

For a long time, there had been a difference of opinion among experts regarding the direction from which the torpedo that crippled the *Bismarck* had been launched. In his book, *Pursuit* (1974), Ludovic Kennedy describes the attack of the Swordfish aircvraft responsible for the mortal hit as coming from the starboard side. Since then, however, several technical experts have gone on record in various publications claiming that the fatal torpedo came from the port side. One of the experts reaffirmed the belief that the torpedo came in from the port side based on his observations of the *Bismarck* during an expedition to the wreck site in July 2001.

The torpedo struck the underside of the hull below the steering compartment and between the twin rudders of the *Bismarck*. The explosion of the torpedo jammed the rudders in their turning position of 12 degrees to port and caused severe flooding of the steering compartment itself. The location of the hit, however, seemed to rule out the possibility of the fatal torpedo coming in from the port side of the ship.

When aircraft attack a surface vessel with torpedoes, they generally launch their torpedoes on a course perpendicular to that of the target to achieve the greatest possibility of a hit, even if the target should begin to turn toward the attacking aircraft or away from it. Since the speed of the torpedo is only slightly greater than that of the ship, the torpedo must be aimed some distance ahead of the target to ensure that the torpedo will reach the same spot at the same time as the ship. The lead distance is dependent upon the estimated speed of the ship.

When a ship turns in the same direction as the torpedo attack, this tends to protect the vital screws and rudders at the stern end of the ship, but when a ship

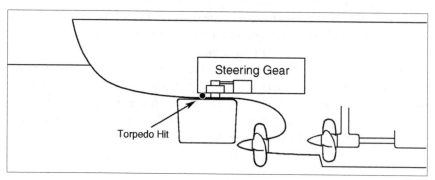

Location of fatal torpedo hit on *Bismarck*.

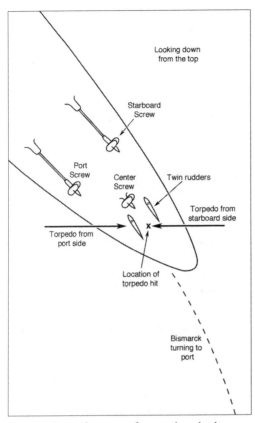

Fatal torpedo coming from starboard side.

turns in the opposite direction, this exposes those critical areas of the stern to an oncoming torpedo. In the case of the *Bismarck*, the ship turned to port with her rudders set at a 12° angle. If the fatal torpedo had come from the port side, it would have been almost impossible for the torpedo to strike on the underside of the hull below the steering compartment and between the twin rudders of the ship. Instead, the torpedo would have most likely hit the hull on the port side of the port rudder or the port rudder itself.

This led the author to believe that the fatal torpedo hit must have come from the starboard side of the *Bismarck*, and not the port side. The *Bismarck's* turn to port would have exposed the stern end of the ship to the oncoming torpedo and the missile could have readily struck the hull in the region where the actual hit occurred. In his first book, "The *Bismarck* Chase" (1998), the author describes the fatal torpedo attack as coming from the starboard side of the ship based upon his own technical analysis of the underwater configuration of the *Bismarck's* stern and the circumstances of the torpedo attack.

The issue was subsequently resolved by the James Cameron expedition to the *Bismarck* wreck site in May 2002. In a more comprehensive exploration of the wreck using manned submersibles in addition to remotely operated underwater vehicles, the Cameron team was able to establish positively that the fatal torpedo hit came from the starboard side based on the clear evidence discovered at the wreck site.

BIBLIOGRAPHY

BOOKS

Ballard, Robert D., *The Discovery of the Bismarck,* Warner/Madison Press Books, Toronto, 1990.

Bercuson, David J., and Herwig, Holger H., *The Destruction of the Bismarck,* The Overlook Press, New York, 2001.

Breyer, Siegfried, *The German Battleship Gneisenau,* Schiffer Publishing, West Chester, 1990.

Breyer, Siegfried, *The German Battleship Scharnhorst,* Schiffer Publishing, West Chester, 1990.

Breyer, Siegfried, *The German Battleship Tirpitz,* Schiffer Publishing, West Chester, 1989.

Breyer, Siegfried, *The German Pocket Battleship Admiral Graf Spee,* Schiffer Publishing, West Chester, 1989.

Brower, Jack, *The Battleship Bismarck—Anatomy of the Ship,* Naval Institute Press, Annapolis, 2005.

Busch, Fritz Otto, *Prinz Eugen im ersten Gefecht,* C. Bertelsmann, Gütersloh, 1943.

Busch, Fritz Otto, *Das Geheimnis der Bismarck—Kampf und Untergang des berühmten deutschen Schlactschiffes,* Wilhelm Goldmann Verlag, Leipzig, 1950.

Elfrath, Ulrich, and Herzog, Bobo, *The Battleship Bismarck—A Documentary in Words and Pictures,* Schiffer Publishing, West Chester, 1989.

Garzke, William H., Jr., and Dulin, Robert O., Jr., *Battleships: Allied Battleships in World War II,* Naval Institute Press, Annapolis, 1980.

Garzke, William H., Jr., and Dulin, Robert O., Jr., *Battleships: Axis and Neutral Battleships in World War II,* Naval Institute Press, Annapolis, 1985.

Grenfell, Russell, *The Bismarck Episode,* Macmillan, New York, 1962.

Hoyt, Edwin P., *Sunk by the Bismarck,* Stein and Day, New York, 1980.

Kemp, Paul J., *Bismarck and Hood,* Arms and Armour Press, London, 1991.

Koop, Gerhard, and Schmolke, Klaus-Peter, *Battleships of the Bismarck Class,* Greenhill Books, London, and Naval Institute Press, Annapolis, 1998.

Koop, Gerhard, and Schmolke, Klaus-Peter, *Pocket Battleships of the Deutschland Class,* Greenhill Books, London, and Naval Institute Press, Annapolis, 2000.

Kennedy, Ludovic, *Pursuit—The Chase and Sinking of the Battleship Bismarck,* Viking Press, New York, 1974.

Müllenheim-Rechberg, Baron Burkard von, *Battleship Bismarck—A Survivor's Story,* Naval Institute Press, Annapolis, 1980.

Müllenheim-Rechberg, Burkard Freiherr von, *Schlachtschiff Bismarck,* Bechtermünz Verlag, Augsburg, 1997.

Preston, Anthony, *Battleships of World War I,* Galahad Books, New York, 1972.

Raven, Alan, and Roberts, John, *British Battleships of World War Two,* Naval Institute Press, Annapolis, 1976.

Raven, Alan, and Roberts, John, *British Cruisers of World War Two,* Arms and Armour Press, London, 1980.

Roberts, John, *The Battlecruiser Hood—Anatomy of the Ship,* Naval Institute Press, Annapolis, 1982.

Rhys-Jones, Graham, *The Loss of the Bismarck,* Naval Institute Press, Annapolis, 1999.

Schmalenbach, Paul, *Kreutzer Prinz Eugen—unter 3 Flaggen,* Koehlers Verlag, Hamburg, 1978.

Schofield, B.B., *The Loss of the Bismarck,* U.S. Naval Institute (Ian Allen), Annapolis, 1972.

Schowell, Jak P. Mallmann, *The German Navy in World War Two—A Reference Guide to the Kriegsmarine, 1935–1945,* NavalInstitute Press, Annapolis, 1978.

Taylor, John W.R., *Combat Aircraft of the World,* G.P.Putnam's Sons, 1969.

Taylor, Theodore, *H.M.S. Hood vs. Bismarck,* Avon Books, New York, 1982.

Whitley, M.J., *Cruisers of World War Two—An International Encyclopedia,* Naval Institute Press, Annapolis, 1995.

Whitley, M.J., *German Cruisers of World War Two,* Naval Institute Press, Annapolis, 1985.

Winklareth, Robert J., *Naval Shipbuilders of the World,* Chatham Publishing, London, and Naval Institute Press, Annapolis, 2000.

Zetterling, Niklas, and Tamelander, Michael, *Bismarck—The Final Days of Germany's Greatest Battleship,* Casemate, Philadelphia, 2009.

ARTICLES

Air Operations of RAF Wick, January–December 1941, Caithness CWS.

Bismarck—Not Ready for Action?, Timothy P. Mulligan, Naval History magazine, February 2001.

Bismarck and the Catalina at Castle Archdale, The, Enniskillen, by seelib, BBC-WW2 People's War.

British Expedition Finds HMS *Hood*, Naval History magazine, October 2001.

Chase of the *Bismarck*, Peter Kemp, Purnell's History of the Second World War, Vol. 2, No. 5, 1967

End of the *Prinz*, George L. Dickey, Jr., U.S. Naval Institute Proceedings, August 1969.

Flying-boats in Fermanagh, Inland Waterway News, Vol. 29, No. 1, Spring 2002.

HMS *Hood*, R.G. Robertson, Warships in Profile, Volume 2, Doubleday, 1973.

HMS *Hood* Asleep in Her Grave, John Ray, The Sun, 24 May 2001.

Hood's Achilles' Heel, Eric Grove, Naval History magazine, 1993.

Hvalfjord Fleet Anchorage and Iceland in the Battle of the Atlantic, Fridthor Eydal, 1997.

I Escaped from the *Bismarck*, Josef Statz, Naval History magazine, January/February 1995.

I Was There!—How Our Catalina Shadowed the *Bismarck*, The War Illustrated: Vol. 4. No. 94, 20 June 1941.

Kriegsmarine *Bismarck*, Paul Schmalenbach, Warship Profile 18, Profile Publications, Ltd., 1972, and Warships in Profile, Volume 2, Doubleday, 1973.

Kriegsmarine *Prinz Eugen*, Paul S. Schmalenbach and James E. Wise, Jr., U.S. Naval Institute Proceedings, June 1961.

Last Hours of the *Bismarck*, Gerhard Junack, Purnell's History of the Second World War, Vol. 2, No. 5, 1967.

Loss of HMS *Hood*—A Re-examination, William J. Jurens, Warship International, No. 2, 1987.

My Return to the Mighty *Hood*, Trevor Grove, Daily Mail, 24 July 2001.

Order of Battle, Operation Cerberus 11–13 February 1942, Richard Hawes, Richard Worth, and John Elrod.

Prinz Eugen Album, Paul Schmalenbach, Warship Profile 6, Profile Publications, Ltd, 1971, and Warships in Profile, Volume 1, Doubleday, 1972.

Seeking the *Bismarck*, Don Walsh, U.S. Naval Institute Proceedings, August 2001.

Surviving the *Bismarck* Sinking, Interview with Heinrich Kuhnt by Ward Carr, Naval History magazine, August 2006.

To Die Gallantly, Jack Sweetman, U.S. Naval Institute Proceedings, Naval Review, 1991.

Troubled History of RAF Kaldadarnes, The, Phylo Roadking, Axis History Forum, March 2010.

Valiant *Hood* Found with Her 1,416 Dead after 60 Years, Padraic Flanagan, Daily Express, 24 July 2001.

Who Sank the *Bismarck?*, William H. Garzke, Jr. and Robert O. Dulin, Jr., U.S. Naval Institute Proceedings, June 1991.

With Gallantry and Determination—The Story of the Torpedoing of the *Bismarck*, Mark E. Horan, World War II—A British Focus.

DOCUMENTS, BRITISH

ADMIRALTY REPORTS:

ADM 116-4351, Report on the Loss of HMS *Hood* (First and Second Boards of Enquiry).

ADM 116-4352, Report on the Loss of HMS *Hood* (Second Board of Enquiry): Evidence of Dr. Godfrey Rotter, Director of Explosives Research, Woolwich. Narrative of Operations Against *"Bismarck"* by Captain J.C. Leach (*Prince of Wales*).

ADM 199-1187: *Prince of Wales* Salvo Plot.

ADM 234-317: Operations against the French Fleet at Mers-el-Kebir, 3–6 July 1940.

ADM 234-509: Admiral Tovey's report covering operations leading to the sinking of the *Bismarck*.

HMS *Suffolk* Operations 23–26 May 1941.

HMS *Norfolk* Gunnery and RDF During Operations Against *Bismarck*.

Gunnery Appendix to Narrative of Operations Against *"Bismarck"* by Captain J.C. Leach.

ADM 267-111, Damage Reports (1941): *Prince of Wales*.

ADM 267-137, Notes on the Sinking of the German Battleship *"Bismarck."*

Admiralty Naval Intelligence Division (NID 2-114/41) Report C.B. 4051 (28), Report of Interrogation of Prisoners of War from German Supply Ships, September 1941.

Air Ministry Report, AIR 14-415: Report on the Sinking of the *Bismarck*.

BRITISH AIR SQUADRON HISTORIES (MAY 1941):

No. 98 Squadron (Battle aircraft) RAF Coastal Command, Kaldadarnes, Iceland.

No. 201 Squadron (Sunderland aircraft), RAF Coastal Command, Sullom Voe, Shetland Islands.

No. 209 Squadron (Catalina aircraft), RAF Coastal Command, Castle Archdale, Northern Ireland.

No. 240 Squadron (Catalina aircraft), RAF Coastal Command, Killadeas, Northern Ireland.

No. 269 Squadron (Hudson aircraft), RAF Coastal Command, Kaldadarnes, Iceland.

No. 612 Squadron (Whitley aircraft), RAF Coastal Command, Wick, Scotland.

No. 800Z Squadron (Fulmar aircraft), Fleet Air Arm, aircraft carrier *Victorious*.

No. 810 Squadron (Swordfish aircraft), Fleet Air Arm, aircraft carrier *Ark Royal*.

No. 818 Squadron (Swordfish aircraft), Fleet Air Arm, aircraft carrier *Ark Royal*.

No. 820 Squadron (Swordfish aircraft), Fleet Air Arm, aircraft carrier *Ark Royal*.

No. 825 Squadron (Swordfish aircraft), Fleet Air Arm, aircraft carrier *Victorious* and RNAS Hatston, Orkney Islands.

British and Other Navies in World War 2, Day-by-Day by Don Kindell:
Royal Navy Ships, January 1941.
Royal Navy Ships, January 1942.

FLEET AIR ARM ARCHIVE 1939–1945:
Aircrew of 810 and 818 Squadrons from HMS *Ark Royal* which Crippled the *Bismarck*, 26 May 1941.
RAF Coastal Command & Naval Air Squadrons.
Roll of Honour and Personnel Register.
Sink the *Bismarck* 1941.

Plot of HMS *Norfolk* and HMS *Suffolk* on 24 May 1941.

DOCUMENTS, GERMAN

Prinz Eugen's Battle Diagram (Gefechtsskizze).
Prinz Eugen's Speed Chart.
Prinz Eugen's War Diary (Kriegstagebuch).
Seekriegsleitung I Op. 410/41, 2 April 1941, Weisung für weitere Unternehmungen von Überwasserstreitkräften (Operational Order for Operation Rhine Exercise).
Stellungsweise des Befehlshaber der Kreutzer, 16 June 1941, Kriegstagebuch des Kreuzers *Prinz Eugen* 18 Mai—1 Juni 1941 (Position statement by the Commander of Cruisers on 16 June 1941, regarding the War Diary of the Cruiser *Prinz Eugen* 18 May—1 June 1941, and responses by theCommander, Naval

Group Command North on 7 July 1941 and by the Fleet Commander on 22 July 1941).

Stellungsweise des erstens Torpedooffizier des Keutzers *Prinz Eugen*, 17 Juli 1941 (Position statement of the first torpedo officer of the cruiser *Prinz Eugen*, 17 July 1941, and response by the commander of the *Prinz Eugen*, 17 July 1941).

DOCUMENTS, U.S.

U.S. Naval Intelligence Report, Serial 1066: Report of Scouting and Search of PBY-5 No. AH545 "Catalina" for Bismarck 26 May 1941, Ensign Leonard B. Smith, U.S. Navy, 9 June 1941.

INDEX